Starting with UNIX

Starting with UNIX†

P. J. BROWN

ADDISON-WESLEY PUBLISHING COMPANY

Reading, Massachusetts · Menlo Park, California · London · Amsterdam
Don Mills, Ontario · Sydney

© 1984 Addison-Wesley Publishers Limited

Typeset by H. Charlesworth and Co. Ltd. directly from magnetic tape supplied by the author using **troff**, the UNIX text-processing system.

Printed in Finland by OTAVA. Member of Finnprint.

OTABIND
PAT. PEND.

Cover design by Marshall Henrichs.

UNIX is a trademark of Bell Laboratories.

ISBN 0-201-10924-7

ABCDEFGHIJ-8987654

To HB

half hard
half soft

Contents

PART I: IDEAS AND CONCEPTS

ACKNOWLEDGEMENTS

The publishers thank the following for permission to reproduce the excerpt on page 177 from the poem "Who's Who" by W.H. Auden published in *Collected Poems*, edited by Edward Mendelson: UK and Commonwealth ©Faber and Faber Ltd, London, US and Open © Random House, Inc. New York.

The publishers wish to thank Dave Farris for the cartoons and Marshall Henrichs for the cover design.

Preface

UNIX provides a powerful and flexible means of getting computers to do what you want them to. Once you have cleared a modest initial learning hurdle, you will find UNIX's philosophy is a fundamentally simple and elegant one. Almost everyone who has made the effort to understand the ideas and the mechanisms underlying UNIX will tell you that the time was well spent: it enabled them to reach a world that is coherent, convenient, even delightful. This book aims to give you such an understanding, and to show enough of the detail of UNIX to get you going. It tries to be light and readable, to be serious without being too solemn.

The book is aimed at the beginner. All we ask of you, the reader, is that you have actually seen a computer and used one for half an hour or so — playing games does not count. Even if you did not really understand what you were doing, you will at least have learned what a computer's terminal and storage media (for example a floppy disk) look like, and how a conversation between a person and a computer may proceed.

You may be intending to use UNIX solely to prepare textual material — reports, essays, letters, books; in this case you may never have written a program in your life and may never plan to do so. Alternatively you may be a skilled programmer who is interested in UNIX as a framework for your programming activities. The book does not assume anything about you other than that you are a beginner to UNIX.

For those readers who already know an operating system our advice is to forget what you know, and start again with a fresh mind. As we have said, UNIX has its own philosophy of how to organize your computing, and if you have fixed and different ideas then you will never strike up a friendship with UNIX. This, in a way, is good news for those readers who have never used any operating systems and are delightfully ignorant of what they are; these absolute beginners, with their open minds, may actually be better placed than those with more experience.

ORGANIZATION OF THE BOOK

Many books start by presenting a detailed account of how to use UNIX. This book adopts a different approach. We firmly believe that it is worth investing a couple of hours in reading about the underlying concepts of UNIX before plunging into details. The book is therefore divided into two Parts: Part I explains the ideas and concepts behind UNIX, and Part II shows how to use UNIX. There are four reasons for this approach.

- once you understand the ideas, the details follow easily. The reverse is not true.
- UNIX itself offers conversational aids that tell you the details of your local system. Thus buying a book covering these same details may be something of an extravagance.
- details change with time, but concepts do not.
- UNIX has been implemented on many different computers and the details vary.

VERSIONS OF UNIX

The last two points are worthy of expansion. The version of UNIX that you use depends upon the vendor, the computer you use and the date of purchase. There are now numerous 'UNIX look-alikes', which have names similar to UNIX. Do not let the variety of names confuse you: most UNIX look-alikes really do look like UNIX, and the concepts described in this book apply to all but the inevitable mavericks. (The version of UNIX that the book assumes is actually the so-called 'Version 7'.)

ACKNOWLEDGEMENTS

I have been fortunate, when preparing this book, to have such a wealth of colleagues to turn to for help and advice. Among those at Kent that I have most imposed upon are: Mike Bayliss, Peter Collinson (above all), Simon Croft, Ursula Fuller, Richard Hellier, Ian Utting and David Wood; among those outside are David Duce, Eric Foxley, Brian Reid, Chris Tavaré, Ken Thompson and Douglas Woodall. I have also been blessed with two fine typists, Judith Farmer and Marianne Kong, who have turned hieroglyphics on paper into coherent bit patterns on disk. Finally I must thank Heather Brown: the worst parts of the drafts of this book were burnt away by the acid dripping from her tongue.

Peter Brown
Canterbury
August 1983

PART I

IDEAS AND CONCEPTS

CHAPTER 1

Introductory background

The rattlesnake is a friendly fellow, but you must deal with him in the right way.
BOOK ON SNAKES

UNIX is an example of an *operating system*: a program that controls the running of a computer. If you wish to exploit any facility of your computer — be it a game-playing program or a fancy printing device — you need to master the operating system first. A popular saying in computing is that the operating system comes between you and your computer. This has the implication that the operating system gets in your way, and actually hinders you in getting at the facilities you want.

Operating systems were first produced around 1950, and since then thousands of different operating systems have been constructed. Many of these were massive, complicated, fussy, and thus a huge barrier to anyone wanting to use a computer. Gradually the designers of operating systems paid more attention to the needs of the human user. Recently the ugly adjective 'user-friendly' has been coined, and used to convey the idea that an operating system helps its users rather than hinders them.

Of the thousands of operating systems that have existed, many have been so unfriendly that they have driven all their users away; then having apparently achieved their aim of banishing the humans they have died of neglect. Nevertheless in spite of the huge mortality there are still hundreds of different operating systems in use today.

KINDS OF OPERATING SYSTEM

Operating systems come in all shapes and sizes. Some are designed to fit onto a tiny computer, others are geared for the huge computers found in, say, head offices of airlines. Some operating systems are geared to a particular class of user, such as military personnel or professional computer scientists. Others, like UNIX, aim to be a Jack-of-all-trades.

Operating systems also differ in their range of availability. An operating system may be tied to one type of computer, or it may be available on many different ranges of computers. UNIX grew up on one type of computer, but because of its success has now been implemented on numerous different ranges of computers. In fact it is probably the most widely implemented operating system in the world today. Its habitat ranges from huge mainframes to relatively modest microcomputers.

In this book, we use the term *UNIX implementation* to describe the version of UNIX on one particular computer. Because of its diverse habitat, UNIX has many variants: indeed there may be differences between UNIX implementations on two identical computers. A consequence of this is that some of the details in this book — particularly those shown in sample terminal sessions——may be slightly different on your UNIX implementation. The differences are not usually of any great consequence.

IS UNIX FRIENDLY?

If you join a new group of people, the first friends you make are probably the more talkative ones: those who approach you readily and tell you everything you need to know about your new environment. As time goes by, you will find that the chatterers bore you and, after a while, become downright annoying. You make new and more solid friendships with the strong and silent types who perhaps were rather forbidding at first. So it is with making the acquaintance of operating systems. You will find UNIX among the strong and silent ones. UNIX is not especially friendly on first acquaintance; it is not unfriendly either — merely somewhat indifferent. As your acquaintance grows, you will find your friendship blossoms — maybe to become firm enough to last a lifetime.

KINDS OF TERMINAL

In the late sixties and early seventies, people conversed with computers using a terminal very much like a typewriter. These typewriter terminals are still available today, though they no longer predominate. When you use such terminals, the characters that you type, as well as being printed on the typewriter's paper, are relayed to the computer. When the computer wants to talk to you, it takes control of the typewriter and prints on the paper.

Nowadays most terminals consist of display screens that resemble television screens — sometimes they are indeed televisions — together with a keyboard. What you type on the keyboard is displayed on the screen, and when the computer wants to talk to you it displays material on the screen. What appears on the screen is almost identical to what would appear on a typewriter's paper.

Some people still prefer to use typewriter terminals, or other sorts of *printing terminal*. They have two advantages: firstly they give you *hard copy*, i.e. printed material you can keep or pass on to someone else; secondly, they do not share the problem of display terminals that only 24 lines of text (or thereabouts) can be shown at any one time.

Many UNIX systems nowadays are primarily based on display terminals but have one printing terminal for use when hard-copy output is needed. (Some systems have a special printer that is used exclusively for printed output and cannot be used as a terminal at all.)

UNIX can be used equally well from a display terminal or a printing terminal. Thus you can follow through the examples in this book irrespective of which type of terminal you are using. A lot of computing terminology is still based on the old typewriter days. In particular, if you have a display terminal, you will have to get used to people saying that the computer 'prints' something on your terminal when they really mean it displays the material on your screen. There are several instances in the UNIX documentation where 'print' means 'display'. In this book we shall keep to the word 'display', and reserve the word 'print' for the cases where material is really printed.

A SAMPLE

In order to give a feel for the use of UNIX, we show below an extract from a UNIX session. We must emphasize, however, that we are not concerned with the details at this stage — such matters are covered in Part II — but with general principles. In our example, material typed by the user is in **bold face**, to distinguish it from UNIX's replies.

```
$ ls
bridgegame    game1        game2        jobletter796
jobletter797  jobletter798
$ cat jobletter798
```

5

Dear sir,

I am sorry I did not turn up for the job interview last
week, but there was a good horror film on the television
and I did not want to miss it.

I am willing to come for a new interview on Wednesday
afternoon next week, though I must leave by 4:30 to
go to the football game.

I am an expurt in UNIX, particularly the game playing
programs, so I would be a grate asset to your company.

    yours sincerely,

```
$ spell jobletter798
expurt
$ ed jobletter798
421
/expurt/
I am an expurt in UNIX, particularly the game playing
s/purt/pert/p
I am an expert in UNIX, particularly the game playing
w
421
q
$
```

To a beginner the above may look largely incomprehensible, but it can be
explained fairly simply.

In the first line, UNIX displays a *prompt*, saying it is ready for the user to type.
The prompt is a dollar sign, followed by a space. The user types **ls**, which is a
command to UNIX to list the names of all his *files*. Files are one of the most
important facilities of UNIX, and we shall discuss them fully later on. For the time
being, think of a file as some information, of any nature you like, kept inside the
computer; each file is identified by a name chosen by the user. In the above example
the user has six files. We shall assume these files arose in the following way. The first
three files, which the user has called **bridgegame**, **game1** and **game2**, are concerned
with games. The other three files contain letters applying for jobs. The user began,
some while ago, by calling his job application letters **jobletter1**, **jobletter2**, etc. He
has had a certain amount of trouble getting a job: the first 795 applications failed.
He has since deleted these files, and their names do not appear on the listing. He has
kept **jobletter796** and **jobletter797**; although these letters have been sent, he is still
awaiting replies, so he keeps the originals for reference. Since there is a chance that
these applications will not be successful the user is now working on a new letter,
jobletter798. This was created earlier in the current session.

To return to the above episode, UNIX, after displaying the names of files,
again produces its prompt, the dollar sign. The user can then type another
command. What he types is

cat jobletter798

The word **cat** is a curious name for a command, but what it does is to display the contents of a given file, in this case **jobletter798**. The user does this to remind himself of what is in the file. After displaying the file, UNIX produces its prompt again.

Just to be certain that the letter is perfect, the user invokes UNIX's program that checks spelling. Unlike **cat**, this command has an obvious name: **spell**. The spelling check on the file **jobletter798** comes up with one mis-spelling: 'expurt'. It is not clever enough to point out the spelling of 'great' as 'grate', since the latter is a correct word. If **spell** were an exceptionally clever program — at the frontier of current research — it would have tried to analyze the meaning of words; if so, it would have pointed out the peculiar use of 'grate'. It is, however, not that smart; it looks at each word in isolation.

The user decides to correct his spelling error by *editing*, i.e. changing, his file. To do this he applies the editor program **ed** to the **jobletter798** file. On being entered, the **ed** program displays the number of characters in the file, in this case 421. The user then types the line

/expurt/

to find the line containing **expurt**. (We shall explain the editor later in the book: you will just have to take its machinations on trust for the moment. One unusual facet of the editor is that it does not produce prompts — the user just types lines at it.) The above line causes the editor to search through the file for **expurt** and display the (first) line that contains it. The user then corrects his spelling error by typing the magic line

s/purt/pert/p

(This actually means substitute **pert** in place of **purt** and print the result.) Having made the change, the user types the lines **w** and **q** to finish off his editing — again the details will be explained later. The editor gives the length of the revised **jobletter798** file. This length is, in fact, the same as before because the alteration made no difference to the length. UNIX then displays its dollar prompt again and the user can issue his next command. Quite likely he will now get the letter typed on some printer attached to his computer; he can then put the letter in an envelope and dispatch it.

Appendix A contains further examples of UNIX sessions. You will not be able to understand all of these yet, but a quick browse through may help give you more of a flavour of UNIX.

COMMANDS AND PROGRAMS

A relationship with a computer is a purely selfish one. You make friends with the system that has most to offer you.

UNIX offers you two facilities. The first is an excellent *file system*, which as its name implies provides a way of storing information in an orderly matter — the UNIX analogue of a filing cabinet. We discuss file systems in Chapters 3 and 4. The second is a rich collection of programs, all written by experts, and all pre-packaged in a form ready to use. Most of the programs are built-in *system* programs that are provided on all (or perhaps nearly all) UNIX implementations. These system programs can be augmented by further programs developed locally for your particular computer. You may eventually write programs yourself to augment UNIX even more, though your initial aim may just be to use what is there, rather than to add to it. The UNIX community, which straddles the world, is a community that shares and exchanges valuable programs and data.

There are 200 or so system programs available under UNIX, and they range from simple aids to comprehensive packages. The programs shown in the above extract were

- **ls**, a program to list the names of files
- **cat**, a program to display the contents of a file
- **spell**, a program to check spelling
- **ed**, an editor.

Examples of others are

- a compiler for the Pascal language
- a program to typeset mathematical equations
- a program to aid in plotting graphs
- a self-teaching program to help you learn about UNIX
- a program to communicate with users on other computers.

As you can see, these are so diverse that it is unlikely that one user would want every one of them. A typical user has a restricted sphere of interest, preparing documents, say, and just gets to know the programs in that area. Nevertheless there is a core of twenty or so UNIX system programs that are so basic that every user must know them. Everyone must know how to display and to copy files, for example. The emphasis of this book is on these core programs, and once you have mastered these, and, of course, mastered the style of UNIX, you will easily be able to master the more specialized programs in your particular field of application. Appendix B gives a list of UNIX commands; this can be used for browsing or for reference.

You select the program you want to use by giving UNIX a *command*. The very word 'command' gives the impression that you are the boss, and that UNIX will do exactly what you want it to. This will, we hope, eventually be the case, but, as you probably know, beginners tend to make mistakes that cause the computer to appear to be an untamed monster. Thus if you mentally substitute 'tentative request' for the word 'command' you may get a better impression of what the world is really like.

When you use a program you are said to *execute* (or *run*) it. In our sample episode we executed the programs **ls**, **cat**, **spell** and **ed**. The word *tool* is often used to describe a program that is an aid to achieving some larger goal. Thus the **spell** program is a tool for writers.

DOCUMENT PREPARATION

UNIX uses the neutral term *document* to refer to any textual material. A document may be a three-line party invitation, a letter, a poem, a report, a list of names and addresses or a twenty-volume book. Documents are normally preserved in files, as we saw in the **jobletter** examples. UNIX provides a large number of tools to aid document preparation. Document preparation overlaps with word-processing, and indeed some people use the two terms as synonyms. The emphasis in UNIX is to provide a general set of tools, which can be applied to documents of any kind and size, and which cover every stage of document preparation from the initial typing of the document through to preparing the finished product for typesetting and/or printing. Word-processing systems are often more specialized, and may be particularly geared to a certain set of tasks performed in offices. These specialized systems excel at their chosen task and are often very easy to learn, but they frequently lack the flexibility and versatility of UNIX's tools.

Although UNIX users are diverse, document preparation is a common thread. To an author, document preparation is an end in itself. To a programmer, document preparation is a means by which he can explain his programs to potential users; programs are useless without documentation.

In this book, we shall often select our examples from the field of document preparation because every reader can then appreciate the examples. We do not however assume that the reader is solely interested in this field.

ON-LINE DOCUMENTATION

Because UNIX is good for document preparation, it has been used to produce its own documentation. Moreover this documentation can be displayed on any user's terminal. Thus if you want information on a particular UNIX feature you do not usually look it up in a printed document. Instead you ask UNIX itself to display on your terminal the relevant page from its documentation.

UNIX documentation is collected together in a massive tome called the *UNIX Programmer's Manual*. Volume 1 of this manual, which describes all the UNIX commands, can be consulted interactively on most UNIX implementations. The only problem with this manual is that it is terse, and not written for beginners. The very purpose of a book such as this, therefore, is to get readers to the stage where they can appreciate the *UNIX Programmer's Manual*; they can then toss the book away.

THE C PROGRAMMING LANGUAGE

UNIX has been implemented using a programming language called *C*. The C language was designed for UNIX, and the development of C and UNIX have proceeded hand in hand. If, like the majority of UNIX users, you are happy to remain an amateur, you do not need to know anything about C.

If, on the other hand, you aspire to be a professional you will need to learn C. Learning C will enable you to change and adapt your local UNIX system and to write system programs. It will also enable you to use some of UNIX's highly specialized system programming tools. In Chapter 12 we give a brief introduction to C, and supply further references for those who are interested.

HISTORY

Operating systems are normally written to satisfy the requirements of an anonymous 'typical customer' identified by marketing men. One of the prime reasons for the success of UNIX is, paradoxically, that there were no marketing men involved.

Work on UNIX was started in 1969 by Ken Thompson, a researcher at Bell Laboratories' Computing Science Research Laboratories in Murray Hill, New Jersey. Ken Thompson's goal was to write an operating system for himself rather than for some anonymous user, and he therefore had a perfect understanding of the customer's needs.

The Murray Hill Laboratory had, and still has, one of the most talented collections of computer scientists in the world. It is certainly in the top five, and in a few areas even comes quite close to the University of Kent at Canterbury.

The promise of Thompson's work attracted some of this talent, and over the years a large number of exceptional people have contributed to UNIX. One of them, Dennis Ritchie, became specially involved and extended UNIX's horizons. The result of Ritchie and Thompson's labours came to light in their prizewinning paper in *Communications of the ACM* (1974 — also reprinted in the January 1983 Anniversary issue). This paper is still excellent reading for all the wisdom it so concisely presents. A confirmation of this wisdom is that the principles of UNIX laid down then still hold good today.

Other people at Bell Laboratories made UNIX even more attractive, by making it portable (i.e. capable of being moved to different computers) and by writing programs that provided more and more facilities.

SMALL-IS-BEAUTIFUL

One of the achievements of UNIX has been to harness all the talent that has gone into producing it. Many past projects involving armies of clever people have ended in absolute disaster. There are two dangers. Firstly the clever people produce something that no-one else can understand. Secondly, the problem of management grows exponentially as teams get bigger — and even one clever person is usually harder to manage than two less talented ones. UNIX has harnessed the talent by adopting a small-is-beautiful philosophy. It is built out of relatively small components, and the power comes from joining the pieces together. Components have been produced by small teams, often one or two people. If a component is small, it is unlikely to be too complicated for ordinary mortals to understand.

The result of UNIX's harnessing of talent, and in particular of its small-is-beautiful philosophy, is that it is one of today's most widely-used operating systems. Its popularity is not the result of the activities of marketing men, of adverts on television, or of free gifts, but simply because UNIX is good.

UNIX users are now an amazingly wide range of people: they encompass writers, businessmen, researchers, scientists and, last but not least, those who use a computer just for the pleasure it brings.

CHAPTER 2

Sharing your computer

A UNIX shared is a UNIX doubled.
OLD PROVERB

UNIX is a *multi-user* operating system. This means that you share the computer with a number of other people, all using the computer at the same time. Each user works on a separate terminal — or, let us hope so, for otherwise you have real problems. Each user has an independent conversation with the computer. The situation is exactly similar to a chess grand-master playing twenty simultaneous games of chess. On some computers the UNIX grand-master may be dealing with many more than twenty simultaneous users; the number may even exceed a hundred on a super-computer. These users may be all in the same building, or, using modern communications systems, may be distributed all over the world.

Most UNIX systems are, however, much more modest: indeed we should really have said that UNIX is *potentially* a multi-user system, as your UNIX may well have only one simultaneous user. A machine which only allows one user at a time is called a *single-user* system (even though there may be several different users who use the machine at separate times). Even if yours is a single-user UNIX it is still worth reading this Chapter, for reasons that will become clear shortly.

The main advantage of a multi-user system is, of course, that hardware costs can be shared. A second advantage is a more surprising one: your first reaction to the idea of having people share a computer with you may be the same as to the idea of sharing your boyfriend or girlfriend; however when people share a computer (where here and elsewhere in this Chapter the word 'share' means 'simultaneously share'), they can communicate with each other — via messages on the computer — and can co-operate in groups to achieve more than any individual can achieve.

Even if you are not convinced by this argument, and are rather fearful of the uncivilized masses who may share a computer with you, you will be appreciative of the third advantage of multi-user systems like UNIX: you can share a computer with the most civilized and reasonable person you know: yourself. This works as follows.

If you set the computer to do a task that will take a fair amount of time, UNIX allows you to get on with another task while you are waiting, instead of just sitting there impatiently twiddling your thumbs. In this case your two separate activities, or more than two if you like, share the computer in exactly the same way as if it were shared by separate users. The only difference is that tasks belonging to the same user all communicate with the same terminal, whereas tasks belonging to separate users normally communicate with their separate terminals. (Hence our previous suggestion that users of single-user UNIX systems read this Chapter.)

The term *task* is actually a jargon word of computing, and is used to mean a program running in the computer. The term *process* is synonymous with the word 'task', and, since UNIX documentation prefers the latter term, we shall use it too.

LEARNING HOW OPERATING SYSTEMS WORK

Large and weighty books have been written on how operating systems work, and on the problems of dealing with numerous simultaneous users. You, as a UNIX user, do not need to know about the principles of operating systems any more than a car driver needs to know the principles of the internal combustion engine. However when you use UNIX, it helps to know what is happening underneath, just as it does when you are using a car, and we shall provide a grossly over-simplified sketch here. (In fact our over-simplified definition of the word 'process' will already have upset operating system gurus.) Nevertheless if you find our explanation hard going feel free to skip this Section and the one that follows. On the other hand, if you are inspired into seeking a deeper understanding of operating systems, a good and comparatively small book is Lister (1979). Another small one, devoted to multi-user systems, is Wilkes (1972); this is comparatively old but still good. A third book, larger and more recent, is by Deitel (1983).

HOW DOES A COMPUTER SUPPORT SEVERAL SIMULTANEOUS USERS?

Surprisingly, when you first use UNIX you are probably not even aware of all the other people who are sharing the computer with you, unless of course they are sitting at adjacent terminals and you can actually see them. The effect is as if you had the computer to yourself. Perhaps, in a similar way, the people simultaneously playing chess against a grand-master each see their world as a single game between them and the master. Only if the computer is heavily loaded in that it has too many users for the power of the machine, does the computer's *response time* become unreasonably slow. (The response time is the time between you typing something and the computer replying.)

Sometimes it is not so much the number of users that loads a computer, but the greed for processing power of a few users.

To explain how UNIX caters for several simultaneous users, we shall change our analogy from a chess grand-master to a juggler. The juggler conveys more of an impression of speed of action, and the need for quick responses. A juggler throws up a ball, and can then deal with other balls for a second or two until the first ball comes down again and it is time to give it another throw.

In a similar way UNIX divides its time into small *time-slots*. The size of a time-slot varies between UNIX implementations; a sample value is one second. UNIX runs one process for a time-slot, and then suspends this process and switches to another. This second process is run for one time-slot and then UNIX switches to a third process. After a few more time-slots, the original process's turn comes again, and it will be resumed where it left off. The algorithm inside an operating system that selects which process to run is called its *scheduling algorithm*. A simple scheduling algorithm is a *round-robin*, which selects each task in turn in a strict order. This is just like the juggler — unless the juggler is pulling a sensational trick whereby one ball overtakes another. Years of study have now been devoted to scheduling algorithms, and algorithms much more sophisticated than the round-robin have been devised. Modern algorithms frequently try to punish greedy people by cutting down on their shares. Most implementations of UNIX attempt to do this, and also to make response time as fast as possible.

Nevertheless if there are twelve users on the computer and each simultaneously starts a process that takes five minutes of computation, even the cleverest scheduling algorithm cannot prevent there being a lapse of an hour before the last one is complete. In fact it will be longer than an hour because of the extra time needed for UNIX to switch between processes. Thus the computer will appear to a user to be at least twelve times as slow as it would be if he were the only user. (This book adopts the convention that users are male but the superuser — a character still to be introduced — is female. While it seems impossible to have any

13

convention that reads well and offends no-one, we hope that this will at least prevent protest marches descending on Canterbury.)

Although we have just cited a case where a process runs twelve times slower than it might we stand by our claim that for most of the time a single user is not inconvenienced by the others. This is because it is extremely rare for all users to be running processes at the same time. There are two reasons for this.

The first is simply a matter of observation. If you take a snapshot of a UNIX system supporting a dozen users, then you might find that six of the users are thinking, three are typing input and the other three are waiting while a process is running. (We assume that the people in the room are trying to do something useful, and are working independently. If they were all playing a spaceship game, then different considerations would apply.)

Even the fastest typist is slow in comparison with the computer's processing speed, so our three people typing are not putting any great load on the computer. Obviously the six people thinking are no load on the computer either, so this just leaves the three people who are running processes.

Of these, we shall assume that one is doing a simple interactive job, which we shall here assume to be editing. The user has typed an editing command and the computer has to execute it. Normally this will not need much computing power — with luck the process can be completed well within one of our time-slots, so this again does not take much power from the computer. Indeed in a great many cases a process will voluntarily relinquish its time-slot before this expires.

The second user, we shall assume, is performing some operation on a file. Files are typically stored on a computer storage device called a *disk*. The second user's process consumes a few time-slots and then needs to input some more data from a file. Input from a file, though faster than input from a terminal, is still slow by computer standards. In order that the industrious computer is not kept hanging around, cursing the slowness of its file input and thinking that it could have checked all the spelling in *War and Peace* during the time it is kept waiting, most computers have an instruction of the form "get on with this filing operation and tell me when it is complete". While the slow filing work is proceeding the computer tackles its other work. In particular it can give a time-slot to our third user.

Our third user has a program that calculates for two hours, and then outputs a single number that is the result of all its labours. (When his program finishes, the user makes a random change to it and runs it for two more hours. By chance, he happens to be a physicist.) His process uses all the time-slots the scheduling algorithm gives it. Its only pause comes when it outputs a line to the terminal. Writing to the terminal is extremely slow, even compared with getting at information stored in files, and gives the chance for others to get some time-slots. Even when this process is not doing any input/output and thus asking for all the time-slots it can get, a good scheduling algorithm should ensure that the other users get their fair share by giving them priority over the greedy person.

In conclusion, therefore, an operating system can support a lot of users because

- at any one time most users are thinking or typing
- most processes pause periodically to do some input/output
- a good scheduling algorithm will keep the greedy users in check

- some processes, particularly the transfer of information to or from a file, can go on in the background while the computer gets on with other processes.

The last point can be expanded: in general, a computer system may be built out of several sub-computers, all of which can be simultaneously working away at different tasks. This is called *multi-processing*. However UNIX gives its users the impression that they are talking to a single entity, so you do not need to worry about such details.

SECURITY AND THE SUPERUSER

Sharing your computer with others would be no pleasure if your 'friends' could change your files or interfere with your UNIX processes. To prevent this, UNIX has a number of security rules, and mechanisms to enforce them.

Most of the rules we live by are laid down by governments. Numerically the most common form of government is the dictatorship. UNIX is also a dictatorship. There is one user who makes the rules by which other users live, and who controls the enforcement of rules. The dictator is called the *superuser*. The superuser controls whether you can use the computer, how much space your files can occupy, which files you can change and even which UNIX commands you can use. She (our convention being to assume a female superuser) does not impose her will by brute strength. You will not find a huge figure glowering over you as you sit at your terminal. Instead the superuser's power lies in her control over certain mechanisms within UNIX. You may not even know who she is.

Generally the superuser is a blessing to you; she performs a host of thankless behind-the-scenes tasks to make your use of UNIX more pleasant. If the superuser were replaced by anarchy, your UNIX system would soon collapse.

LOGGING IN

Immediately you try to use UNIX you become aware of the superuser's power. She controls who can use the UNIX she manages. Each user has to have a *login name*, which the superuser (or her agent) allocates. Typically your login name is your initials or your first name. Login names must be unique, and hence if there is already a **peter** using your UNIX, you cannot be **peter** too.

The word 'login' comes from a computer jargon term. Each time you use a multi-user operating system you must first make yourself known to the computer. This is called *logging in*. Once logged in you can then use the system until you say good-bye by *logging out*. The period you spend logged in is called a *session*. Assuming your superuser permits it, a session may last anything from a few seconds to several hours. Moreover you might have a number of sessions in a day.

There may be limits on the number of users who can be simultaneously logged in, i.e. using the computer. Obviously, since each terminal can only support one user at a time, the physical limit on the number of simultaneous users is the number of terminals that can connect to a UNIX system, but sometimes the superuser sets the actual limit lower than this. For a personal UNIX system there may be only one terminal and hence one simultaneous user. A small shared UNIX might, for example, have a limit of a dozen users. The total number of users of the system may still number hundreds, since the limit only applies to the number of people logged in at the same time.

To prevent imposters each UNIX login name has an associated secret *password*. Every time you log in you need to type both your login name and your password. Normally every character you type at the keyboard appears on the screen. This does not, however, happen when you type your password: if the password appeared on the screen its very purpose, secrecy, would be lost; thus UNIX suppresses it. Even so, beware of the sneaky person who watches your fingers when you type your password.

In Chapter 6, when we introduce the details of using UNIX, we shall show an example of logging in.

Your password is something you control; once logged in you can change it to anything you like. Do not try to be too clever. The most humiliating experience in computing is to forget your own password, and have to crawl to the superuser (assuming you know who she is) and ask her to give you a new password.

FINDING ANOTHER USER'S PASSWORD

Human ingenuity the world over has been devoted to finding other people's passwords.

The first approach is through psychology. A large number of people chose as their password the name of the thing they most love in the world: their girlfriend or boyfriend, a sports team or perhaps themselves. It is amazing how often a guess along these lines is correct.

A second approach, open to those who are programmers, is to write subtle programs that deceive the innocent. A particularly simple and appealing one runs as follows. You write a program that displays on the terminal the exact prompt that UNIX would give when it expected someone to log in. You then leave your program in this state and vacate your terminal. After a while your prey appears. He follows the normal logging in procedure, typing his login name and password. What your program does is to write these to a file, output a message to the user such as 'wrong password' and log out. The real UNIX logging in prompt then appears. Your prey thinks he mistyped his password and indeed when he tries a second time all goes well, so he thinks no more of it. Later on you log in and examine the file that your sneaky program created, and you have the password. If you are really lucky you will catch the superuser. Once you have her password, all the power of the system is yours. You log in as superuser, change her password and the bloodless coup is complete. The superuser's login name is, by the way, nothing flamboyant like Napolean or Thatcher; it is simply **root**. We shall see why later.

If you are not a programmer you may not have understood the above explanation. Nevertheless, if you work in a UNIX environment where people delight in playing tricks on one another, our explanation will have served a purpose if it simply puts you on your guard.

PROTECTION BETWEEN PROCESSES

Although UNIX may be running several simultaneous processes, you can safely assume that other people's processes will not upset yours. For example there is no danger, when someone else uses the **spell** program at the same time as you, that their spelling errors will get mixed up with yours.

You may, if you get to be an advanced user of UNIX, intentionally create two different processes of your own which communicate with one another. However such matters are beyond the scope of this introductory book.

The important point to remember is that when you start with UNIX you will not need to use such facilities, and thus can sleep soundly.

PROTECTING FILES

Although your processes are safe from interference by other users, the material you keep in your files might not be. Indeed if you are working in a team you may be quite happy for other members of the team to change your files. For example, our user in Chapter 1 might even be happy for his friends to try to change and improve his **jobletter** files. However you normally want protection, and UNIX provides a means of achieving this. It does not, of course, protect you from the all-embracing powers of the superuser, who can change or delete anything she likes.

ACCOUNTING

UNIX, like any other multi-user system, may keep records of how much of the computer's resources each user has consumed. These resources include file space, processing time and connect time (i.e. the time for which you are logged in to UNIX, irrespective of whether you are thinking or doing something).

On some UNIX implementations users pay real money for the resources they use, and the computer's accounting information is used to calculate the charges. If you are lucky enough to be using a UNIX system with no charges, the accounting figures still come in useful for managing the system. This is because of the phenomenon that *if a computing resource is freely available, and pleasant to use like UNIX, then users will swamp it*. Thus the space for files, however large, soon becomes exhausted; similarly, processing power, however great, gets lapped up until response time becomes slow and further users are driven away.

Because of this phenomenon, there must be firm management to punish the greedy and protect the unselfish users like you. This is done by the superuser, and, at the second-to-second level by the scheduling algorithm, using the accounting information that UNIX provides.

ELECTRONIC MAIL

If a computer system has a fair number of users they will want to communicate with one another. To facilitate this, UNIX supports a system of *electronic mail* whereby users can send each other messages. Messages sent to a user who is not currently logged in are preserved until he next does so; he can then display his mail. Often the first message that UNIX displays when you log in is 'You have mail'.

On some of the bigger UNIX implementations, which support large and diverse user populations, electronic mail has become the preferred method of communication, to the detriment of written notes or the use of the telephone.

Indeed the term 'mail' comes to mean electronic mail rather than ordinary mail, a convention we shall adopt in this book. Some UNIX users log in once or twice a day just to read their mail.

The nature of messages sent obviously depends on the user community. On some implementations, special interest groups flourish and use UNIX to exchange information on, say, wines. On others the mail is predominantly concerned with administrative matters or with availability and use of information ("My address list has now been updated to include your suggestions", "You have eight copies of similar information, delete some of them".)

CHAPTER 3

Files

I know I put it somewhere safe, but now I can't remember where.

All the information you keep inside the computer is put into files. The word 'file' is in fact a rather inappropriate one. The word is derived from the sort of file you put in a filing cabinet; such files tend to contain a lot of separate pieces of paper: letters, bills, reports and so on.

When you start to use UNIX files do not try to put entirely separate entities, such as a letter and an invoice, in the same file. Instead if two pieces of information are different in nature, create separate files for them. You are always free to combine files later on, when you have more experience of managing your information.

This is not to say that you cannot create big files in UNIX; files can be up to a billion characters, and a single file could therefore contain a mailing list of millions of names and addresses. Nevertheless, in line with UNIX's small-is-beautiful approach, it is still often best to split such large files into a collection of smaller files, particularly if you are going to work on individual parts separately. Thus a long report might be divided into separate chapters, each in a different file.

Any information you want preserved from one UNIX session to the next needs to be stored in files. (You may also use 'temporary' files that you throw away at the end of a session.) Even modest users find that they soon build up a collection of tens, perhaps hundreds, of files. In fact as a UNIX user you tend to generate more files than if you use other operating systems. One reason for this is the small-is-beautiful philosophy; a second reason is that, because UNIX has so many excellent facilities, you use it for many more purposes that you first imagine. For example if you use UNIX mainly for writing Pascal programs you will also use UNIX to produce documentation for your programs, and perhaps to keep records of your modifications and to build up statistical information about performance.

Do not concern yourself at this stage about how UNIX files are actually stored. All you need to know is that UNIX provides a *file system* which looks after all your files for you. Your only task is to choose a name, the *filename*, by which you will know each file you create. UNIX allows any sequence of characters to act as a filename but we shall keep to sequences of letters and/or digits (except for *extensions* — see later), and we recommend you do the same.

We saw six examples of filenames in our sample session in Chapter 1. Further examples are **mailinglist**, **f** and **division2**.

BINARY AND CHARACTER FILES

The majority of files contain documents, where we use the word 'document' to cover any material represented by a sequence of characters. Thus a document could be anything from a love poem to the textual version of a program. Files that contain documents are called *character files*. UNIX does not, of course, know or care what a file represents. When you look at a file, you may rhapsodize over its beauty as a poem, or alternatively you may admire its elegance as a program, but inside the computer all files are just sequences of characters. The end of a line is represented as a special 'newline' character, and this character is treated by UNIX just like any other. Thus the beautiful love poem

I adore
you even more
than Southampton's superb
Football Clerb.

is represented by the sequence of characters: 'I', space, 'a', 'd', 'o', 'r', 'e', newline, 'y', 'o', 'u', space, ...

In addition to these character files, UNIX supports *binary files*. If you are not a programmer you will not be interested in creating these, but you should at least know what they are. If you are little the wiser after reading this Chapter, do not worry too much — you can try reading it again after you have had a little more experience.

As you may know even if you are not a programmer, programs are often converted from their textual (or *source*) form to a sequence of individual bits that can be directly executed by the computer. It is convenient to store this binary form of a program in the file system, as well as the source form. This saves re-translating the program to binary form each time it is used. When you use a UNIX system program, such as **ls**, you use its binary form directly.

Some programs are only issued in binary form, because their originators want to keep the source form secret (sometimes for commercial reasons, sometimes because of shame). In addition it is common practice to store certain data in binary form. Thus high-level programming languages such as Pascal provide ways of reading and writing data in binary form.

Even within character files, although we have pretended these are represented as sequences of characters, each character is really stored as a numeric code. The numeric codes are defined by some coding system. There are a number of different standard coding systems (if it is not a contradiction in terms to speak of different standards) of which ASCII (American Standard Code for Information Interchange) is the most popular. Another popular code, ISO, is very similar to ASCII. Each character is stored as a *byte*, which consists of 8 bits. In this book we are certainly not interested in talking about individual bits — indeed some readers may not know what a bit is. It is quite adequate to think of a byte as representing a decimal value in the range 0 to 255. If we assume the ASCII code our poem would be stored as the sequence of bytes

    73 32 97 100 111 114 101 ...

No wonder that UNIX is often gruff and grumpy, given that it sees romance as a series of numbers.

One of the most pleasant properties of UNIX is that *all files are treated in the same way*. This is one of the many features of UNIX that you do not really appreciate unless you have used another operating system, where different types of file require different commands. To UNIX every file is simply a sequence of bytes, and you can, for example, use the same command to copy a file irrespective of whether the file contains a poem or a program, and irrespective of whether it is a character file or a binary file. This freedom to do what you like with any file nevertheless has its dangers in that you are free to do silly things as well as sensible things, as we shall shortly see.

Fortunately most users need not be concerned with coding systems and bytes. However some apparently peculiar behaviour of your computer may become clearer if you realize that even character files are actually encoded inside the computer as numbers. When UNIX displays a file it converts the numbers back to character form, using the coding system in reverse. As a result the internal numbers come out on a display as the characters you expect. Your freedom to do what you like with any file allows you to try to decode and display a file that is not a character file but a binary file. In other words you can try to convert to characters some bytes that do not represent characters at all. What comes out when you do this is an apparently random sequence of characters. (The characters may, by chance, represent a coherent sequence of words, but the chances of producing the complete works of Shakespeare are not great.) A random sequence of characters is not particularly dramatic, but the fireworks begin when one of the character codes you are trying to display happens to correspond to a code that changes the behaviour of your terminal. Such codes may cause the screen to clear, to go into reverse-video, or a sound to be produced. With luck you may get a *Son et Lumière* show.

PHYSICAL DEVICES

One of the greatest services that UNIX provides is to disguise from its users the intricacies of the physical devices on which files are stored. In this Section we show some of these unseen favours that UNIX performs.

Your files will probably be stored on such devices as disks and tapes. These physical devices place a large number of nasty constraints on their usage. Typically files must be divided into blocks of information — a block might, for example, consist of 512 bytes. There are huge problems in keeping track of which pieces of storage are in use, and which are free. There are further problems in 'fragmentation': sometimes the unused parts of storage might consist of lots of very small pieces, whereas it is desirable (or perhaps necessary) to store information in one large contiguous piece.

In early operating systems for mainframe computers the poor user was put in the front line to battle with these problems. The same is true for some modern operating systems that run on very small computers. UNIX does all the fighting for you. To you, the user, a file is simply a sequence of characters (bytes). As a UNIX user you are completely unaware of such matters as block size and the layout of information. Indeed you can be completely unaware of what physical medium is used to store your files. If you are a woodworker and think of a file as a tool for rubbing away your wood, then you could be under the incredible illusion that computers stored their information as tiny scratches on wood. This illusion would not prevent you using UNIX effectively. More to the point, even though storage technology is constantly changing, the UNIX user's view of a file remains constant. It may even be that the next dramatic advance in storage technology will indeed be to store information as scratches on wood. The wood may even be removable, so that the terms 'log in' and 'log out' will have literal meanings.

You do not even have to worry about the size of each of your files. UNIX will reserve room for each file however big it is; UNIX does not mind if the file subsequently changes in size. The only limits are the total size of physical storage and the less-than-onerous requirement than a single file cannot exceed a billion characters — since most systems do not have a billion characters of storage anyway this requirement is similar to one than says that no individual may own more than a thousand tons of gold.

PERMANENT AND REMOVABLE FILE SYSTEMS

Although you need not concern yourself with the physical details of your storage media, there is one general property you must know about file systems: whether they are *permanent* or *removable*.

All UNIX systems provide some permanent file space. This is stored on devices such as fixed disks that are always attached to the computer. Permanent file space could even reside on a disk that was potentially removable but was never in fact removed. To exploit the full power of UNIX you need a reasonable amount of storage for files: most systems provide millions of characters and some provide hundreds of millions. This therefore is a radically different environment from a small microcomputer with floppy disks.

In some UNIX implementations, all the file system is in permanent storage. On others, the permanent storage is supplemented by removable storage. The removable storage may be a largish disk that is *mounted* (i.e. put into the computer) when a certain group of users is active, or it may be a relatively small disk that belongs to one user and is mounted when he logs in and dismounted when he logs out.

The permanent file system may be spread over several different physical disks, but you the user are not concerned with this any more than with the characteristics of the disks themselves. To you the UNIX file system is one uniform whole. For a removable file system, on the other hand, you need to know something about where your files are stored in order to know what to mount.

SHARING AND PROTECTING FILES

Just as you share your computer with others you share its file system. It is through the file system that you can gain by the presence of other users. UNIX allows you to access files belonging to other users, and on the majority of UNIX implementations a co-operative spirit has blossomed. People use each other's files, whether they are job application letters, drafts of books, programs or data, and as a result everyone is more productive.

Sad to say, societies based on free and open sharing rarely work. In few communities do people leave their houses open with their possessions available to all, though somewhere in the world there may still be societies — doubtless dubbed as 'primitive' — in this happy state. Instead the majority of people have locks on their doors.

UNIX, too, provides its locks. You can protect your files so that others cannot change them or, if you want to be really protective, cannot look at them at all. Doubtless you will need to put these protection locks on some of your own files, but try to keep your UNIX community as open as possible. Significantly, Bourne (1983) reports that few people within Bell Laboratories itself protect their files; this is not unrelated to the success of UNIX as a co-operative project.

In the next Chapter, we shall cover some details about file access and protection.

Not only may you want to access files belonging to other users, but you will also definitely want to access some files provided by UNIX itself. UNIX provides a large number of public files. They include all the built-in programs available to you — these are generally made available in binary form. They also include the files that provide the interactive documentation of your UNIX system.

Thus the file system is an amalgam of your files, public UNIX files and other people's files. All of these are provided as an integrated whole.

MANAGING A LOT OF FILES

After using UNIX for a year, you might be the proud possessor of a hundred different files. If you have no system for organizing your files, the time will soon come when you forget which file relates to which of your projects. (If you have ever used floppy disks, you may have been forced into a partial solution of this problem. A typical floppy might contain 10 to 20 files; if you have a hundred files, and thus require 5 to 10 different floppies, you are forced into thinking how your files are best divided up into separate families — one family for each floppy.)

Irrespective of the physical media on which files are stored, operating systems should help you manage your files by providing an overall structure which allows you to divide your files into small families, and to see how the families relate to one another.

REQUIREMENTS OF A FILE SYSTEM

In the first part of this Chapter we discussed the underlying details of the way individual files are stored. To summarize, what the user needs to know is that

- files may represent character or binary information, but all files are stored inside the computer in an identical way: as a sequence of bytes. Details of the precise coding system used for character files are not important
- on some UNIX implementations, files may be removable

In the second part of this Chapter we discussed the way files are used. This was in preparation for the next Chapter, which is concerned with how files relate to each other. We have identified the following requirements of a file system.

- it should provide some overall structure to help you manage your files
- it should allow you access to your own files, to other user's files and to public UNIX files
- it should provide a protection mechanism
- it should cover all files, even removable ones

As a trailer to the next Chapter, we can say that if you have used files on other operating systems you are due for a pleasant surprise. The UNIX file system is so simple and uniform that you may well wonder why your previous operating system was so complicated.

CHAPTER 4

File structure

You cannot say 'trees' without smiling.
CONSERVATION SLOGAN

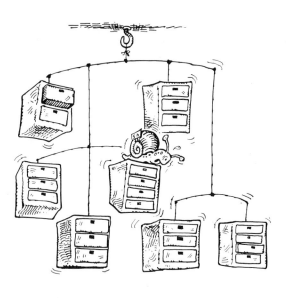

Providing a good file system was the first aim of UNIX, and its file system is the cornerstone of the whole operating system.

The fundamental mechanism which succeeds, single-handedly, in meeting most of the requirements we outlined at the end of the previous Chapter is the *hierarchical* file structure. The basic building block of this hierarchy is the *directory*, so we shall start by explaining this.

DIRECTORIES

Every file system must keep records of the names of all existing files and where they are stored. This is called a *directory*. Directories may also contain further information about each file, such as a specification of who can use it.

On some operating systems, file systems have one directory for each user, while on others there is one directory for each disk or tape. UNIX, since it does not concern the user with physical media, uses the former approach. However the concept is considerably generalized. A directory is treated as an ordinary file; in particular it has a name just like any other filename. (A directory is actually a binary file because, although filenames within the directory are stored in character form, information about files is represented in binary form.)

Since a directory is an ordinary file, one or more of the files within a directory can themselves be directories. This simple statement is the foundation of the entire UNIX file system.

We shall explain why by first considering a separate application: a personal telephone directory.

A PERSONAL TELEPHONE DIRECTORY

Assume you spend a lot of time making telephone calls and in particular in looking up people's numbers in a massive telephone directory. To save time, you decide to write on a small card the names and telephone numbers of the people you most frequently call. This card is placed beside your phone, and serves as your personal directory. After a while your directory card gets full so you decide to expand your system to several cards. When designing this new system you ponder on why you use the telephone and conclude that you use it for four separate activities

- flirting
- seeking information
- arguing
- seeking reassurance

You therefore create four directory cards labelled **flirts**, **boffins**, **arguers** and **flatterers**, and write the appropriate names and telephone numbers on each directory card. Some names may be in more than one directory. These four new directories are sub-directories of your main directory. Your main directory is revised to contain only the names that you call very often indeed, plus references to the sub-directories. The main card might therefore read

anne	**7699**
arguers	*see separate directory*
boffins	*see separate directory*

derek	7698
flatterers	*see separate directory*
flirts	*see separate directory*
mother	01 – 999 – 9999

The main directory is normally beside your phone. However if you are in the mood for arguing you put the **arguers** directory beside your phone, in place of the main directory. After a happy hour spend arguing you may well return to the main directory again, and perhaps then select another sub-directory card.

If this system works well you can extend it to deeper levels. Assume the **arguers** directory gets full. You then divide it into two sub-directory cards, **aggressive** and **sarcastic**, say, and only leave in the **arguers** directory your favourite (i.e. most hated) contacts — the ones you phone almost every time you feel the urge to argue. Your **arguers** directory now reads

aggressive	*see separate directory*
heather	7550
sarcastic	*see separate directory*

.
.
.

Now this may or may not be a sensible way to organize your personal telephone directories, but it is a good way to organize a file system, and it is the method UNIX uses.

ORGANIZING UNIX DIRECTORIES

When you use UNIX you have, at all times, a *current directory*; this is analogous to the card that is currently beside the phone. You can change your current directory as often as you wish.

When you first log in, your current directory is a directory called your *home directory*, the analogy of the main telephone directory card. You place in your home directory the files you use almost every time you log in. In our case we shall assume that there are two such files: our love poem, in a file called **lovepoem** and, more cherished still, the file **reply**, which is the reply from the loved one. For each of our projects we create sub-directories of the main directory. In particular we have a directory **model** which contains the files for the economic modelling system we are building, and a directory **articles**, which is the magazine we edit. The **model** directory contains two files: **program** and **data**; the **articles** directory contains three files: **comment**, **news** and **reviews**. The structure of our directory is shown in Figure 4.1.

Indeed the structure might be extended further if names such as **reviews** were themselves directories.

You can give different files the same name, provided they are in separate directories. Thus we could extend each of our directories to include a file **lovepoem**, where each of these **lovepoem** files contained a different love poem.

It is also possible to do the opposite: to have the same file referenced from separate directories. In this case the file can go under the same name in each

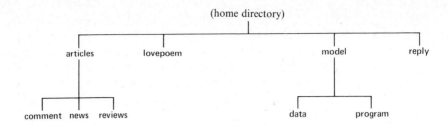

Figure 4.1 The directory tree of a user

directory, or it can be referred to under separate names in separate directories. (An analogy would be that **bugfixer** in our **boffins** telephone directory was the same person as **grumpy** in the **arguers** directory.) The process of referring to the same file in separate ways is called, in UNIX, *linking*.

ADVANTAGES OF DIRECTORIES

Is it really worth structuring your files into separate directories? The first point to emphasize is that you do not lose anything by doing so. Irrespective of your current directory, you can still refer to all the files stored in other directories. The way you do this is through a *pathname*, which we shall explain later.

There are therefore no significant disadvantages in using separate directories; more to the point, there are four solid advantages, as follows.

- *small-is-beautiful*. One of the most common operations in UNIX is for the user to display the names of all the files in a directory. You are regularly doing this to keep track of what files exist, and perhaps to remind you of their names. If a directory is small it is much easier to find a given filename, and much harder to overlook an error such as a file you do not really want.
- *protection*. Since directories are ordinary files you can attach protection to them. Thus you can prevent others changing, or even looking at, your economic model, simply by putting the appropriate protection on the **model** directory. (The alternative is to identify every individual file that needs protecting, and to protect each one in turn.)
- *management*. It is well known that on any computer project much more time is spent on maintenance than on undertaking the project in the first place. In a programming project maintenance consists of making small changes and corrections over the time your programs are used. One prime reason why maintenance is so time-consuming is that if you come to make changes after a six-month absence from the project, you take a huge amount of time trying to figure out what your programs are doing and how they fit together. Even if your project is concerned with document preparation rather than programming, you will still spend a large amount of time on the equivalent of maintenance: changing existing documents, splitting them up, and collecting them together in new combinations. Irrespective of whether you are a writer, a programmer, or both, the directory structure you use has a small but significant effect on mainten-ance. When you plan a directory structure ask yourself this question: "If I

come back to this project after a six-month gap, will the purpose of each file be readily obvious?" Clearly, your choice of filenames is crucial to this question; if your imagination only runs to names like **file1**, **file2**, etc., then your maintenance problems will be huge. However, the choosing of a good directory structure, based on a hierarchy that reflects what you are doing, is just as important as your choice of filenames. People who fail to create a comprehensible file structure pay a penalty later when they waste hours printing out all their files to try to figure out the purpose of each file, and how it relates to other files.

- *ease of adaptation.* Related to the question of maintenance is that of adaptation: changing to a new environment. Someone else takes over the reviews section of your magazine; alternatively your economic model is to be applied to the economy of a different country, and, although your modelling program still works, all the data need to be changed. One crucial factor in determining whether you will be able to adapt successfully is the nature of your directory structure. If the structure reflects the natural sub-divisions of your project, you will be as successfully adaptable a species as the house-sparrow, the rat or the FORTRAN.

BEING A PIONEER

Most of us who use computers are great conservatives, perhaps from bitter experience. We master a few simple facilities that appear to work well for us and then try to stick with these for the rest of our lives. Even if you are convinced by our arguments about the merits of a hierarchy of directories, you are still likely to shun actually creating them — until tomorrow, perhaps. However, just for once try to be a pioneer. A small initial investment in your time will reap great rewards later. An excellent way of getting yourself to think about structure is to make a rule that none of your directories should contain more than a dozen files. This will force you to explore the world of structured file systems. After exploring the world, you may indeed return home and modify your original self-imposed rule. But, unless you explore the world, you will never have the experience to make decent decisions on what is best for you.

It may be helpful to think of the UNIX directory rather than the UNIX file as the equivalent of the file you put in your filing cabinet. Each is a small collection of related documents.

You might be beginning to think that we are overdoing our hard-sell of the merits of directories — and there is more to come. If so, you may be right, but the fact is that in practice they are a resource that beginners to UNIX fail to exploit, and this is to their ultimate loss. When, in the second Part of this book, we introduce the practicalities of UNIX, we shall soon start creating new directories.

TREE STRUCTURE

The structure in which UNIX keeps its files is called a *tree*. The reasons for this are obvious. A structure with branches that split into sub-branches is just like a living tree.

Trees are an excellent way of imposing structure (we are persevering with our hard-sell). Most companies, for example, are managed as trees. Indeed the commonest way of showing how a company is organized is to present the information in the form of a tree.

Tree structures are widely used in computer science to represent the structuring of data. Thus the idea of using a tree to represent a file system is not new; it is an application of a method well proved over time. UNIX's use of a tree-structured file system has been so successful that the idea has been adopted by others and has almost become a norm for all but the simplest file systems.

If you want to read more about the uses of trees, a good book is Knuth's (1973) *The Art of Computer Programming*, Volume 1, one of the classics of computing. This contains a wealth of information, of which the material on trees is only a small part.

Computer scientists, being perverse folk, tend to draw their trees upside down. We shall follow this convention — indeed our earlier picture of a directory structure was drawn as a tree with the root, the home directory, at the top. UNIX has a terminology which is based on taking the file system tree to be a family tree. Thus a directory within a directory is said to be a *child*, and similarly the child looks on the directory above it as its *parent*. Hence in our example **model** is a child of the home directory, and the home directory is the parent of **model**. (Each child has only one parent, so the UNIX view is actually of a family tree of a uni-sexual species.)

THE OVERALL TREE

We have now covered one of the requirements of a file system stated at the end of Chapter 3: providing a structure that helps you manage your files. It is time to move on to two other requirements: accessing other files and catering for removable files. Both of these are satisfied by an extension of the tree structure we have just described.

We have so far confined ourselves to a small part of a complete tree. Your home directory is actually a sub-directory of a larger structure, which is a *single tree representing the whole of the UNIX file system*. The root of this tree is a directory called **root** — you can, perhaps, begin to see why **root** is the login name of the superuser. The **root** directory contains a number of sub-directories, one of which is called **usr**. (UNIX liks to b concis so it oftn lavs out lttrs such as 'e'. Many of us considr this xcssiv.) The **usr** directory contains all the files created by UNIX users. The public files built into the UNIX system are in other sub-directories of **root**; one of these sub-directories is called **bin**, and contains binary versions of the UNIX programs you might want to use. UNIX file systems are often structured so that the **usr** directory consists solely of a number of sub-directories, one for each user; each sub-directory is a user's home directory and has as its name the user's login name. Thus if your login name is **you** and another person's login name is **him**, the tree will be as shown in Figure 4.2.

The advantage of this structure is that you can refer to any file in the file system, simply by giving its pathname from the **root**. To reference the file **lovepoem**, for example, the path is defined as follows

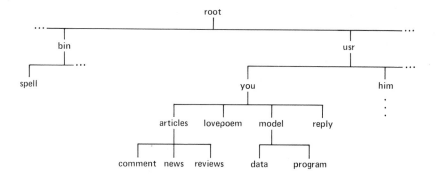

Figure 4.2 The complete directory tree

- start at the **root**
- go to the directory **usr**
- then go to directory **you**
- the file **lovepoem** is in this directory

This is written as the UNIX pathname

/usr/you/lovepoem

The '/' at the beginning is an abbreviation for **root**. This pathname could be used by you or any other user to refer to **lovepoem**, irrespective of the current directory. If **lovepoem** is in the current directory, this relatively verbose pathname is unnecessary. The name **lovepoem** suffices. Similarly, if you recall our sample UNIX session back in Chapter 1, the **jobletter798** file was in our current directory, so it was unnecessary to refer to it using a full pathname.

The overall tree structure offers the same advantages as each individual user's tree structure, but magnified. Thus it becomes easier not only to see how each user's files relate to one another, but also to see the interrelationship of all the files in the UNIX system. Directories can be kept small. There may be thousands of files in a UNIX system but the very biggest directory might only contain a hundred files. Small directories make searching for files quicker.

REMOVABLE FILES

The overall tree structure offers a further advantage: it covers the requirement to cater for removable files.

If you look at our sample tree displayed in Figure 4.2, and delete from it the directory **you** and everything below **you** (i.e. remove all your files) then the result is still a valid tree structure. The same is true of any other sub-tree of the main tree. Thus if the files within each removable unit are organized as a tree, then this sub-tree can be connected and disconnected from the main tree as units (e.g. disks) are mounted and dismounted. A complete tree on a removable unit is itself called a file system. Thus the main UNIX file system can itself contain subsidiary file systems, just as a directory can contain subsidiary directories.

To make the same point in a different way, if all your files are stored on a removable disk then the tree growing from **you** is a separate file system stored on this disk. It can be incorporated into the main file system when you log in and mount your disk.

Even if the file storage in your UNIX is all permanent it may still be split up into separate file systems. If, for example, your UNIX implementation has four permanent disks then each might be given a separate file system. The advantage of the separation is that if a tragedy befalls one disk then only one file system is lost. This is no consolation if the lost one is the main file system or the file system containing your files, but otherwise you may not be greatly inconvenienced. Taken as a whole, the total sum of the misery is less than if a disk crash had knocked the whole system out. In fact on many UNIX implementations, a single permanent disk may be divided into several file systems, in order to give still more resilience.

All this is really the concern of the superuser rather than the average user. Boundaries between subsidiary file systems are quite invisible to the normal user; the entire UNIX file space appears as a single tree. The only impact it has on the average user is that there is a restriction that you must not link (give two names to the same file) across file systems. This is such a minor restriction that many people have used UNIX for years without ever realizing that their system's permanent disk storage was divided into separate file systems.

In fact, by including the above discussion, we have probably come too much under the influence of our friend Dudley Detail. Whichever UNIX implementation you use you will soon meet Dudley. He knows all there is to know about UNIX, and even if you go to him for the simplest piece of advice, he will give you the benefit of a twenty-minute monologue about the finer points of UNIX. The only problem is that you come away not quite knowing what the answer to your simple question really was.

INTRODUCTION TO PROTECTION

We have now seen that UNIX's hierarchical file store, by itself, covers three of our requirements for a file system: providing a structure for managing your own files, allowing access to other files, and catering for permanent and removable files. Our last requirement, a protection system, requires a further mechanism and we shall now concentrate on this. Two concepts that are important in UNIX's protection system are those of an 'owner' and a 'group'.

OWNERS AND GROUPS

Every UNIX file has an *owner*. Normally the owner is represented by his login name. If you create a file you own it for life. This applies even if the file is moved into someone else's directory. If another person makes a copy of one of your files then certainly they may own the copy, but the original — the one that will fetch the high price with the antique collectors of the year 2100 — is still yours. Files that are created as part of the UNIX system, rather than by an ordinary user, are owned by **root**, the superuser; now, perhaps, you can understand her true power.

UNIX allows users to be formed into *group*s. These are normally people working together on the same project, often being groups of friends as well. UNIX is a formidable dictatorship. You do not decide who your friends are; the superuser defines your friends for you by fixing which group you belong to. Some users are loners and do not even bother to find out if they belong to a group; others derive benefit from groups by allowing members of their group to have privileges, in the form of access to files, denied to the world in general.

As well as their use in protection, groups may also be used for accounting. If groups are regarded as an important part of your UNIX implementation you may find that your home directory is not a child of the **usr** directory but is a child of a group directory that comes between **you** and **usr**.

Some UNIX users have several different login names. You may, for example, be a part-time librarian and keep the library records on the computer. In this case it would be sensible to have a separate login name, **librarian** say, for your library work, and to keep the login name **you** for the rest of your work. The advantage of this dual identity is that if somebody else subsequently takes over your library work, then he can simply take over the **librarian** login name. You just tell him the password. He then owns all the **librarian**'s files, but you still own the rest of your files. (If a computer is used by a single person, she might still have several different login names to represent different sides of her character — one of which is, of course, the superuser.) If you have several different login names these need not even be in the same group.

PERMISSIONS

The basis of the UNIX protection system is that you can attach to each file some *permissions*, which control who can do what with the file. There are three kinds of permission

- permission to read
- permission to write (i.e. to change)
- permission to execute (i.e. to use the file as a program — see below)

(A few readers may be unfamiliar with the computer jargon of reading and writing. The terms correspond closely to their normal English usage. Reading means looking at the contents of a file, and writing means altering a file in any way, i.e. creating a file, deleting it or changing its contents.)

The three kinds of permission are controlled independently, though certain combinations, such as a file that can be written but not read, are rather odd.

In addition these three kinds of permission can be applied to each of the three classes of user

- the owner
- other users in the owner's group
- users not in the owner's group — we call these users 'the rest of the world'

If a class of user does not have permission to, say, write a file then UNIX prevents such users from doing so and thus the file is protected from writing. As an example of the use of permissions to achieve protection, if you own a file you can set its permissions so that

- you can both read and write the file
- members of your group can only read it
- the rest of the world cannot even read it

Since there are three kinds of permission, and three classes of user that each permission can be applied to, there is a total of nine independent permission attributes attached to each file. (Dudley says there is a tenth one, used by UNIX system programs, and he is very willing to explain it to you in full, if you have an hour to spare.) Since a directory is an ordinary file, permission attributes can be applied to directories too.

The terminology on what we call permissions varies: some people use the term *access rights* to mean the same thing. Moreover UNIX documentation uses the word *mode* to mean the set of permissions attached to a file, but we shall try to avoid using this somewhat meaningless term. We shall use the natural terminology, also used by UNIX documentation, that *read permission* means permission to read, *write permission* means permission to write, and *execute permission* means permission to execute.

There are no rules, of course, for the ultimate dictator, the superuser. She can examine or even delete all your files whenever she likes, and your permission mechanisms are not worth the bytes they are written on.

The initial permissions, when you first create a file, are defined by the UNIX system. Often these will allow you to read and write, but all others only to read. You are, however, free to change the permissions at any time for each file you own — but not for files you do not own. If you are interested in changing the initial settings of permissions you may find this more difficult; start by looking at your local UNIX documentation under the somewhat unlikely heading of *umask*.

Execute permission is only applicable to three kinds of file
- binary versions of programs
- files of commands (see Chapter 7)
- directories. In this case the meaning of 'execute' is rather different, as we shall explain shortly.

If a file is not one of these it should never have an execute permission set. Permission to execute a file that, by its nature, cannot be executed is like permission to commit suicide (by execution?).

THE GREAT PEST

That fine book *The Small Garden* by C.E. Lucas Phillips (Pan, 1980) is full of wisdom about gardening. (The next edition will contain a special warning to computer scientists to stop them planting their trees upside down.) One of the book's most apt statements is that of all the pests that damage the garden, the most dangerous one is you yourself. The same applies to file systems. You can make elaborate arrangements to prevent others deleting your most valuable files, but the most likely person to delete them, albeit accidentally, is you yourself. Thus the protections that you can set against yourself are quite appropriate. We shall be more specific later.

Meanwhile ruminate on the sad fact that, lurking within each of us, lies a powerful and immortal Great Pest, ever ready to spring when we are off our guard.

EXAMPLES OF PROTECTION

To show how you might use UNIX's protection mechanisms we shall present two specific examples.

Example 1

You have developed a superb new chess playing program, which, whatever the quality of its human opponent, puts up a great fight but always just loses. Such a program would have millions of buyers and is certain to make your fortune. Although you are happy for people in your group to use the program you do not want anyone to steal it. What you do, therefore, is to prevent anyone other than you, the owner, from even reading the file containing your source program. However you create a second file, which contains the binary form of the program, and give your group execute permission for this binary file. You do not give them permission to read it, since otherwise they could make a copy of it.

Example 2

When you produce your best selling novel using UNIX, you put each different chapter into a separate file. (Later on we have a specific example where we do just this.) You give the rest of your group read permission for each chapter. Assuming there are young children outside the group you give the rest of the world permission to read only those chapters that do not contain torrid love scenes.

PROTECTION FOR DIRECTORIES

You notionally 'execute' a directory D when you use it to find one of the files within D. Hence if a person is to be able to get at any of these files, or any files in sub-directories of D, he must have execute permission for D. Permission to read just gives the ability to display the names of the files in D, but not to get at the files themselves. Permission to write to a directory allows someone to add new files to the directory; he can also delete any file in the directory for which he has permission to write (on some UNIX implementations he does not even need that).

The permissions attached to a directory need not be the same as the permissions for files within that directory. Thus you may allow everyone to read and execute a particular directory, but they may be prevented from looking at individual files in the directory. Indeed all the files in the directory could have permission to read denied, thus making the permission to read and execute the directory an almost empty privilege.

If you deny the rest of the world permission to execute and read your home directory, then you have a secret set of files (except, of course, to the superuser). When another user examines the UNIX file system it will appear to him that the tree is cut off at **you**, and nothing below this is apparently present. This user in turn could cut you off from his home directory so that you would not see his part of the tree. Each user therefore sees a tree that is a subset of the tree that is really there. Two different users may well see different subsets.

PROTECTION FROM YOURSELF

Some people's handwriting is so awful that it is hard to believe they can read it themselves. Nevertheless there does not seem much of a case for files that the owner cannot even read.

Many people, as a defence against the Great Pest, protect themselves from writing their own files. Assuming the files have permission to read, they are then 'read-only' files. Owners create read-only files by giving write permission to nobody, not even themselves. This works because UNIX recognizes such files as a special case. When you, as owner, try to write to such a file UNIX does not give its normal response of "No, you cannot"; instead it asks "Do you really want to write to this read-only file?" (though in reality it puts the question more tersely). If your answer is an explicit 'yes', UNIX proceeds to write. You do however have the chance to say 'no' if you got it wrong and were just about to destroy your most valued possession. We shall give an explicit example of this 'second chance' technique in Chapter 6.

RUNNING OUT OF FILE STORAGE

No-one ever wants to throw away a file. There is always some chance that it may come in useful in the future, if only to a historian interested in the primitive things people used to do with computers.

Nevertheless you will one day have to face up to deleting files, particularly if your UNIX is based mainly on permanent storage. By its very nature this is of a fixed total size. To delay the unhappy day, and to make it less unhappy when it does come, it is well worth adopting the discipline that at the end of each session you delete files that you do not really need. There will always be files of intermediate results, or early versions of documents that have subsequently been superseded, such as the first 795 job letters in Chapter 1. If you keep these files for too long and, by their very nature, do not use them, you will forget what they are. You will then be afraid to delete them in case their usage, now forgotten, is actually something vital. This may sound fanciful to you, but it happens all the time.

Even when the unhappy day comes, some UNIX implementations alleviate the heartache by providing an *archiving system*. In such a system you can preserve files on a back-up medium such as magnetic tape. Then if you really need the file after you have deleted it from the main file system it can at least be retrieved from the archive, though you may need to give an hour's or even a day's notice to do so. Some large UNIX implementations, for example, may have human operators remote from the users, who mount the archiving tapes at some set time each day. (If you read about archives in UNIX documentation, beware a double use of the term: a special UNIX convention is that 'archive' means a library of program fragments; this contrasts with the normal use of 'archive' to mean back-up copies of files.)

Magnetic tapes are cheaper than disks (though magnetic tape drives are expensive), and it really costs little to keep huge amounts of material in an archive, and to keep it for years.

CHAPTER 5

Input and the shell

Sweet Echo, sweetest nymph, that liv'st unseen
Within thy airy shell.
MILTON

The purpose of this Chapter is to explain how you type your input to UNIX, and how UNIX interprets what you have typed. We assume your input device is a keyboard, but similar principles are likely to apply to other input media, even to speech input.

KEYBOARDS

If you look at a number of different makes of computer keyboard you will find they are much the same in terms of the printable characters they offer. There may be small variations, such as a dollar-sign on one keyboard where there is a pound-sign on another, or an acute accent in place of a double-quote, but these variations are comparatively trivial. What is not trivial is the difference in *control characters*: the keys with labels such as DEL, ESC, BREAK etc. which perform a function rather than display a character. These vary greatly between keyboards. Operating systems are designed to cater for as many types of terminal as possible: they assume that certain functions will be available, but the key used to achieve a given function may vary between keyboards. You will therefore need to find out what key your particular terminal uses for some of the functions described in this Chapter.

NETWORKS

It is becoming increasingly common for computers to be connected together in networks. One advantage is that it may be possible to send electronic mail to other users all over the network; several businesses are totally based on such mail as the primary method of circulating information. On some networks you only have access to one computer, and electronic mail might be the only means of communicating with the rest of the network. On other networks there may be a variety of alternative computer systems that you can use, provided you have valid login names, and these might run different operating systems. (In some environments it is even possible to use several different operating systems *simultaneously* from the same terminal. For a beginner, though, one operating system is quite enough.)

Networks are good for users. They offer variety, and extra facilities for communication with both humans and computer files. Nevertheless they add a small extra complication to your communication with UNIX. Before logging in to UNIX you may have to identify which computer you wish to use, and indeed you may have to log in to the network first. After you have logged in you may find that the software which controls the network imposes extra rules on the control characters on your terminal. Ideally this effect should be minimal as a good network is invisible to its users.

In this book, we ignore any possible extra complications imposed by networks, but clearly if you are communicating with UNIX via a network you will need to find out about your local rules before you can even begin your acquaintance with UNIX itself.

TYPING

UNIX normally communicates with you one line at a time. There are certainly some programs that run under UNIX which take their input in *raw-mode*, i.e. one character at a time, but these are the exception rather than the rule.

Thus in general UNIX does not analyze the line you have typed until you type the RETURN key to indicate the end of the line. A beneficial consequence of this is that if you make a typing error and notice it, you can correct your error before UNIX acts on what you have typed. (Terminals are notoriously variable in what they call the RETURN key: the key could be labelled CR or NEWLINE, for example, rather than RETURN.)

There are two ways of correcting typing errors. By far the most commonly used is to erase the last character you typed. You do this by typing the key that serves the function of 'erase'. On your particular terminal it might well be the BACKSPACE key, the DEL key or the '#' character. We shall simply call it the *erase key*. You can press the erase key as many times as you like. Thus by pressing it five times you erase the last five characters you typed. You cannot, of course, erase more characters than you have typed on the current line.

If you make a real mess of typing a line you can 'kill' the line by typing another special key, the exact position of which depends on your terminal. You can then start a fresh attempt at typing the line.

As an example assume that the erase key is '#' and the kill key is '@' and consider the following input

My first thoughts@
My seconk#d thug##oughts

Here the first line was killed and UNIX automatically started a second line, to give a fresh start. In the second line the characters 'k' and 'ug' were erased. At the end of the line we assume that the RETURN key was typed to feed the line to UNIX. The overall effect is exactly as if the following single line was typed

My second thoughts

In addition to the erase and kill keys, some terminals may provide further 'local editing' facilities, such as insertion of extra characters at any desired point in the current line.

SCROLLING

If you are using UNIX from a conventional display terminal, you may have a problem when a command outputs more than a screenful of information. An example would be a command that displays a long file. It is likely that the information will be output so fast that you will not have time to read it before it vanishes off the top of the screen. There are two frequently used ways of solving this problem. On some implementations, UNIX stops at the end of the first screenful of information to give you a chance to read it. When you are ready to proceed you type a key, and the next screenful duly appears. A common rule is that the RETURN key advances one line, and any other key advances to the next screenful. This is an instance of *scrolling* — a term used because of a resemblance to unrolling a scroll.

An alternative 'solution' to the problem is to leave you to do the work. Most terminals have special control characters that cause the display to freeze and unfreeze. Typically you can freeze a display by holding down the CONTROL key and typing 's' (in a similar way to holding the SHIFT key down if you want a capital 'S'). We shall, in this book, follow the popular practice of using $\wedge x$ to mean the character x typed with the CONTROL key held down. When you type $\wedge s$ the display freezes so that you can read it before the information disappears; typing $\wedge q$ unfreezes the display so that information starts flashing by again.

Some UNIX implementations have programs called **more** or **page**, which can be used to browse through long files.

FULL-DUPLEX AND TYPE-AHEAD

Almost certainly your terminal will be connected to UNIX in a *full-duplex* manner, which means that you can talk to UNIX at the same time as it talks to you. In general, having both parties talking at the same time is no way to conduct a civilized conversation, but there are three circumstances where simultaneous talking can be valuable.

The first can be exemplified thus: you are browsing round the filing system and find that Dudley has a file called **hints**. Thinking this may contain useful advice on UNIX, and noticing that he generously allows everybody permission to read this file, you display it. Unfortunately it turns out to consist of a host of trivial detail, and, worse, it goes on and on. UNIX has displayed fifty pages and there is no sign of an end. To cater for emergencies such as this, UNIX has a *break-in key*. If you press this key — again it is a terminal-dependent key — while UNIX is talking to you it will (in general) shut up immediately and ask for the next command. You can use the break-in key to stop UNIX when it is not producing output, but silently executing a very long command; this is particularly useful when you belatedly discover you typed the wrong command in the first place. Before you start to use any operating system find out what the break-in key is on your terminal, since it can be a godsend. Indeed it is a pity that humans are not fitted with break-in keys too.

The act of breaking-in is called, in the UNIX documentation, an *interrupt*. We shall, however, continue to use the term break-in, since in the general world of computing the word interrupt has a wider meaning than a user-inspired break-in.

The second use of simultaneous talking is that you can type ahead. Thus if your current UNIX process is taking a long time, you can type further lines of input while you are waiting. These lines must anticipate what UNIX requires. Thus if you know the next thing UNIX will do is to ask a yes/no question, you can answer 'yes' before the question is asked. Similarly, if you know UNIX will next ask for a command you can type the next command you want done. You can, within reason, type ahead as far as you like. UNIX simply takes the lines you have typed when it is ready for them. Since you can type ahead even while UNIX is producing output, it can be an example of simultaneous talking. Obviously, you will only type ahead when you have become quite familiar with UNIX.

The third instance of simultaneous talking occurs when you set UNIX doing several processes at the same time. While you are talking to one process, another process might talk back to you. This can result in a confusing jumble on your display; we shall discuss in Chapter 7 how to curb such anarchy.

TERMINAL CHARACTERISTICS

We have said that the erase key, the kill key and the break-in key are dependent on your keyboard. There is a host of other *terminal characteristics* concerned with either your input device (e.g. keyboard) or your output device (e.g. display). These include size of screen, cursor movements and graphics facilities. Some UNIX implementations have a special file which describes the characteristics of each of the types of terminal attached to the system. Using this information, UNIX programs with special requirements, such as graphics, can adapt their behaviour to reflect the type of terminal they are using, so that their appearance is as uniform as possible. Sometimes, however, UNIX gets the wrong idea about a terminal and, if this happens, communication with the user is at best garbled and at worst non-existent. Solving such problems usually needs expert help.

Users do, however, have some control over their terminal's behaviour. There is a command called **stty** which can be used for such purposes as changing the erase key. We discuss this further in Chapter 13.

THE SHELL

Let us assume you have successfully mastered your terminal, have logged into UNIX, and are confidently ready to type lines of input. Having done all this it comes as something of a shock to learn that UNIX itself does not look at the lines you type. Instead UNIX is surrounded by a *shell*, which, like that of a tortoise or snail, protects it from people outside.

The shell is actually your friend. It converts the commands you type into an internal form which UNIX programs expect. As a result it offers a powerful and pleasant way of specifying your commands.

A further potential advantage of this intermediary shell is that each user can have his own shell. Your shell is just an ordinary program which translates the commands you type into UNIX's internal format. In practice, however, most users have the same shell, though some second-class UNIX citizens may be given a restricted shell that only allows a limited number of commands. We shall assume the standard shell in this book (though, to be exact, there are several different variants of this 'standard' as we shall explain in Chapter 7).

DEVICE-INDEPENDENCE

Output from UNIX normally comes to your terminal. This applies, for instance, to all the output in the example in Chapter 1, such as the list of files and the job letter. Sometimes you may want to send the output from one of your commands to a file rather than to your terminal; you can then view this file at some time in the future. For example if the **spell** program had come up with a hundred spelling errors, you might well wish to preserve the errors in a file, so that you could deal with them later — when you had a couple of hours to spare. To accomplish this you add to your command an indication to *redirect* the output to the place you want. The shell takes care of the redirection for you, and indeed the UNIX underneath knows nothing about it. A similar principle applies to redirection of input.

The way this redirection is implemented is as follows. Three notional files always exist:

- the *standard input*
- the *standard output*
- the *standard error output*

These all normally correspond to your terminal. Thus the concept of input/output to a file is generalized to include input/output to a terminal, as well as to a real file in the file system. Obviously terminal files cannot be used to store information — this must be done in real files. By default, each command takes its input from the standard input and sends its output to the standard output — hence the names. When you redirect the input or output the effect is temporarily to redefine the standard input and/or the standard output to be something other than your terminal. Redirection is usually applied to a single command, but it can be applied to a sequence of commands.

The importance of the standard error output arises when the standard output is redirected. Even if you redirect your output to a file you still want error messages (for example a message from UNIX that you have typed an incorrect command) to come to your terminal. This is why the two types of output are kept notionally separate. The standard error output is only redirected away from the terminal in unusual circumstances; doing so effectively says "Do not tell me if something goes wrong; just make a note of it somewhere".

As well as your terminal, you may have other input or output devices attached to your computer. If so, you can use the redirection mechanism to communicate with them. We shall give some precise details in Chapter 13. However, the most common such device is a printer, and communication with this is normally done through the 'spooling' mechanism that we are just about to introduce.

SPOOLING

Assume you have a printer on your UNIX system. This will usually be shared by all the other users of your system. It does not mean, however, that if another user starts printing something while you are also using the printer, then the two sets of printing are garbled together and you have to get to work with scissors cutting out the parts that are yours. UNIX prevents this problem.

Moreover UNIX does not even require you to wait until your printing is finished before you can get on with something else. Instead it copies all material to be printed to a special internal file of its own. Individual requests for printing are kept separate to remove the subsequent need for scissors. A separate process prints out the material that is in the special internal file, but the process works away in the background while the users are getting on with their ordinary work. You can even ask for a file to be printed while the printer is temporarily out-of-action. UNIX simply keeps the material to be printed in its internal file, and does the printing when the printer becomes available again.

In all cases the only delay the user at the terminal sees when he asks for printing is the time taken for UNIX to copy the requisite material to its internal file. This time is not usually even noticeable.

The mechanism UNIX uses to accomplish this magic is called *spooling* (where 'spool' stands for Simultaneous Peripheral Operation On Line, though the acronym is unlikely to leave anyone the wiser). Spooling can be applied to other input/output devices besides printers. It can also be used in the provision of facilities such as electronic mail to be sent round a network. Here spooling mirrors a Post Office that piles up mail in the sorting office for several days before doing anything about it, though hopefully UNIX delays are seconds rather than days.

PIPES

We now come to one of the finest features of UNIX. It is a feature that is valuable to both writers and users of UNIX programs. We shall start by introducing a problem that faces the program writer, and shall then go on to describe a facility that helps solve this problem. The solution has the happy property that it makes all UNIX programs easier to use, irrespective of whether they are built-in programs or programs written by users.

If you provide a program that is used by others you might expect to become some kind of hero. However in reality, far from being a hero, you are continually attacked and harassed with an insidious weapon called a *WIBNI*. WIBNIs arise because everyone knows that programs in general, and yours in particular, are flexible and can easily be changed. Thus whenever one of the users of your program comes across a feature that is lacking, or a feature whose design is not to his taste, he asks you to change your program accordingly.

To take a specific example, assume you yourself have implemented a UNIX program called **keats** which takes as input the dullest of prose and turns it into the finest of poetry. You think you have done your bit for the world by producing this magic program, but no. One user says it would be nice if lines of the poem could be numbered; another says it would be nice if the prose input could be in encrypted form (to thwart the plagiarist), while a third says it would be nice if the poems were put in a form for a typesetter. You then understand what WIBNI means: "Wouldn't It Be Nice If ... ?"

If you implemented all the WIBNIs, your **keats** program would get larger and larger, and more and more cumbersome to use. The result of such an exercise is frequently that as a program is 'improved' to provide more and more facilities it actually gets worse.

The writers of UNIX programs faced these WIBNIs, just like everyone else. However they came up with an answer that enabled them to retain their small-is-beautiful philosophy but still to fend off the WIBNIs. The answer is a *pipe*. (The word is a reference to a pipeline, rather than to the offensive weapon some people put in their mouths and drive others away by polluting the atmosphere with smoke fumes.)

Figure 5.1 illustrates a pipe containing two programs.

Figure 5.1 The form of a pipe

Here the standard output from *program1* acts as the standard input to *program2*. A UNIX user can connect any desired programs together in a pipe. (Obviously the programs must be ones that have input and/or output, in order that the pipe connections be made.) The user of **keats** can create the pipe shown in Figure 5.2.

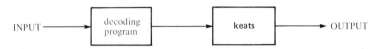

Figure 5.2 A pipe that decodes the input to **keats**

The input to this pipe is some encrypted prose. The *decoding program* converts it to ordinary prose and passes this directly to **keats**, which turns it into poetry, the final output. Thus the overall effect of the pipe is to turn encrypted prose into poetry.

UNIX designers are rightly proud of pipes, and their use pervades the whole design philosophy of UNIX programs. The philosophy can be summarized as "Do not write large and complicated programs. Instead provide small modular components, each of which does a single job and does it well." The user can then connect these modules together in any desired manner to achieve the function he requires. In our example **keats** is good at poetry but knows nothing of encryption. The decoding program has the opposite properties. Combined together in a pipe they provide good encryption together with good poetry.

Pipes can be as long as you like. UNIX has a typesetting program **troff**, which we shall describe later; unlike **keats**, which sadly is hypothetical, **troff** is a real UNIX program, as perhaps you guessed by its supremely unmemorable name. **Troff** can be added to our pipe, as shown in Figure 5.3.

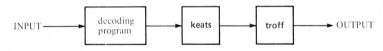

Figure 5.3 The pipe extended to typeset the output from **keats**

In this pipe the input is some encrypted prose and the final output is some poetry, presented in a form that can be fed to a typesetting machine.

If your UNIX has a program that prefixes line numbers to lines of text, this too could be added to the above pipe, thus satisfying all the WIBNIs we cited above.

Pipes are so important and so valuable in UNIX that some programs are designed mainly with a view to being a component of a pipe, rather than to be used by themselves. Such programs are known as *filters*. A typical filter would be a program to delete all blank lines from a file.

The only real limitation on pipes is that you cannot build a complicated network where several programs feed into one. Entrepreneurs will, however, be glad to know that you can go as far as building a form of T-joint in a pipe; those interested should examine their UNIX documentation for the **tee** program.

SOFTWARE TOOLS

If you are a programmer and are interested in exploring further the ideas of building programs out of small modules, then you cannot do better than to read *Software Tools* by Kernighan and Plauger (1976). (The examples in that book are expressed in the language RATFOR, an extension of FORTRAN. If you prefer the examples to be in Pascal there is an alternative form of the book: *Software Tools in Pascal*. Whichever book you read, the ideas apply to all programming languages.) The book is one of the wisest and best written books in computing. Remarkably for a book written by two people, there is a perfect uniformity of style and content. To give you a flavour of the style the following is an extract from the introduction.

"Whenever possible we will build more complicated programs up from the simpler; whenever possible we will *avoid* building at all, by finding new uses for existing tools, singly or in combinations. Our programs *work together*; their cumulative effect is much greater than you could get from a similar collection of programs that you couldn't easily connect. By the end of the book you will have been introduced to a set of tools that solve many problems you encounter as a programmer."

UNIX is an excellent base on which to implement the ideals of *Software Tools*, and indeed these very ideals permeate almost all of UNIX itself.

SUMMARY

This ends Part I of the book. We hope you are now well prepared to assimilate the practical details of UNIX that are to be described in Part II, and then to experiment with UNIX itself — knowing what you are doing.

Some people learn by reading, some learn by doing. Successful people do both. When you get deep into Part II you may wish to refer back to Part I. Above all we hope that the two Parts of the book form a complementary partnership: we hope that an understanding of the concepts — even an incomplete understanding — will help you to master practical details, and we hope that practical experience will help clarify concepts.

PART II

APPLYING THE IDEAS

CHAPTER 6

A sample session

When I play with my **cat**, who knows whether I make her more
sport than she makes me?
MONTAIGNE

We begin this Part of the book by following through a sample UNIX session. You can take two alternative approaches to such sample sessions. The first is simply to read them just like the other parts of the book. The second is to log in to your UNIX implementation — assuming one is available to you — and follow the sample sessions through, perhaps making a few variations of your own. The first approach is probably better, but it is a matter of personal taste. Whichever approach you take, it is important at some stage to have a comprehensive 'getting to know you' session with your UNIX — explore its tree, experiment with its protection mechanism and try out its commands. The only question is whether there is merit in following a sample script or whether it is better to give rein to your own imagination.

Remember that UNIXes vary, though the principles are much the same. Thus some of the details of our examples may be different on your implementation. This particularly applies to the format of information output by UNIX. Even the prompt that UNIX displays when it is ready for a command may, on your UNIX, be a '%' sign rather than a '$' sign.

Our sample sessions show what should appear at a terminal. We follow the convention of Chapter 1: material typed by the user is in **bold face** to distinguish it from material output by UNIX. (Do not worry if you have forgotten all the details of the brief example in Chapter 1; we start again from scratch here.) The way we follow through a session is to show an episode consisting of a few commands and then to give a verbal explanation of what happened in the episode. We then go on to the next episode. The point of resumption is indicated by a line of form

> *directory name*

The *directory name* is the name of your current directory, and is included to remind you where the previous episode left off. If at any stage you want to remind yourself of the nature of a particular command, or to find out more about it, consult Appendix B.

You start by logging in. UNIX will display the prompt 'login:'. To get this prompt it may be necessary first to wake your terminal up to your presence. Do this by hitting it, just as you would wake up a person. For a terminal you hit it on the keyboard. The keys to hit vary between systems, but repeated pressing of the space, BREAK or RETURN keys jolt many systems from their slumbers.

Before proceeding any further, check that your terminal is set for lower case typing — we certainly hope you have not got an upper-case-only terminal. Thus make sure that keys such as SHIFT LOCK or ALPHA LOCK are not set. UNIX is a fanatical devotee of lower case typing; all its commands and other built-in filenames are (almost) exclusively made up of lower case letters. To start with, it is best to go along with UNIX's fanaticism; later on you can perhaps use the odd upper case letter in a filename. The *contents* of your files can, of course, be in upper or lower case according to your aesthetics. If you type your login name in upper case, UNIX assumes you are a lost soul with an upper-case-only terminal, and thereafter expects you to type everything in upper case.

You log in by typing your login name and password. When you type these lines, as with every other line of input to UNIX, do not forget to type the

RETURN key at the end. In fact as a general rule if your UNIX appears to go dead, then a likely cause is that it is still waiting for you to type the RETURN.

Our log in proceeds as follows

```
login: me
Password: cleverme
```

The password will not, we hope, actually be displayed on the screen.

On logging in, we may get some messages and/or some mail. A common message is one requesting everyone to delete some of their files because the permanent disk space is nearly full. There may be a threat that if people do not delete their own files, the superuser will do it for them. In our case we do not have any files yet, so we can, for once, laugh at the superuser's threats.

UNIX will then display its *command prompt*, asking you to type a command. In our sample session the command prompt is '$'.

Brian Kernighan (1978) has written an excellent introductory tutorial entitled *UNIX for beginners*. In this the user starts by asking UNIX what the date is, and, apparently satisfied, gets involved in writing a book. Since Kernighan's paper, almost every UNIX tutorial session has started with the user asking for the date, and later going on to his book. We shall continue this fine tradition.

Our first action, therefore, is to use the **date** command. We then ask for a listing of all the files in the current directory by using the **ls** command. (The name **ls** means List Sorted — the names are sorted into alphabetical order.) The current directory when we log in is our home directory, which has no files in it since we have not used UNIX before. We assume the name of our home directory is **/usr/me**.

```
/usr/me
```

```
$ date
Fri Nov   11 15:16:49 GMT  1983
$ ls
$
```

You can see that the **date** command, as a bonus, displays the time as well as the date. The time is normally the local time; in our case it is Greenwich Mean Time, as represented by the GMT.

A REVELATION

Notice how, in reply to our **ls** command, UNIX says nothing at all. Our current directory is empty, so the contents is null. UNIX does not say "Your current directory is empty, so I have nothing to list"; instead it simply lists nothing, since that is exactly what we asked for.

It can now be revealed for the first time that there was a third person, in addition to Thompson and Ritchie, who was responsible for the original design of UNIX. He is a hermit who does his very best to avoid human conversation. Because he shuns publicity his contribution to UNIX has been overlooked, but it was he who designed nearly all the parts of UNIX that interface with the user.

This hermit prefers to be known (if he has to be known at all) by the name *hrmt*. The silent response to **ls** is typical of hrmt's work, as is the very name **ls** — though hrmt would have preferred the command to have a one-character name rather than its outrageously long two-character name; his view was unfortunately overruled.

FORMAT OF COMMANDS

The general form of a UNIX command consists of the command name optionally followed by a list of one or more *arguments*. Each argument is a string of characters preceded by a space (or by several spaces and/or tabs if you really want to make the command look a long one). An example of a command with one argument is

> **ed jobletter798**

Here the argument, **jobletter798**, specifies which file is to be edited by the **ed** program. The only commands used so far in this Chapter, **date** and **ls**, were not given any arguments, but we shall soon show some examples of commands that are. In the UNIX documentation arguments are often referred to as *word*s.

In order to force UNIX to say something when we next use **ls**, we shall create some files. This can be done with the **cat** command. In order that you can have fun with **cat**, rather than vice-versa, we shall devote some time to explaining it in detail — thus making you the master.

The **cat** command is a fine example of the economy of UNIX in covering a wide range of functions with a single command. It is also an example of hrmt's sense of economy in names: **cat** stands for 'concatenate' (i.e. join together). The **cat** command, therefore, can be used to join a lot of files together. It copies each of these files to the standard output, leaving the original files intact. As we have said earlier, the standard output corresponds to the terminal, unless it is redirected elsewhere.

Cat can be used to concatenate a single file; the output is then a copy of this file. Hence **cat** can be used as a command to copy a file. The name of the file to be 'concatenated' is supplied as an argument to **cat**. For example

> **cat x**

copies the file **x** to the terminal, i.e. displays it. Thus the general command to concatenate files also serves to display a single file — indeed this is its most frequent usage.

The generalization of **cat** is carried one stage further. If you do not specify any file at all to be concatenated, i.e. just type

> **cat**

then UNIX takes this null specification to mean that the 'file' is to be taken from the standard input, again the terminal. The result is that this minimal form of **cat** takes lines of input from the terminal, and copies them back to the terminal. (It is a quirk of **cat** that in this case it does not produce the output until it has had a reasonable gulp of the input. Thus it does not echo each line as it is typed.)

To summarize the behaviour of **cat**:

(1) **cat** on its own simply copies back what is typed on the terminal
(2) **cat** of a single file copies that file
(3) **cat** of several files makes a copy consisting of all the files concatenated
(4) by default the output goes to the terminal but you can redirect it to a file.

In our sample session we shall start by exploring case (1) — not a very useful facility but it lays the groundwork. In order that we do not go on typing forever we need a way of indicating when our input is finished. (We could use the break-in key, but this should be reserved for an emergency stop rather than a planned one.) In UNIX you indicate the end of input by typing ∧ **d** (the letter 'd' with the CONTROL key held down).

/usr/me

```
$ cat
I hate parrots
I am not talking to you any more
∧ d
I hate parrots
I am not talking to you any more
$
```

Usually the ∧ **d** is not echoed on the display screen, though certain UNIX systems display something like '(EOF)' — meaning End of File — in its place.

Look at the second, third and fourth lines of the above episode. You will see that UNIX gave no prompt at all for these lines, which were the input to **cat**. This silence is the normal practice of UNIX when it is asking for data from the standard input, but it can be disconcerting to beginners.

Now let us do something more useful by redirecting the output from **cat** to a file. We do this by writing the '>' sign followed (without the need for spaces in between) by the name of the file we want to create.

/usr/me

```
$ cat >scores
Southampton          9     Tottenham            0
Unikent Computing    6     Rest of the world    1
∧ d
$ cat scores
Southampton          9     Tottenham            0
Unikent Computing    6     Rest of the world    1
$
```

Here our first use of **cat** is still case (1) but with the output redirected to the file **scores**. The second use of **cat** is case (2); it displays the file **scores** that we have just created.

We shall now create a second file, the start of the best-selling thriller we are writing.

/usr/me

```
$ cat >bestseller
Greg Daimler entered the room. There were seven bodies on
the floor. He coughed. A body fell from the top of the
bookcase. He looked up. He saw ten more bodies stuck to
the ceiling.
^d
$
```

Our apologies for stopping this just as you were becoming riveted to the story, but you cannot expect to get two books for the price of one.

If we now type **ls** it will have something to tell us.

/usr/me

```
$ ls
bestseller        scores
$
```

On your UNIX the format of the listing of filenames might be different from the above. In particular each filename within the directory may be displayed on a line by itself, e.g.

```
$ ls
bestseller
scores
$
```

Once files are created, then, unless you explicitly delete them, they will last until the dying day of your UNIX system — or at least they should do. In particular if you now logged out, and logged in again a month or even a year later then an **ls** should still give the above result.

Before proceeding to further matters, we shall finish our exploration of **cat** by giving it the rare pleasure of actually doing some concatenating.

/usr/me

```
$ cat scores bestseller
Southampton        9      Tottenham          0
Unikent Computing  6      Rest of the world  1
Greg Daimler entered the room. There were seven bodies on
the floor. He coughed. A body fell from the top of the
bookcase. He looked up. He saw ten more bodies stuck to
the ceiling.
$
```

OPTIONS

When we have used the **ls** command we have not given it any arguments. It can, however, have arguments. In particular the argument −**l** means that you want a 'long' listing of the files in the directory. An argument that begins with a minus sign is called an *option*. Options cause a command to act differently from normal; we discuss this further later in this Chapter. For the **ls** command the 'long' option gives you extra information about each file in the directory.

```
/usr/me
```

```
$ ls  −l
total 2
−rw−r− −r− −      1 me      182 Nov 11 15:25 bestseller
−rw−r− −r− −      1 me      076 Nov 11 15:22 scores
$
```

As you can see, there is a lot of information here. The first line output by **ls** gives the total number of storage units (they are called *blocks*) occupied by our files. Since our files are small, each occupies one block and so the total is two. The remaining lines of the listing give details about each of the files **bestseller** and **scores**. We shall explain the former.

The line about **bestseller** starts with the ten-character string

```
−rw−r− −r− −
```

This tells you the permissions for **bestseller**. Within this string the minus sign effectively represents 'no'. The first character of the string has a special meaning: here a **d** says the file is a directory. Since neither of our files is a directory, they both have a minus sign for the first character. The remaining nine characters are divided into threes. The first three give the permissions for the owner of the file.

r   means allowed to read
w   means allowed to write
x   means allowed to execute

Thus we can read and write **bestseller**, but not execute it. (It would be ludicrous to execute it as it is not an executable file.) The next three characters, an **r** followed by two minus signs, give the permissions for members of our group, and the last three characters, also an **r** followed by two minus signs, give the permissions for everyone else. A complete analysis of the ten-character string is therefore

−	not a directory
r	owner can read
w	owner can write
−	owner cannot execute
r	other members of the owner's group can read
−	other members of the owner's group cannot write
−	other members of the owner's group cannot execute
r	non-members of the owner's group can read
−	non-members of the owner's group cannot write
−	non-members of the owner's group cannot execute

These permissions, the initial ones set when the file is created, are fixed by UNIX itself. Your UNIX may be different from ours but the above permissions are reasonable, though perhaps over-protective.

The next piece of information about **bestseller** is the number '1'. This is the 'number of links' — a concept we explain more fully later in this Chapter; broadly speaking it means the number of filenames that are synonymous with this one. Since **bestseller** is stand-alone, like most files are, the number of links is 1.

After the '1' comes the owner of the file. Since we created the file, we are the proud owner. It is possible to have in your directory files that are owned by other people and are, as it were, on loan to you.

After the owner comes the size of the file in characters. You can verify the figure 182 by counting the characters yourself — do not forget the newline character on the end of each line.

The last field in the listing is the time at which the file was last changed. This is called a *datestamp*.

"In addition to −l, there are seventeen other alternative options to the **ls** command on my UNIX," said Dudley. "If you are interested in the i-numbers of your files, you can ... ."

EXPLORING THE TREE

The **ls** command can be used to look at directories other than the current one. You do this by supplying the directory name as an argument; if no directory name is supplied as an argument, as in our previous use of **ls**, the current directory is assumed. The directory at the very top of the tree, the **root** directory, is known by the very simple name of '/'.

```
/usr/me
```

```
$ ls /
bin      dev      etc      lib      mbox      usr
$
```

This lists the names of the files in the **root** directory. (Remember two points: firstly each argument must be preceded by a space, so there must be a space between the above **ls** and the '/' which follows it; secondly, the contents of the root directory will vary among UNIX systems so what you see on your UNIX may differ in detail from the above.)

RELATION OF OPTIONS TO OTHER ARGUMENTS

We have seen there are two possible kinds of argument to the **ls** command

ls −l	gives a long listing
ls *directory name*	lists a different directory from the current one

In general there might be ambiguity between these two kinds of argument and UNIX may not be able to tell whether a given argument represents a directory name or not. UNIX resolves this ambiguity by its rule that arguments which represent options must start with a minus sign. Thus −l specifies the 'long listing' option. We recommended earlier that you constructed your filenames out of letters and digits. Doubtless you will break this rule sometimes, but whatever you do, do not start a filename with a minus sign. If you had a directory called −l, it would be indistinguishable from the option −l.

Among the other options for **ls** alluded to by Dudley are

a   list all the files in the directory — this includes some normally hidden files used by UNIX itself

r   reverse the order of the listing

You can write a sequence of these letters in your list of options, e.g. −**alr** would ask for all the three options we have mentioned. (The order in which you write the sequence is immaterial; hence −**ral** is the same as −**lar**.)

In general, arguments that represent options are written before those that do not.

The use of options is illustrated below.

```
/usr/me

$ ls −lr
total 2
−rw−r−−r−−    1 me     076 Nov 11 15:22 scores
−rw−r−−r−−    1 me     182 Nov 11 15:25 bestseller
$ ls −r /
usr     mbox    lib     etc     dev     bin
$
```

CHANGING PERMISSIONS

It is simple to change the permissions on files. Let us assume we want to make our file **scores** readable and writable by members of our group, but completely inaccessible to everyone else. We do this with the **chmod** command. **Chmod** has two (or more) arguments: the first consists of a sequence of digits; the remaining arguments are the filename(s) to which the new permissions are to apply. The three digits in the first argument correspond to the three types of user:

the first digit describes the owner
the second digit describes the group
the third digit describes the rest

Each digit is constructed by adding together the numbers

4 for read permission
2 for write permission
1 for execute permission

Thus if the first digit is 6 this means the owner has read and write permission.

```
/usr/me
```

```
$ chmod 660 scores
$ ls −l
total 2
−rw −r − − r − −   1 me        182 Nov 11 15:25 bestseller
−rw −rw − − − −   1 me        076 Nov 11 15:22 scores
$
```

You can see how the permissions for **scores** have been changed.

You may find the numerical argument to **chmod** a bit baffling. If so consult your UNIX documentation and you will see there is an alternative way of writing this argument. It may however be arguable whether the notation is any better than the horrible numeric one. The only merit of understanding the numeric one is that the numbers may appear in certain UNIX error messages.

MAKING A DIRECTORY

There is something wrong with our novel: not, of course, in the text, but in the way we have organized the files.

Since the novel itself will eventually be a long file it is much better to plan to split it up into separate files. A chapter is a natural unit. We will work on one chapter at a time, and will want to apply operations such as printing and spelling checking to each individual chapter we finish, rather than to the current text of the whole novel. Thus we shall put each chapter in a separate file.

Given that the novel will consist of many different files it is highly desirable to create a separate directory for these files, rather than to mix them up with all our other files. This is done by the **mkdir** command. The argument to **mkdir** is the name of the new directory you want.

```
┌──────────┐
│ /usr/me  │
└──────────┘

$ mkdir novel
$ ls −l
total 3
−rw −r − − r − −   1 me        182 Nov 11 15:25 bestseller
drwx r − x r − x   2 me        032 Nov 11 15:39 novel
−rw −r w − − − −   1 me        076 Nov 11 15:22 scores
$
```

Notice how, in the listing of files, the line for **novel** has a **d** at the start, showing that it is a directory. Its permissions allow everyone to execute it, as shown by the three occurrences of **x**. Remember that executing a directory means using it to access a file within that directory. A useful way of remembering this is that the letter 'x' represents eXecute permission or, for a directory, permission to aXess files within that directory. Directories are useless without execute permission, and thus **mkdir** automatically gives execute permissions to every directory it creates.

(You may also have noticed that the 'number of links' field for the directory is given as 2. You need not be greatly concerned with this. Dudley will tell you that the 'number of links' field for a directory has a value two more than the number of sub-directories in that directory; as **novel** has no such sub-directories — indeed at the moment it is totally empty — its number of links is two.)

Although we have just created a new directory, our current directory has not changed. The current directory is still our home directory, where we have been since we logged in. We can display the pathname of our current directory by using the **pwd** command — this is hrmt's term for Print Working (i.e. current) Directory. To change our current directory we use the command **cd**, and supply as its argument the name of the new current directory we want to use.

```
/usr/me
```

```
$ pwd
/usr/me
$ cd novel
$ pwd
/usr/me/novel
$ cat  >introduction
Any resemblance between the characters in this book and
real people is entirely coincidental. I would like to
thank my wife Heather for proof deading the manuscipt.
∧d
$ ls
introduction
$ spell introduction
manuscipt
$
```

Here we have used **pwd** twice in order to illustrate the change in our current directory from our home directory to its **novel** sub-directory. Having changed our current directory to **novel** we created a file within it, called **introduction**. When we used **ls** we were shown the state of this directory. Finally we applied the oft-mentioned **spell** program to our new file. It output the one word 'manuscipt' that it thought (rightly) was a spelling error. It did not object to 'deading' — which shows how foolish it is to put too much faith in spelling correction programs.

The tree structure of our part of the file system is now as follows.

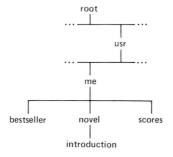

Figure 6.1 The tree structure associated with **me**

59

Now that we have re-organized our file structure we can move our file **bestseller** into the new directory **novel,** and rename it **chapter1.** To do this we need to widen our horizons, since the file **bestseller** is outside our current directory, **novel.**

PATHNAMES

We have already explained that the pathname is the mechanism that you can use to refer to any file in the file system. The pathname for our **bestseller** file is

/usr/me/bestseller

This works irrespective of our current directory. The path starts from the **root,** which is signified by the '/' on the front. As a particular example of this notation a pathname consisting of the one character '/' represents the root directory, and that is why earlier in the sample session

ls /

gave a listing of the root directory.

Pathnames starting at the root can, within large file systems, become very verbose, so UNIX offers a second way of specifying pathnames. This is to start from your current directory instead of from the root. If you do not put a '/' on the front of a pathname it means that this second form is to apply. The following table shows some examples of pathnames to your **introduction** file, assuming various different directories are your current directory. Do not forget you can change your current directory to any directory in the entire file system (provided, as always, that the permissions allow you to reach it). Similarly other users can set any of your directories as their current directory.

Current directory	*Pathname for* **introduction**
novel	**introduction**
me	**novel/introduction**
usr	**me/novel/introduction**
root	**usr/me/novel/introduction**

All these examples go down the tree (i.e. away from the root) from the current directory to a file. However when we left our sample session our current directory was **novel**, and we wanted to refer to the file **bestseller** which is up the tree from our current directory.

This can be done using a special extra name UNIX provides in each directory it creates: this is the name '..' and it refers to the parent (i.e. the directory) above the current one. Thus when our current directory is **novel** we can refer to **bestseller** as

../bestseller

This is shorter and more convenient than using a pathname starting from the root.

You can extend this '..' notation, though not, as you might expect, by writing more than two dots. If you want to go up two levels, i.e. to refer to a file in the **usr** directory, you can refer to it as

../..lfilename

As an example, the fatuous pathname

../../me/novel/introduction

would be identical to saying **introduction**, since you go up two levels and then come back down to your current directory again.

Everywhere in UNIX where you write a filename as argument, e.g. when using the **cat** command, you can specify a pathname instead. Thus all the UNIX commands that work with files can work with any file that you can access in the entire file system.

MOVING FILES

The **mv** command will move a file from one place to another. It is *not* equivalent to copying a file since the original instance is destroyed; it is more like renaming a file. (To be exact, an **mv** is equivalent to renaming a file unless the new name is in a different file system from the old — in which rare case a new copy of the file is made.) The first argument to **mv** is the existing filename and the second is the new filename. We can use **mv** to get **bestseller** into our current directory, **novel**.

```
/usr/me/novel
```

```
$ mv ../bestseller chapter1
$ ls  −l
total 2
−rw−r−−r−−     1 me       182 Nov 11 15:25 chapter1
−rw−r−−r−−     1 me       165 Nov 11 15:41 introduction
$ ls ..
novel    scores
$
```

The permissions remain unchanged when a file is moved. Notice our second **ls** above. This gives a listing of our home directory, as '..' means the parent of our current directory. You can see that **bestseller** has gone from this directory.

COPYING FILES

The command **cp** is like **mv** except that it actually makes a copy. (You can often do the same thing using the **cat** command, but **cp** can be more convenient.) Thus if our friend **aper** wants to make a copy of our introduction in his home directory he can say

cp ../me/novel/introduction beginning

He now has a file **beginning** which is an independent copy of our **introduction**.

Just as you can read files outside your current directory you can also write them. Thus we can create a file **morescores** in our home directory by

```
/usr/me/novel
```

```
$ cat >../morescores
Somerset   650 (Botchards 310)
Kent   246 (Tavaré 61)
∧d
$
```

DELETING FILES

In our session so far we have been steadily creating files, starting from nothing. It is now time to talk about destroying them.

There are two ways of destroying the contents of a file. One is to write some other material on top of the previous contents; in this case the file itself still exists but its contents have changed. The other is to delete the file altogether so that its name no longer appears in the directory. In both cases the original contents of the file are lost forever.

UNIX commands vary in their attitude to writing to a file that already exists. UNIX implementations vary too, and there can be further variations depending on individual user's profiles (see later). On our system, for example, if you **cp** to an existing file, the previous contents are overwritten without ceremony. On the other hand, if you redirect output to an existing file (say when using **cat**) then UNIX refuses to overwrite the file. You have to delete the file explicitly first. Commands that share **cp**'s attitude are an encouragement to the Great Pest. If you write to what you think is a new filename, and you have inadvertently chosen a new name that corresponds to an existing file, then the contents of the original file are lost.

The way to delete a file completely is to use the **rm** command, supplying as arguments the names of the file(s) you want to delete. In any usage of the computer you will continually be creating new files. If you do not regularly delete files you are in an unstable, continually expanding, state and you will inevitably crash against some size limitation. In any stable UNIX system the total user population must be deleting files as often as they create them.

We shall therefore be public-spirited and delete our **morescores** file. (Before it goes we should explain that it represents scores in a golf competition; no reader would surely be foolish enough to think that a cricket match would finish with Kent losing so heavily.)

/usr/me/novel

```
$ ls ..
morescores       novel            scores
$ rm ../morescores
$ ls ..
novel   scores
$
```

You can see that after the **rm** the file **morescores** has gone. You can also see that, although our current directory is **novel**, we can still quite freely work with files in another directory; in this case we work in the parent directory by using the '..' notation.

At this point our spies tell us that **aper** has taken a copy of our **introduction** file and called it **beginning**. We decide to delete this copy. To do this we can change our current directory to his home directory, find out what is there, and delete the copy of our introduction.

```
/usr/me/novel
```

```
$ cd /usr/aper
$ ls −l
total 3
−r w −r w −r w −   1 aper      165 Nov  11 15:18 beginning
−r w x r − −r − −   1 aper      343 Aug  13 12:18 end
−r w x r − −r − −   1 aper      377 Oct  30 17:58 middle
$ rm beginning
rm: /usr/aper/beginning  not  removed
$
```

When we used **rm**, UNIX replied with an error message, telling us that our attack had been repulsed. The defensive weapon that **aper** must have used was to deny us write permission on his directory; you need to change the directory when you delete a file, so our attempted deletion was not accepted. Notice how UNIX uses the full pathname when it refers to a file in an error message.

We are not, however, totally defeated. **Aper** has persuaded a friend to help him improve our introduction, and to allow this friend to work on the **beginning** file, he has set its permissions so that everyone can write to it. We can exploit this loop hole. Given that we have write permission for **beginning**, we can copy anything we like on top of its previous contents.

```
/usr/aper
```

```
$ cp /usr/me/scores beginning
$ cat beginning
Southampton          9      Tottenham           0
Unikent  Computing   6      Rest  of  the  world  1
$
```

We have therefore destroyed the contents of **beginning** by writing **scores** on top of it. We can now withdraw from our successful foray.

```
/usr/aper
```

```
$ cd /usr/me
$
```

We are now back in our home directory. (We could have achieved the same effect by simply typing

cd

on its own. If you do not give **cd** an argument, this is taken to mean that you want to return to your home directory.)

Although directories are files, you cannot use **rm** to remove a directory (unless you use a special option). Instead you use the command **rmdir**. The directory must be empty before you delete it.

Before finishing our discussion of **rm** we must re-emphasize our previous warning: when you delete a file it is lost forever, so beware. It would be the meanest of practical jokes to tell a beginner to UNIX that **rm** stood for **re**ally **m**andatory, and was a way of telling UNIX to treat a file with the utmost care.

LINKING

Let us assume that another author, **dickens**, having seen the excellence of our novel, wants us to help with his work. In particular he wants us to co-author **chapter5** within his book, **olvrtwst**, a new novel written in the UNIX style. The rule we agree is that both co-authors can write to the **chapter5** file within his **olvrtwst** directory, so he gives us (as a member of his group) write permission.

We can reference his **chapter5** file using a pathname. This however, is somewhat long-winded and if we are going to access his file a lot it is more convenient to have a synonym facility. To accomplish this we use UNIX's linking mechanism. It is possible to link any number of filenames, perhaps belonging to separate users, to the same actual file; in this case all the filenames are synonyms.

We decide to use the name **withdickens** as the synonym for **chapter5** of the **dickens** novel. To accomplish the linking we use the **ln** command.

```
┌──────────┐
│ /usr/me  │
└──────────┘
$ ln /usr/dickens/olvrtwst/chapter5  withdickens
$ ls −l
total 12
d r w x r − x r − x   2 me          64 Nov 11 16:04 novel
− r w − r w − − − −   1 me          76 Nov 11 15:22 scores
− r w − r w − − − −   2 dickens   4766 Aug 25 13:33 withdickens
$
```

Notice how the total blocks of file storage is now 12. This is because **withdickens** is a relatively long file (4766 bytes) and takes ten 512-byte blocks on our UNIX.

The entry for **withdickens** in the listing shows a number of interesting properties. Firstly the owner of the file is **dickens**, not ourselves, and the permissions are controlled by him; he has given write permission to his group, so we are all right. Secondly the number of links is now given as two. (All people linked to a file see it in the same way — indeed there is only one file to see. Thus if **dickens** did a **ls** he would see an identical line to our line for **withdickens**, except that he would see the name as **chapter5**.)

The 'number of links' field provides a further advantage of linking, which makes it better than a straight synonym facility. It is a means of preventing one of the sharers of the file deleting it and thus upsetting the others. What **rm** does is, in fact, not to delete a file but to *unlink* it, i.e. to do the opposite of linking. Only if, after this unlinking, the number of links has became zero does the file disappear.

Thus assume that **dickens**, either deliberately in a fit of depression, or inadvertently as a result of the Great Pest within him, deletes his **chapter5**. We do not lose our **withdickens** file. The only change in it that we may notice is that its number of links is down to one. Thus files that we link to can be regarded exactly like any of our other files. (The only proviso is that if you do not own a file you cannot change its permissions. In this example if we want the permissions changed we will have to persuade **dickens**, who still owns the file even though he has deleted it, to link to it again and make the change; alternatively we can copy the file in such a way that we own the copy.)

There are two restrictions on linking. Firstly, although in most of UNIX a directory is treated as an ordinary file, you cannot link to a directory. Thus we could not have created a link to **olvrtwst**. Secondly you cannot link to a file in a separate file system. ("It is all connected with i-numbers, which are ... ", said Dudley.)

SIMULTANEOUS WRITING

In UNIX you can read a file that someone else is simultaneously writing. This happens quite naturally with directories. For example you can at any time read the **usr** directory and it may happen that while you are reading it a new user is being added to the directory. UNIX takes care of this without any fuss. At some point during the reading of a file that is being written to by someone else you will switch from the old version to the new version. In most cases the switch will not be noticeable to you, unless the writer has changed the files radically, such as replacing soccer scores by a John Milton poem.

It is also possible to have several people simultaneously writing to a file. However in our **withdickens** example it would be desirable to have some informal agreement with **dickens** to prevent anarchy.

COMBATING THE GREAT PEST

We shall finish the sample session by illustrating two features that were discussed when we introduced files in Chapters 3 and 4. The first is the displaying of binary files. If we now typed

cat novel

we would get a peculiar output on our terminal. This is because **novel** is a directory file and is in fact a mixture of character information (the filenames) and binary information about each file. The resultant output, which we have not shown above because it varies so much between terminals, would be a mixture of file names and random characters — a puzzling concoction if we had not realized what we had done.

The second, and more important, matter to be illustrated is the way we deny ourselves write permission on our own files.

```
/usr/me
```

```
$ cd novel
$ chmod 440 introduction
$ ls −l
total 2
−r w −r − − r − −      1 me      182 Nov 11 15:25 chapter1
−r − −r − − − − −      1 me      165 Nov 11 15:41 introduction
$
```

You can see that neither we nor anyone else now has write permission for **introduction**. If we really do need to write to **introduction** we can change its permissions to allow writing again, but the current permissions prevent accidents.

Suddenly the Great Pest appears and tries to overwrite, and then to **rm** our **introduction**.

> **/usr/me/novel**

```
$ cp ../scores introduction
cp: cannot create /usr/me/novel/introduction
$ rm introduction
rm: override protection 440 for introduction? n
$ ls
chapter1          introduction
$
```

UNIX did not allow the Great Pest to **cp** on top of our existing file. When he tried the **rm** UNIX gave us a second chance, and our better self took control and typed **n** for no deletion. The Great Pest has been thwarted, as you can see from the above listing, which shows **introduction** to be still in existence.

Happy with our triumph, we log out.

> **/usr/me/novel**

```
$ ∧d
$
```

The use of ∧d to log out is sometimes a nuisance: you may type it accidentally, believing that you need to terminate some data. Thus some UNIX implementations instead provide explicit commands to log out, e.g. **logout**.

It is important to log out before leaving your terminal. If you do not

- you may still be charged for the time you are 'using' the system
- anyone else who takes over your terminal does not need to log in. The terminal is logged in for you, and he can thus delete all your files.

If you are using UNIX over a phone line, hanging up the phone may count as logging out.

Finally, some UNIX implementations have a *time-out* mechanism. If your terminal is inactive for, say, fifteen minutes you are assumed to have dropped off to sleep and are logged out.

CHAPTER 7

Commands and the shell

I have accidentally deleted all my ∗ files.
ANGUISHED CRY

In Chapter 5 we introduced the idea of the 'shell' which comes between you and the UNIX programs that you use. In the sample session in the previous Chapter, the existence of the shell was barely evident. Commands were typed and some action was performed. We did not care whether this was done by the shell itself or by other UNIX programs to which it passed control; our concern was that our commands were performed, not with who was responsible. As it happens, the main contribution of the shell to our sample session was to redirect the output on a few of our commands; otherwise we did not exploit its talents.

In this Chapter we consider some further features of the shell, and here it does help to consider the shell as a separate entity.

Before we proceed further, however, we shall introduce one more UNIX command, **grep**, which has a particularly happy symbiotic relationship with the shell. The command

> **grep** *pattern* *file*

displays all the lines of the *file* which match the given *pattern*. Often the pattern is a single word, e.g.

> **grep Daimler chapter1**

displays all the lines of **chapter1** that contain the word **Daimler**. The **grep** command is useful in itself but, coupled with some extra features of the shell, it is a real winner.

STYLE

It is easier to understand the shell if you appreciate the style which pervades UNIX commands.

Every language for communicating with computers imposes a style upon the user. If you are familiar with the programming languages BASIC and Pascal, you will know that each has a very distinct style. If you were shown a single statement from a program, even if you were totally unfamiliar with that kind of statement, you could immediately say whether that statement was in BASIC or Pascal.

Similarly UNIX encourages a certain style for writing commands. The advantages of a style are two-fold:

- *easy learning*. Once you know the style, you can usually guess how to use each command. You do not keep having to refer to documentation.
- *use of tools*. If all commands follow a similar style, there can be automatic tools for helping to write commands. Such tools provide positive feed-back. If the tools are good, then this provides further encouragement to conform to the style; the more the style is adopted the more easy it is to provide further good tools.

Any language for communicating with computers encompasses both of the following

- *syntax:* the grammatical rules on what you can write in the language
- *semantics:* what the language means, i.e. what actions the computer is made to perform

The style for UNIX commands covers both their syntax and some aspects of their semantics.

A command that epitomizes the UNIX style is our favourite **spell** command. Its full syntax is

spell *options filename1 filename2 ... filenameN*

Thus the name **spell** is immediately followed by some *options* — these, as the name strongly implies, are optional. After this comes a list of N filenames. The **spell** command is applied to each of these files in turn. If N is zero, i.e. there are no file names, then the convention is that input is taken from the terminal. We could thus type

---

any directory

```
$ spell
Try some words
harrass harass
grumpy grumpey
precede preseed
∧d
grumpey
grumpy
harrass
$
```

Here we typed input directly to **spell** in order to find out how to spell 'harass', 'grumpy' and 'precede'. We deliberately chose these examples to reinforce a warning we made earlier: use **spell** as an aid, but do not trust it too far. **Spell** works by looking up words in a built-in dictionary. There are gaps in this dictionary: perhaps in order to emphasize what a happy friendly family UNIX users are, the word 'grumpy' was not even in the dictionary in our UNIX, and so **spell** thought it was a spelling error. **Spell** also tries to match words by applying common prefixes and suffixes like dis-, pre-, iso-, -ing, and -ation. It will sometimes accept nonsense words as correct if they are built using these prefixes and/or suffixes. For example our **spell** accepted 'preseed', because it is the word 'seed' with the prefix 'pre-' applied.

Returning from this digression, you may have noticed that the style of writing a list of filenames as arguments to **spell** follows an identical pattern to the style of the **cat** command, which we used during the sample session in the previous Chapter. This is no accident, and indeed helps to confirm the uniformity of the style. It was the very reason we explored **cat** at some length. In fact we would have chosen **cat** as our example here except that (at least on some UNIX implementations) it is atypical in that it has no *options*.

OPTIONS

We explored options when we covered the **ls** command. The typical UNIX command has about three options, each indicated by a lower case letter. The convention that each option is represented by a single character is fairly uniform throughout UNIX commands, but there is great variation from the norm of three. Some commands have no options while others have so many options that they use all the 26 possible lower case letters, some upper case letters and some other characters too.

On most UNIX implementations, **spell** is close to the norm of three. For our examples here we shall use just one option:

$-$**b** means use British spellings — thus 'realize' becomes 'realise'

The much improved version of **spell**, available tomorrow, will have British spellings as standard. Perverse souls can, if they really want to be a centre of ridicule, use American spellings. In this case they must use our new $-$**w**(rong) option.

In the meantime we must be content with the present imperfect **spell**. Samples of its use are

(1) **spell**
(2) **spell** $-$**b**
(3) **spell chapter1**
(4) **spell** $-$**b chapter1**
(5) **spell chapter1 chapter2 chapter3**
(6) **spell** $-$**b chapter1 chapter2 chapter3**

Examples (1) and (2) take their input from the standard input, normally the terminal. Examples (5) and (6) apply spelling checks to the three files **chapter1**, **chapter2** and **chapter3** (in that order — though for **spell** the ordering does not have any effect).

We could extend any or all of the above examples by redirecting the output to, say, a file.

Other examples of UNIX commands which follow an identical style to **spell** are **rm** and **ls**. Samples of the use of these are

ls $-$**l directory1 directory2**
rm chapter1 chapter2

EXTRA ARGUMENTS

Before we say more about arguments to UNIX commands we should make a general point: one reason for the richness of UNIX is the diversity of people who have contributed to it by implementing commands. Generally all these implementors have kept to the overall UNIX style, but when it comes to the finer detail practices have inevitably diverged.

This comes out in the specification of options. We said in the previous Chapter that options begin with a minus sign to distinguish them from filenames, and that options are normally written at the start of a list of arguments. This is true, but there are some commands which have the added flexibility of allowing options to be changed *within* a list of filenames; moreover some commands even allow the minus sign that precedes options to be optionally omitted. Such details are largely in the realm of Dudley so we shall not worry about them here.

Some UNIX commands have other arguments, in addition to options and filenames. The normal UNIX convention is that these come after the options (if any), and before the filenames. An example we have already encountered is the **chmod** command. Another is the **grep** command, which, as you will have guessed because of UNIX's uniformity of style, can be applied to a list of filenames. Examples of **grep** are

    grep kill chapter1
    grep kill chapter1 chapter2 chapter3
    grep −n kill chapter1 chapter2 chapter3

These commands all search for the word 'kill'. The option −**n** means that output lines should be prefixed with the line number of the corresponding input line (thus you might find out that 'kill' was used in lines 150 and 296 of **chapter1**).

The first argument to **grep** (not counting the options for the moment), which is the pattern to be searched for, must always be present. Thus our argument **kill** is not interpreted as a filename, even if we happened to have a file with this name.

If, however, **kill** were an optional argument there would be a problem with ambiguity. Furthermore such an optional argument could not be represented by a single character, and therefore does not readily come under the *options* mechanism. UNIX has no uniform convention to solve this ambiguity problem. However a popular device is to use the *options* mechanism to indicate whether certain subsequent arguments are present.

All this sounds complicated, so we had better show an example. We shall choose a facility that is present in our dream of the UNIX of the future. This is a weapon to eliminate authors who use certain words that rile us. The weapon is an optional *hated-word* that can be supplied as an argument to **rm**. If you say

    rm conceptualize /usr/crass/document

then this new **rm** tests if the **document** file in the home directory of the user **crass** contains the word 'conceptualize', and, if so, not only does it delete the offending file, but it also deletes all other files in **crass**'s home directory — irrespective of whether the requisite permissions are given. For good measure, this imaginary **rm** changes **crass**'s password to a random combination so he will not be able to log in again.

Now this **rm** has one draw-back: its syntax is ambiguous, in that the *hated-word* is an optional argument. Thus it is not clear whether **conceptualize** is a filename or a *hated-word*. To resolve the ambiguity, the revised syntax is

    rm −h conceptualize /usr/crass/document

The −**h** option has the effect of saying that the next argument is a *hated-word*, not a filename.

(A final thought on the matter: this book now contains the word 'conceptualize' — in fact several occurrences of it. We had better be a tiny bit careful when our dream of the new **rm** is realized — and also indeed when our new **spell** is realised.)

SUMMARY OF STYLE

To summarize the style of UNIX commands:

- options come first and are prefixed by a minus sign.

- any arguments that are not filenames come next. If a command has optional arguments options can be used to say what arguments are present.
- a command ends with an arbitrarily long list of filenames. If the list is missing, the standard input is assumed.

A command may also include instructions to redirect the standard input/output. We discuss this later in the Chapter.

Obviously there are some commands that do not quite fit the style. Examples are **mv** and **cp** which, by their very nature, always require two filenames as arguments. ("This is wrong." said Dudley. "There are alternative forms of **cp** and **mv** covered in pages 1096 to 1214 of my *Notes for UNIX users*, which ... ".) However, these exceptions are a small perturbation of the overall uniformity of style.

NOTATION FOR SPECIFYING SYNTAX

Most UNIX documentation has a standard notation for describing the general form of each command. An example is the following description of the **ls** command.

> **ls** [*options*] *file* ...

The notation is simple to understand as there are just two conventions.

[*xxx*] means that the argument *xxx* may optionally be omitted

xxx ... means that there can be indefinitely many arguments of the form *xxx*

Thus the above description of **ls** says that the *options* may be omitted, and that there can be indefinitely many *file*s. Similarly the description

> **chmod** *mode file* ...

specifies that the first argument to **chmod** is something called a *mode* and this is then followed by an indefinitely long list of *file*s. Obviously, the documentation of **chmod** must explain what a *mode* is, and similarly the documentation of **ls** must explain what its *options* are.

Since UNIX programs, and their documentation, are written by so many different people there tends to be a certain looseness in the use of conventions. However it is almost invariably true that if an argument is described as *file*, *name* or *filename* then that argument is indeed the name of a file.

The brackets '[' and ']' can actually be nested, as in

> **abc** [−[**p**] [**q**] [**r**]]

This says that the argument to **abc** can optionally consist of a minus sign, and if this is present, then the minus sign may be followed by a **p** and/or a **q** and/or an **r**. Thus all the following are valid

> **abc**
> **abc** −
> **abc** −**p**
> **abc** −**pqr**

Actually most of the UNIX documentation adopts the somewhat naughty approach of writing the above as

    abc [− **pqr**]

which, taken literally, means you either can write − **pqr** or nothing at all; however readers guess that it really means the same as our original specification of the **abc** command. Indeed many UNIX commands carry the flexibility further by allowing options to be specified one by one, e.g.

    abc −**p** −**q** −**r**

The brackets and the dots used in the notation to specify commands can, if desired, be combined, i.e.

[*xxx*] ...   means that *xxx* can be repeated any number of times, including zero times

Again UNIX documentation is loose and

    xxx ...

is often used to include the possibility of zero repetitions of *xxx* — indeed our earlier **ls** example did just this.

Nevertheless such blemishes do not detract from the overall picture. Given an understanding of the UNIX style, and of this simple syntactic notation, you should find it easy to read UNIX documentation and master the commands that are useful to you.

DIFFERENT SHELLS

There are several popular shells used on UNIX systems. One that emanates from Bell Laboratories is the so-called Bourne shell, named after Steve Bourne. Steve Bourne is the author of a UNIX book called *The UNIX system*, which is a much more sophisticated work than the one that you are reading now. Another good shell is the C shell, which is syntactically related to the C language. The C shell comes from another centre of UNIX excellence: the University of California at Berkeley. The Bourne shell is called **sh** — a request from hrmt that conversations should be quiet and short — and the C shell is called **csh**.

Everything we have said about style, and nearly everything we say later in this Chapter about the details of the shell, applies both to **sh** and to **csh** (and to the numerous variants of each). On the few occasions where we need to be specific we shall assume **sh**. Generally you only have to know which shell you are using if you write elaborate shell programs, which are beyond the scope of this book.

WILDCARDS

We have said that uniformity of style goes hand in hand with tools to make commands easier to write. We can now show a specific tool provided by the shell which makes it much easier to specify both individual filenames and lists of filenames.

The tool is a method whereby the shell fills in your filenames for you. It does this by assigning a special meaning to the following characters.

?	means any single character
*	means any sequence of characters (including the null sequence)
[abc]	means either *a* or *b* or *c*

These special characters are called *wildcards*. If you use wildcards in any argument to a UNIX command, the shell expands the argument to consist of a list of all the filenames that could match the argument. It is easiest to appreciate this by examining a specific example.

Assume that our current directory, relating to a magazine we edit, contains the filenames

**advice   article0   article1   article2   article3
comment1 comment2   comment3   commerce**

Then the following examples show how we could refer to files in this directory.

Example 1

cat c*

is equivalent to

cat comment1 comment2 comment3 commerce

Example 2

spell comment?

is equivalent to

spell comment1 comment2 comment3

Example 3

chmod 644 article[23]

is equivalent to

chmod 644 article2 article3

Example 4

cat *r*[3e]

would **cat** any filename containing an **r** and ending in **3** or **e**. Hence it is the same as

cat article3 commerce

Example 5

grep kiss article[1 − 3]

indicates a further feature. The **1 − 3** within the brackets means anything between **1** and **3** inclusive and hence is equivalent to

grep kiss article1 article2 article3

Example 6

   rm *

deletes all files in the current directory.

Example 7

   rm /usr/aper/*

removes all **aper**'s files, provided, of course, you have permission to remove them. This example shows that you can use the wildcard mechanisms in all directories, not just the current one.

   Note that the lists of filenames generated by the shell are in alphabetical and numerical order (e.g. **a** comes before **b** and **1** before **2**). Strictly speaking, the ordering is determined by the ASCII code or whatever other code your UNIX uses for storing characters. The ordering is a natural one because it is the same as is used by **ls**.

   Note also that the shell tries to expand wildcard characters in all arguments — it does not know which arguments are supposed to be filenames. Thus if you write

   grep c* advice

to find occurrences of **c*** in the file **advice** the shell gratuitously turns it into

   grep comment1 comment2 comment3 commerce advice

Grep then assiduously searches for the word **comment1** in each of the four specified files. The chances are it does not find it, so in the true UNIX tradition it says nothing. The result is that, if you are not awake to what the shell does behind the scenes, you are left thinking that the file **advice** does not contain the string 'c*', which may be far from the truth.

   Thus there are times where you want the shell to leave you alone, and the shell, very charitably, provides a mechanism for doing this. Anything enclosed in quotes is treated literally by the shell. Thus we should have written our original **grep** as

   grep 'c*' advice

This use of quotes can surmount a further problem. If you wanted to search for 'he said' in **article1**, then

   grep he said article1

would search for **he** in the (non-existent) file **said** and in **article1**. Instead you can say

   grep 'he said' article1

MORE ADVICE ON FILENAMES

A consequence of the existence of wildcards is that it is all the more advisable to take care in the choice of filenames. An acquaintance of ours accidentally created a file called '*'. He decided to delete it, and the Great Pest within him typed

rm *

He spent the next three weeks re-creating all the files he had accidentally deleted. He should, of course, have typed

rm '*'

Alternatively he could have used another UNIX feature: this is that if a character is preceded by '\' — this is called a *backslash* — the shell assumes that you really mean that character. (If you really mean a backslash you have to type two backslashes.) Thus an equivalent of the above **rm** is

rm *

If you have a friend who is always boasting of his UNIX prowess, create a file called '*' in one of his directories (if you are allowed to), and place in the file the message

You do not really understand UNIX

When he rushes to delete this outrageous message he will, if he forgets to use quotes or the backslash, confirm that the message was in fact true.

There is another, more positive, way that wildcard facilities of the shell can influence your choice of filenames. If you are preparing a book or report there is some advantage in calling the chapters **chapter1**, **chapter2**, etc. You can then simply say

cat chapter*

to display the whole book. If you have an introduction, there is even some advantage in calling this file **chapter0** rather than **introduction**, so that it can be caught by the same mechanism. If you have more than nine chapters you have another naming problem. If you use the name **chapter10** for your tenth chapter then the order in which files are displayed by the above **cat**, being strictly alphabetic, is

chapter1
chapter10
chapter2
.
.
.

This would be a bit sad if **chapter10** revealed who the murderer was. If you called it **chapter91**, on the other hand, it would come out in the right place.

Nevertheless there comes a stage where such tricks of naming cause more problems than they solve, and sensible filenames must take priority over trickery.

Many UNIX users employ the '*' wildcard to gain the convenience of long, and hence more meaningful, filenames without the penalty of extra typing. Thus you could have a filename **division3scores**; if you did not happen to have, in the same directory, any other filename containing the character '3', you could just use to refer to **division3scores**, thus saving a bit of typing. Again, this kind of trickery is best kept within bounds.

EXTENSIONS

There is one character besides letters and digits that is commonly used in UNIX filenames. This is the dot. It is common practice to put, on the end of a filename, a dot followed by a few characters to show what type of information is in the file. This is called an *extension*. Examples of extensions are

average.p   a Pascal program
average.c   a program in the C language
average.spec   a specification of the **average** program

This convention has the following advantages

- some UNIX programs insist on certain extensions, in order that they are not sent rubbish. Thus the compiler for the C language insists that source programs are stored in files with a **.c** extension.
- some UNIX compiling programs (e.g. the compiler for the C language) use the extension to identify the type of a file, e.g. **.o** might mean an intermediate binary file as distinct from a source program. We discuss these matters in Chapter 12.
- the use of extensions fits well with the '*****' wildcard. Thus

     *.p

refers to all the Pascal programs in the current directory.

Note however that the extension mechanism is simply a naming convention, and has no effect on how the file is stored. There is nothing to stop you giving a **.p** extension to something that is not a Pascal program, though the UNIX programs that use extensions — e.g. the Pascal compiler — might be a bit upset with you.

README FILES

It is something of a defect of UNIX (and, indeed, other operating systems) that directories contain only the names of files, and there is no facility for a user to put a comment against a name, in order to say more about the purpose of the file. The extension mechanism is merely a poor excuse for a proper commentary facility. To combat this defect, and generally to make UNIX more friendly, a convention has grown up to define files called **README**. You put a **README** file in each directory that merits further explanation. The file contains a short verbal explanation of the directory and the files within it (e.g. "this is the November issue of the magazine; articles are collected in files ... . To run off a copy of the magazine, do the following: ..."). All the capital letters in the name **README** must greatly offend UNIX's sensibilities, so some users employ names such as **readme** or **read.me**. The advantage of the capital letters is that they stand out in a listing. Also, for what it is worth, **README** can usually be unambiguously referenced as '**R***'.

SUMMARY OF ADVICE

To summarize our advice to beginners on the choice of filenames:

- if you write programs use extensions to show the nature of your files
- only use letters and digits in filenames (together with the dots that herald extensions)
- select systematic filenames with a view to the use of wildcards
- be an antihrmt and choose meaningful, and hence sometimes long, filenames; when reasonable, use wildcards to abbreviate the long names
- create **README** files to explain what you are doing

THE ECHO COMMAND

UNIX supports a command **echo** which just outputs its arguments, e.g.

```
┌────────────────┐
│ any directory  │
└────────────────┘
```

```
$ echo hello there
hello there
$
```

This in itself may not strike you as the great facility you have always needed, but **echo** is useful in showing how the expansion of wildcards works. (It also has further uses which we cover later.) Assuming the magazine directory we used previously, the following examples show **echo** in action.

```
┌────────────────────┐
│ /usr/me/magazine   │
└────────────────────┘
```

```
$ echo Current articles: article*
Current articles: article0 article1 article2 article3
$ echo '***' [a−g]?????
*** advice
$
```

In the second **echo** above, the three asterisks at the start of the argument are enclosed in quotes and are therefore copied literally. The rest of the argument is a pattern to find all filenames that begin with a letter between **a** and **g**, and then consist of exactly five further characters. The filename **advice** is the only one that follows such a pattern.

REDIRECTION

We have already seen the use of the '>' character to redirect output, e.g.

   cat >**scores**

If you want to add to the end of an existing file you can use '>>' instead of '>'. For example

   cat >>**scores**

appends to the end of **scores**. (If **scores** does not already exist, UNIX creates a new file called **scores** and so the effect of ' > >' is then no different to '>'.)

You can redirect input by using the '<' symbol, e.g.

cat <existingfile

takes the input to **cat** from **existingfile** rather than the standard input. You can, however, say

cat existingfile

to do the same thing, and thus redirecting input does not enable **cat** to do anything it cannot do already. The same applies to most other built-in UNIX commands, and the main people who use input redirection are those who write their own programs (see Chapter 12).

All redirection is done by the shell rather than the UNIX underneath. You can confirm this by typing

echo hello >t

What the shell does is to strip off the >**t** from this command, and ask **echo** to perform its task on the argument **hello**. It duly copies this to the standard output, but the shell intercepts this output and sends it to the file **t**. If you then display the file **t** you find it contains the text **hello** and not the text

hello >t

Since the shell strips off your redirection instructions, it follows that it is immaterial what order you write these instructions in. Thus the following are all equivalent

grep kiss <existingfile >t
grep kiss >t <existingfile
grep >t <existingfile kiss

(Also identical is

grep kiss existingfile >t

Thus with **grep**, as with **cat**, the redirection of input does not gain you anything you cannot do already.)

CHICKENS

If you are beginning to find this Chapter hard going, feel free to opt out at this point. We still have some important topics to cover — notably the way UNIX implements some concepts we outlined in Part I, such as pipes and background processes. However you can get by for your first month or so with UNIX without consciously using these. Hence if you are now shell-shocked you might do better to save what is left of your mental energy for the next Chapter, which contains material everyone needs to know from day one.

PIPES

For those intrepid readers who remain, there is the reward that our next topic, the pipe, is realized in an extremely simple way. You just write a sequence of commands separated by the '|' symbol. For example

ls | spell

tests if all your filenames (not the contents of the files) are spelled properly. The effect is that the output from **ls**, instead of going to the terminal, is redirected to act as input to the command **spell**. The above command is thus equivalent to the two commands

ls > tempfile
spell < tempfile

but is, of course, much faster and more convenient. Specifically the pipe has the advantage that **ls** and **spell** work together in parallel rather than in sequence.

Performing a spelling check on your filenames is a curious thing to do. In order to provide some more realistic examples of pipes, we shall introduce some further UNIX commands which are suitable for use as filters, i.e. components of pipes. These commands, all of which do something to the standard input and send the result to the standard output are

sort	sort into alphabetic order
uniq	delete each line that is identical to the previous line
tr *string1 string2*	translate each occurrence of a character in *string1* into the corresponding character of *string2*

"The **sort** command is a very interesting one," said Dudley. "It has lots of options for sort keys and merging and sorting backwards and upside down and ... ".

The strings supplied as arguments to **tr** can use ranges of characters, e.g. **a**−**f** for the letters **a**, **b**, **c**, **d**, **e** and **f**. Two examples of **tr** — both of which work on the standard input and send the result to the standard output — are

tr AB 78	turns each **A** into **7** and each **B** into **8**
tr A−**Z a**−**z**	turns each **A** into **a**, **B** into **b**, etc., i.e. turns all upper case letters into lower case

Given these three new additions to our armoury, we can provide some more useful examples of pipes.

Assume a file **names** contains a list of all the people in a town. Each line of the file consists of a first name, a second name and an age, e.g.

Fiona	Hawkins	9
Fred	Brown	12
Charles	Smith	33

The file is sorted in ascending age. The following operations show commands that can be applied to the file.

Example 1

grep Smith names

displays all the lines of **names** that contain **Smith**.

Example 2

    grep Charles names | grep 33

displays all the lines of **names** that contain both **Charles** and **33** (in either order —
though as we have it the age always comes second).

Example 3

    grep Charles names | grep 33 | uniq

is the same as Example 2 except that duplicate lines are deleted (e.g. if there were
two Charles Smiths aged 33).

Example 4

    We find that some names are entirely in lower case (e.g. **charles smith**), some
very important people are exclusively in upper case (e.g. **CHARLES SMITH**),
whereas others use a mixture (e.g. **Charles Smith**). In our previous examples only
the last of these three was recognized. If, in Example 2, we want to find instances
of each Charles aged 33 irrespective of whether the name is in upper or lower case,
we extend our pipe to be

    tr A − Z a − z <names | grep charles | grep 33

Example 5

    Finally our last pipe finds all the Smiths and sorts them according to first
name, deleting duplicates.

    tr A − Z a − z <names | grep smith | sort | uniq

EXPLOITING PIPES

We hope you can begin to see from the above examples that if you have a file of
information and want all or part of this information extracted and presented in a
different form, then the chances are you can achieve your objective using a single
pipe. This is a confirmation of the success of the 'software tools' philosophy of
UNIX: to provide a set of modular components and to allow users to combine
these together to build a command tailored to solve the problem in hand.

    Pipes are an unfamiliar concept, even to experienced computer users new to
UNIX, and it takes time to realize what a powerful aid they are. If you find you
are creating numerous files to hold intermediate results, there is a good chance you
should be using pipes.

EXECUTING COMMANDS IN THE BACKGROUND

If you want to execute a command in the background, so that you can get on with
something else while it is doing its work, you simply append an **&** to the command,
e.g.

    /usr/me/novel

```
$ spell chapter* >t&
7654
$
```

Here we apply the spelling correction program to every chapter of a long book and redirect the output, the list of wrong words, to the file **t**. UNIX replies by saying 7654 (it gives you a different arbitrary number each time), and outputs a command prompt so that we can proceed normally while the background command is being executed. At this point we are using two separate processes inside the computer: the execution of the background command and our normal 'foreground' dialogue with the shell. If there are other users on the machine they could be executing background processes too, in addition to their normal foreground process. Thus the number of processes in existence might be much greater than the number of users on the machine.

The arbitrary number 7654 is the *process ID* (or, as hrmt calls it, *PID*) of our background process. This number uniquely identifies that process among all the others. Most of the time you ignore process IDs — they are more the province of Dudley; however the process ID is useful if you want to 'kill' a process. Not only do computer scientists draw trees upside down, but they also have a jargon where 'kill' means to stop execution.

Assume you suddenly decide you do not want to apply spelling correction to your book because it is written in Latin; thus **spell** would reject almost every single word. You therefore decide to kill your background process to save wasting computer time, and creating a huge file **t**. To do this you use the command

kill 7654

and the process identified by 7654 dies (i.e. ceases execution).

If you want to look at all your processes you can use the **ps** command. If we had typed **ps** before killing our 7654 process we would have got a display such as

```
PID    TTY    TIME   COMMAND
6005   tty11  0:06   sh
7654   tty11  0:10   spell chapter1 chapter2 chapter3
```

(The exact format varies between UNIX implementations.) The last line of the above tells us that our background process to use **spell** is indeed numbered 7654. It is controlled from **tty11**, which is the name UNIX gives to our terminal (see later), and has been running for 10 seconds. Notice how the **spell** command being executed is shown in the expanded form generated by the shell, i.e. the asterisk notation has been expanded to give a list of file names. (Thus the internal UNIX view of your command may in general differ from your view, so do not worry if **ps** comes up with a peculiar interpretation.) In addition, the **ps** shows we are running a second process, numbered 6005. This is the shell, called **sh**, that we talk to all the time.

Some UNIX users find amusement in continually typing **ps** to monitor the progress of their background process. The above ten seconds might, for example, have changed to eleven if we typed **ps** a second time. However if you spend your foreground time continually looking over your shoulder at the background this defeats the object of the background process.

You are not confined to running one process in the background. You can run as many as you wish, so that the output from your **ps** may fill half the screen.

A few more facts about background processes:

- if you type the break-in key this only halts the foreground process, not the background process.
- on some UNIX implementations a background process may continue even if you log out; on others logging out kills all your processes.
- on some UNIX implementations background processes may not communicate with the terminal.
- on some UNIX implementations you can move processes from the foreground to the background, or vice versa, while they are still running.

Our apologies for the repetitious 'on some UNIX implementations', but you really do need to consult your local documentation on such matters.

Most of us find it hard to carry on several conversations at the same time. Therefore, unless you are lucky enough to have a super terminal that has several separate 'windows' on UNIX, it is usually best to confine your UNIX conversation to the foreground process, and to redirect the input and output from background processes so that it does not appear on your terminal.

USE OF A PRINTER

In Part I we introduced the idea of 'spooling', whereby material for input/output devices such as printers is run off in the background, while you get on with other work. The command

    lpr *file* ...

copies the given *file*(s) to the printer spooler. The spooling process to do the actual printing is automatically placed in the background, so there is no need to put an '**&**' on the end of the **lpr** command.

A popular use of **lpr** is to put it at the end of a pipe, e.g.

    grep plumber traders | sort | lpr

This searches for all lines within the file **traders** which contain the word 'plumber', sorts the lines found, and finally prints them. On some implementations **lpr** is called **opr**.

DEFINING YOUR OWN COMMANDS

Assume our custom is to put an explanatory **README** file in each of our directories. Our normal action on entering a directory we have not visited for a while is to type the two commands

    cat README
    ls

Given that we type this pair of commands very frequently, we can make our future life slightly more convenient by putting these two commands into a file, called, say, **info**. We do this as follows

```
 /usr/me/somedirectory

    $ cat  > info
    cat README
    ls
    ∧ d
    $
```

We have now written a program, albeit a modest one: the file **info** contains two shell commands and represents a *shell program.*

Whenever we want to execute our pair of commands we can execute the contents of the **info** file instead of typing the commands each time.

EXECUTING SHELL COMMANDS

Before we explain how to execute the shell program in the **info** file, we should explain an important and powerful property of the shell itself. The shell is an ordinary UNIX program that normally reads the commands that you type at your terminal, and causes these commands to be executed. As with other UNIX programs, the shell can be made to take its input from a file instead of from the terminal (the standard input). Thus to execute our **info** file we can say

sh <**info**

This can be slightly abbreviated by writing

sh info

The shell, like many other UNIX programs, allows a list of filenames to be supplied as arguments; in such a case it takes its input from each of these files in turn, in just the same way as the **cat** program. In the above example there is just one file, **info**.

When the **info** file is fed to the shell the two commands within it are executed exactly as if they had been typed on a terminal.

The above use of the shell is interesting for a second reason. Our command line

sh info   (or   **sh** <**info**)

was interpreted, like all command lines, by the shell. This command line, however, has the unusual property that it invokes the shell. Thus we have used the shell within the shell. UNIX happily supports such 'nested' use of programs to any desired depth (e.g. a shell within a shell within a shell ...). The use of the shell within the shell is most obvious to you if you type

sh info&

Here you manifestly have an instance of the shell running in the background with the **info** file as its input, while your normal shell process talks to you in the foreground.

MAKING FILES EXECUTABLE

We can actually do even better than our above way of executing the shell program in the **info** file. We can upgrade **info** into a UNIX command that can be used in the same way as the built-in UNIX commands such as **date** and **ls**. This is done in an extremely simple way: all we do is change the permissions on **info** so that it becomes an executable file. The appropriate command is

```
/usr/me/somedirectory

$ chmod  755  info
$ ls  −l  info
− rwxr − xr − x      1  me            14 Nov 29 14:41 info
$
```

We performed the **ls** to confirm that **info** is now indeed executable — if you give **ls** an argument that is a non-directory file it just lists the properties of that file. Now we have made **info** executable, it has become our own local UNIX command to augment the built-in commands. We can therefore use **info** just as we use built-in commands such as **date** and **ls**, i.e.

info
We get a printout of the current **README** *file*
and a listing of the current directory

Although **info** now appears as a single UNIX command, it achieves its effect behind the scenes by using the two underlying commands **cat** and **ls**. This is an instance of a familiar happening in UNIX, e.g.

- a directory can itself contain directories
- a tree can itself contain trees, and, following on from this, a file system can itself contain file systems

It should be no surprise therefore that a command can itself be made out of commands. The technique of building things out of themselves is one of the reasons for the power and elegance of UNIX.

Readers who are programmers might be interested to know how shell programs are differentiated from programs that they might write using their favourite programming language; we shall therefore say a little more about the concept of executable files.

Executable files are either binary programs that were generated using some programming language such as C — we cover such matters in Chapter 12 — or they are shell programs. The former have a secret mark put on them by the 'loader' — again a topic that we shall discuss in Chapter 12. In our case the **info** file has no such secret mark and is therefore taken to be a shell program. When you type

info

UNIX simply takes it as

sh info

85

REDIRECTION ON SHELL PROGRAMS

When you define your own UNIX commands, these have all the facilities of built-in UNIX commands. In particular you can redirect their input and/or output, and you can use them as components of pipes, e.g.

> **info > t**
> **info | lpr**

It is worth exploring the first example above further. Here we make a nested call of the shell to execute our **info** command, and for this nested call, the standard output is the file **t** rather than the terminal. The **cat** and **ls** within **info** therefore send their output to **t**. If, however, **info** contained a command that explicitly redirected its output to a file **t1**, this would carry redirection one level deeper and would use **t1** to override the standard output **t**.

BIN DIRECTORIES

We still have not finished with our **info** command. We can go even further in upgrading its status to that of a fully-fledged UNIX command. We do this by using a device called a **bin** directory. To explain the UNIX convention of **bin** directories it helps to go back to first principles and look at the format of some UNIX commands:

> **ls**
> **cat x y**
> **info**
> **spell chapter1**

In all four cases the *command name* (i.e. **ls**, **cat**, **info** or **spell**) is simply the name of a UNIX file; this is an executable file and the act of executing it defines the action of the command. Thus execution of the shell program in the file **info** defines the **info** command. Similarly there is, somewhere in the UNIX file system, an executable file called **spell**; this file contains a program to perform spelling checks.

Of all the four command names above, only the **info** file is ever likely to be in our current directory; nevertheless in the other three cases we do not have to write pathnames to show which directory contains the desired file. The reason is that, for command names only, UNIX uses a predefined method of searching for the filename; this is called a *search path*. The search path normally starts at the current directory, and, if the command name is not found there, the search proceeds to other directories which are known to contain executable files corresponding to commands. By convention all these directories are called **bin**.

If you look at the root directory of your UNIX you will find it has a directory called **bin**, and if you then look inside **bin** you will find its filenames indeed correspond to built-in UNIX commands. Most UNIXes actually distribute the built-in commands among several **bin** directories. In particular the **/usr** directory usually has a **bin** sub-directory which contains further built-in commands. We shall assume in this book that all the built-in commands are stored in either **/bin** or **/usr/bin**.

Users can create their own **bin** directory, and place in it commands that they have defined themselves. By convention this **bin** directory is a sub-directory of the user's home directory.

We could therefore create a **bin** directory, if we did not have one already, and move our definition of **info** into it. To see the advantage of doing this we shall first examine how a search path is defined. If x is the current command name and the user is **me** then a common search path is

- first look for x in the current directory
- if this fails, look for x in **/usr/me/bin**
- if this fails, look for x in **/bin**
- if this fails, look for x in **/usr/bin**
- if this fails, give an error message
- in all cases give an error message if x is not an executable file

Your default search path is defined by the superuser. It is likely to be as above, except that the directory **/usr/me/bin** may not be there. If it is not, then when you first create your own **bin** directory you will need to add **/usr/me/bin** to your search path. You can also add other directories to your search path, such as a friend's **bin** directory. We shall explain later how to change your search path; in the meantime, assume that **/usr/me/bin** is indeed in the path.

The advantage of moving **info** to our **bin** directory is that, once there, it is recognized as a command name *irrespective of the current directory*, since **usr/me/bin** is always in our search path. If **info** is stored in a directory that is not in the search path it is only recognized when that directory is the current directory.

Some commands are essentially local to a directory and are best left there. However any command that is globally useful is worth putting in a **bin** directory on your search path.

Lastly there are three further points about search paths:

- if you want to execute a file that is out of the current search path you can give its full pathname. For example the command name

  /usr/me/info

  would execute the **info** program in the directory **/usr/me**, irrespective of the current directory and search path. (The exact rule is that if you put a '/' in your command name this is assumed to be part of a pathname and the normal search path is not used.)

- if you move a file into your **bin** directory then on some UNIX implementations you will need to log out and log in again for the new command to become effective. The reason for this curious behaviour is that UNIX can be more efficient if, at the start of a session, it 'freezes' certain internal tables used to look up command names. (As an alternative to logging out there may be a special command to re-freeze the tables in their new form.)

- there is no inherent difference between commands defined by users and built-in commands. UNIX simply follows a search path, and is quite unconcerned as to who defined the command.

A SORTIE AGAINST DUDLEY

We can use our new-found knowledge of shell programs and search paths to implement a command that has the double advantage of serving as an illustrative example and silencing Dudley for a while. Our action is

> **any directory**

```
$ cat > /usr/dudley/bin/cat
echo The dreaded file-moth has struck
∧d
$ chmod 777 /usr/dudley/bin/cat
$
```

The effect of this nefarious attack (which takes advantage of Dudley's generosity in allowing us write permission on his **bin** directory) is that when Dudley next uses the command

> **cat** *filename*

he will get the output

> The dreaded file-moth has struck

The impression is therefore that the contents of all his files have been overwritten by this fatuous message.

What really has happened is that we have, for Dudley, defined the **cat** command as

> **echo The dreaded file-moth has struck**

Since Dudley's search path will look at his **bin** directory before the built-in **bin** directories (or so we assume), the new **cat** will be recognized rather than the true **cat**. The principal illustrated by this example is therefore that you can, if you wish, redefine existing UNIX commands — though usually you do this for your own benefit rather than a friend's.

THE SHELL PROGRAMMING LANGUAGE

The shell actually offers a quite comprehensive programming language, supporting most of the concepts you have come across if you have used, say, BASIC. In particular there are variables, assignment statements, IF statements, loops and so on. Such matters are beyond the scope of this book, but you might be interested in the following sample, in order to get a flavour of shell programming. The level of detail in this example is such that it is very much tied to the Bourne shell rather than the C shell.

```
if test X$1 = X−w
then
  shift
  /usr/bin/spell $*
else
  /usr/bin/spell −b $*
fi
```

This new command realizes a dream, or, to be exact, realises a dream. It is our new **spell** command with the British spellings. It is in a file called **spell** in our **bin** directory, and thus overrides the bad old **spell**, which is in the **/usr/bin** directory.

Shell programs can refer to arguments of the current command. The first argument is referenced as **$1**, the second as **$2**, and so on; **$*** means all the arguments. Thus the first line of our program tests if the first argument is −**w**. (The reason for the X character is too complicated to explain here; it is a feature of shell programming that, if you are a tyro, you tear your hair out trying to find unusual ways of combating apparently irrational shell behaviour; the X is written by a bald programmer.) If the first argument is −**w** the shell command **shift** is called to shift the arguments up; the −**w** argument is shifted away, and what was the second argument to our **spell** becomes the first. The old **spell** is then called, and the arguments to our **spell** (less the −**w** argument) are passed on to it.

If the argument −**w** is not supplied the **else** part of the above **if** is used: this calls the old **spell** with the −**b** option, thus requesting British spellings, and passes on all the arguments to our **spell**. The outcome is that our new **spell** program has the desired effect: if the user does not say −**w** he gets British spellings.

The Bourne shell supports a wealth of other facilities not covered by this example. Perhaps the one of most interest to relative beginners is the facility for built-in variables with fixed meanings. In particular

HOME means the name of your home directory
PATH is your search path

These two variables are part of the *environment*, which defines the way you use UNIX. If you type the command

set

you get a print-out of your environment. This includes the values of **HOME** and **PATH**, the name of the shell you are using, the characters used as prompts, etc.

You can change the environment by giving a new value to a variable in the environment. For example you can set a new **PATH** by assigning it a value which consists of a sequence of directory names separated by colons. This is done, assuming you are using **sh**, by the command

PATH = . : **$HOME/bin** : **/bin** : **/usr/bin**

This sets the search path to consist of the sequence
(1) the current directory — it is a UNIX rule that this is indicated by '.'
(2) the **bin** directory in your home directory — **$HOME** inserts the name of your home directory
(3) **/bin**
(4) **/usr/bin**

When you type the above command, *leave the spaces out*; we should not really have put them there but it does aid readability.

USER PROFILES

The chances are that the very first act you performed when you started to use UNIX was to execute a shell program. This is because each user normally has a shell program called **.profile** which is automatically executed every time he logs in. Your particular **.profile** file may define your search path, your home directory, the characteristics of the terminal you normally use, and so on.

On some UNIXes you may also have a **.logout** file which is automatically executed every time you log out; this file might, for example, clear up your files by deleting all files with certain names. (Some UNIX implementations have further shell programs of this nature; alternatively they may use different names to ours, such as **.login** instead of **.profile**.)

You may wonder why, if you have files such as these, you have never seen them on an **ls**. The reason is that **ls** treats any filenames starting with '.' as unmentionable. Thus the internal mechanisms of UNIX which use **.profile** files and the like are hidden from the innocent user. If you want to see the unmentionable files you give the − **a** option (meaning 'all') to **ls**. Then if you are in your home directory, you might get a listing such as

```
  .        ..        .profile  file1    file2    file3
```

whereas without the − **a** you would only see

```
  file1    file2    file3
```

Of these three unmentionable files

.	is your current directory
..	links you back to the parent directory
.profile	is the file executed every time you log in

You can, if you wish, edit your **.profile** file. You could add to it the command

echo Hello beautiful

to make UNIX, however reluctantly, type

```
  Hello  beautiful
```

to you every time you log in.

More to the point you can make **.profile** set variables in the environment to tailor UNIX to your preferred way of working. Thus you can set **PATH** so that your **bin** directory, and perhaps your friend's too, is automatically included in your search path.

SUMMARY OF THE SHELL

Compared with most operating systems, the UNIX shell offers enormous power and flexibility. To start with you may limit yourself to its simpler facilities, such as redirection, pipes and background processes. However if you aspire to be a professional UNIX programmer it is well worth spending an hour or two battling to understand the documentation of your shell; the documentation may not give in easily, but eventually you may conquer it and learn of the riches locked away.

CHAPTER 8

Editing

Silence is golden.
PROVERB

Silence is.
HRMT

The tasks to be performed by an editor are absurdly simple: the inserting and deleting of characters in a file. It is an unfortunate characteristic of all of us that the more trivial a matter is, the more we argue about it and take up truculent positions. Thus everyone has their own fixed views about editors, and all designers of operating systems have implemented their own editor, different from any other. In addition users of operating systems have often added editors of their own design, and thus on any one machine there might be an 'official' editor plus several unofficial ones.

There are basically two types of editor. The difference lies in how the user identifies the point at which he wants to make an alteration (a deletion or an insertion). In one type of editor the user moves a cursor round the screen until it points at the desired place. Such *screen editors* are popular on micros. In the other type of editor, the position to change is identified by context (e.g. "I want to change the word 'to' in the line that contains the word 'unpalatable' "). *Context editors* — also called *line-based editors* — are popular on mainframes, and indeed many mainframe terminals do not allow free cursor movement, so there is no possibility of a screen editor.

The 'official' UNIX editor is a context editor called **ed**. Some UNIXes also provide an 'official' screen editor called **vi**. In addition, your UNIX implementation may have legion alternative editors to these. Some of the alternative editors are based on **ed**; they often have similar names to **ed**, e.g. **em** or **ex**. Others are totally different. If you want to use one of the latter, good luck to you. We understand, of course, that the use of any editor is a temporary measure; you will eventually decide that you should design a new editor, different from all the others, and better too. Until this is available, you will have to live with the current inferior products.

In this book we shall concentrate on **ed** since it is available on all types of terminal. Furthermore the **vi** editor contains the facilities of **ed** as a sub-set, so a knowledge of **ed** is valuable even if you subsequently use **vi**. (In fact one of the variants of **ed**, called **ex**, is actually the same program as **vi**.) At the end of the Chapter we give a brief introduction to screen editors.

A NOTE FOR BASIC USERS

If you have written programs in the BASIC language, then you will know BASIC's editing facilities. This knowledge is, however, no use in your learning about general-purpose editors such as **ed.** Editing in BASIC depends on each line having a number on the front, e.g.

    100 PRINT "HELLO"

These numbers are fine for BASIC, but it is neither necessary nor desirable to put numbers on the front of lines of, say, our best selling novel. Because of this, it is necessary to use a different sort of editing.

Indeed, very few programming languages apart from BASIC have numbers built into lines. For most programming languages, including Pascal, C and FORTRAN, you use a general-purpose editor to change your program. Thus **ed** has been designed to cater for editing programs as much as for editing English text.

THE ED EDITOR

P.J. Plauger, in a review in the February 1982 issue of *Computing Reviews*, sums up **ed** perfectly as "an editor geared for dumb terminals and smart people". (Dumb terminals are terminals with no fancy features — dumb means 'stupid' not 'silent'.)

There must be a lot of dumb terminals and smart people about, because **ed** has been widely copied and is now used with lots of operating systems besides UNIX. Needless to say each copy was implemented by people who had their own ideas on how **ed** could be improved. Thus **ed** now has hundreds of children and grandchildren all over the world, all bearing a resemblance to one another, but no two the same. Your UNIX may support one of these offspring of **ed** rather than **ed** itself, so be prepared for variations on what is described here.

The real **ed** contains some of the finest examples of hrmt's work. Every element of your conversation with **ed**, whether your instructions or its error messages, gives the impression that each character typed is worth a bar of gold. Many editing instructions, though already brief, can be further shortened by taking advantage of default assumptions built into **ed**.

When you enter **ed** you leave the shell and start typing editing commands rather than shell commands. There are several other UNIX programs with a similar property: thus if your UNIX has a BASIC system then when you enter this you start typing BASIC commands rather than shell commands. When you quit from **ed** (or BASIC) you go back to the shell again.

When **ed** wants you to type a command it issues hrmt's favourite prompt: nothing. You therefore do not wait for an invitation to type: you just get on with it.

THE BUFFER

Ed's first action is to make its own copy of the file to be edited. This is called the *buffer* copy. The buffer is (normally) kept in fast storage, so that editing will be quick. All edits are applied to the buffer, not to the original file. At the end of an editing session, you should write the buffer back to a file. Normally you will write the buffer back in place of the original, but there is nothing to stop you writing it to a new file or even in place of some other file. If you have made an appalling mess of your edits, you do not need to write the buffer at all; instead you can simply exit from the editor and no harm will have been done to your file, only to your self-confidence.

In addition to using editors to change existing files, people also use them to create new ones. In such cases the buffer is initially empty.

At any time during editing you have a *current line*, which you can think of as a pointer that identifies one line in the buffer. Initially the current line is the last line of the buffer. When you specify a change, this is made to the current line. The simplest way of editing is to do it in two stages:
(A) move the current line to the line you want to change
(B) make the change

There are three ways of moving the current line:
(1) by specifying a number. This is taken to be a line number within the buffer. Thus if you specify 45 you get the forty-fifth line of the buffer. By an **ed**

convention, if you specify a dot, this stands for the number of the current line; another rule is that a dollar means the last line of the buffer.

(2) by a context search. Here **ed** searches for lines containing a given *string* (i.e. sequence of characters), and sets the current line to the first such line it finds. The rule of **ed** is that strings must be enclosed within '/' characters, thus **/pig/** searches for lines containing **pig**. (In most programming languages, on the other hand, strings are enclosed in quotes, e.g. 'pig'). The context search for a string begins with the line beyond the current one; if the search reaches the end of the buffer without finding its quarry, it starts again at the beginning and continues until it gets back to the current line. This is called *wrap-around*. Only after it has done a full lap does it give up.

(3) by relative numbers. You can extend cases (1) and (2) by appending a plus or minus sign and a number. For example

> **/pig/ + 2**

means two lines beyond the next occurrence of **pig** and

> **/Summary/ − 12**

means twelve lines before the next occurrence of **Summary**. It is particularly useful to use line numbers relative to the current line. Thus **. + 3** means three lines beyond the current line. Indeed this is so commonly used that hrmt allows you to omit the dot and just type **+ 3**. We shall not, however, use this shorthand here as its initial impact might be confusing.

Beginners are always tempted to use method (1), the line number. This temptation, like all temptations, is best resisted but never is. The problem with line numbers is that they are only suitable for very short files. If you want to change a big file it is highly unlikely that you will know that your point of change is, say, line 1597. There is, moreover, a secondary problem: line numbers change. Thus if you insert an extra line before line 3, the previous line 3 becomes line 4, line 4 becomes line 5, and line 1597 becomes line 1598.

If you are ever going to use UNIX in more than a trivial way, avoid the temptation of line numbers and get into the habit of finding lines by context.

In order that you have a sound understanding of how to set the current line we shall show some samples of this alone — we shall not, as yet, make any changes in the buffer.

The simplest **ed** commands consist of a setting of the current line followed by a *command-name*. The command-name is normally a single letter.

A SAMPLE SESSION

We shall show the editor being used on the file **chapter1** of our book. Assuming this file has remained intact since we created it two chapters ago, it still contains the text

> Greg Daimler entered the room. There were seven bodies on
> the floor. He coughed. A body fell from the top of the
> bookcase. He looked up. He saw ten more bodies stuck to
> the ceiling.

To start our editing we type

$ **ed chapter1**
182

The number typed back by **ed** is the number of characters (or, on some implementations, the number of lines) in the file. We call the file being edited, in this case **chapter1**, the *current file*.

The most common action of a beginner is to display the current line. Indeed this is the only action we shall perform in this introductory exploration of **ed**. Because it is so common, it is represented by the briefest **ed** command-name: the command-name consisting of zero characters, i.e. the *null* command-name. (Alternatively you can use **p** for 'print' as the command-name if you want to be verbose — **ed** uses the word 'print' to mean 'display on the terminal' and we shall follow the same convention within this Chapter.) Hence if you simply set the current line, e.g. by typing **16** or **/pig/**, you get a display of the new current line.

We shall now start our editing session. We shall break up the session into small fragments in order to explain what is happening. Each fragment begins with a line of form

☛ *text of current line*

so that the current line is readily obvious. Note, however, that this is a feature of the book, not of **ed** itself. At the very start, as we have said, the current line is the last line of the buffer.

☛ the ceiling.

```
.
the ceiling.
1
Greg Daimler entered the room. There were seven bodies on
/ten/
bookcase. He looked up. He saw ten more bodies stuck to
.-2
Greg Daimler entered the room. There were seven bodies on
```

Here we print four different current lines. Firstly we type a dot to examine the current line without moving it. This prints the last line of our file, where the current line is initially placed.

We then move the current line to line 1 — just to tempt you with the forbidden fruit. (Actually line 1 is the only line number that is regularly used even by people devoted to context searching; it is often necessary to refer to the first line of the file and this is a natural way to do it.)

Thirdly we use context searching. **Ed** advances the current line to the next line that contains **ten**. Note that **ed** simply regards the buffer as a collection of lines, and all characters within the lines are treated equally. A line is *not* regarded as a collection of words: thus if you search for **ten**, you might not get a line containing the word 'ten'; instead **ed** might match **ten** against 'tennis' or 'stench'. In our example, however, we do indeed find the word 'ten'.

Lastly, we set the current line back two lines, and, in fact, it is now back to line one again.

We shall now show three more examples of context searching in order to illustrate some specialized points.

☞ Greg Daimler entered the room. There were seven bodies on

/k t/
bookcase. He looked up. He saw ten more bodies stuck to
/body/
the floor. He coughed. A body fell from the top of the
/body/
the floor. He coughed. A body fell from the top of the

The first line shows how all characters are treated equally: in particular a space is no different from any other character and can therefore be included in a context search. The string

/k t/

searches for a **k** followed by a space followed by a **t**.

The first search for **body** shows the wrap-around feature of searching : when we started our search we were at the third line of the buffer, but the search has to go to the end of the buffer and then start again before it finds its quarry in the second line.

When we search for **body** again we do a full circle. There is only one line containing **body** (as distinct from **bodies**), so the search goes right round until it gets back to the same current line again.

Finally we shall make some mistakes and show the power of **ed**'s error messages.

☞ the floor. He coughed. A body fell from the top of the

gold
?
/gold/
??

In the first line we intended to write **/gold/** but typed **gold** by mistake. This is not an **ed** command so **hrmt** replies with a derisive '?'. We then search for a string, **gold**, that does not exist within the buffer. Hence **ed** does a full lap round the buffer and still fails to find its target. Hrmt, enraged by this wasted search, is twice as voluble as before.

The two messages '?' and '??', plus certain messages concerned with files, are the limit of **ed**'s conversation. You will never get any other error message (unless your **ed** is an adapted version). Thus be sure you well understand the syntax of **ed** before you use it; you will not get any help if you go wrong. Indeed that is the very reason why, although we are deep into the Chapter, we have just finished covering the preliminaries to editing and are only now ready to describe how to make changes to the text in the buffer.

SOME CHANGES

There are two kinds of change you can make to the buffer

- you can insert or delete complete lines
- you can substitute one string for another within a line

We shall explore the former first.

There are four commands for changing complete lines:

d   delete the current line
i   insert before the current line
a   append to the current line (i.e. insert after)
c   change the current line, i.e. delete it and put other lines in its place

For all but the first of these you need to specify the lines to be added. In all cases you can add as many lines as you like. To indicate the end of the material to be added you type a line consisting of a single dot.

We shall illustrate these by first adding some new lines to the end of our buffer.

☞ the floor. He coughed. A body fell from the top of the

```
$
the ceiling.
a
At this point a door opened.
A tall and exceptionally beautiful girl entered the room.
She was wearing a low-cut and very tight dress.

.
```

Here we set the current line to the last line of the buffer by typing a dollar sign, and then append three further lines. After text has been added to the buffer, **ed** resets the current line to the last of the newly added lines.

You can see that **ed** has two modes of working. Most of the time it is in *command mode*, where it takes the lines you type as commands (e.g. to move the current line or to make a change). After you type an **i**, **a** or **c** command, **ed** changes mode and takes your lines of input to be additions to the buffer. When you type a dot, **ed** returns to command mode. (It is a feature of **ed** that when it needs a character with a special meaning, its first choice is a dot: we have already seen that a dot as a line number means the current line, and a dot on a line by itself terminates text to be added to the buffer. There is a further use of dot still to be explained.)

Ed contains two especially slippery banana skins that cause beginners to tumble. One is the dot to terminate inserted text. The undoing of many beginners — and experts too — is that they periodically forget the dot.

☞ She was wearing a low-cut and very tight dress.

```
.-2
At this point a door opened.
i
The clock struck three.
```

Here we insert a new line, crucial to the plot of the novel, before the current one. Having (apparently) done this we then remember that it is also crucial to the plot that the tractor stopped before three o'clock, so we further insert the line.

i

The tractor outside stopped its engine.

.

Fortunately at this point we decide to review our handiwork and print the buffer. We then see

Greg Daimler entered the room. There were seven bodies on
the floor. He coughed. A body fell from the top of the
bookcase. He looked up. He saw ten more bodies stuck to
the ceiling.
The clock struck three.
i
The tractor outside stopped its engine.
At this point a door opened.
A tall and exceptionally beautiful girl entered the room.
She was wearing a low-cut and very tight dress.

(We shall shortly explain how to print the buffer.) The buffer is not what we expect, and the full insidiousness of the banana skin is revealed: we slipped into another world without knowing it. The reason why this happened is that we forgot to type the dot after our first insert, with the result that the second insert is taken as part of the data for the first.

We remedy this by deleting the line that just contains the letter **i**; this line is one before the current line (we assume that the current line was restored to its previous position after printing the buffer). After deleting the **i** line, we delete the line about the tractor as well.

☛ The tractor outside stopped its engine.

.−1
i
d
d

After a **d** the current line is set to the line after the deleted one. Hence repeated typing of **d** deletes successive lines.

We now re-insert the tractor line in its intended place, before the line about the clock striking.

☛ At this point a door opened.

.−1
The clock struck three.
i
The tractor outside stopped its engine.

.

The buffer now contains

Greg Daimler entered the room. There were seven bodies on
the floor. He coughed. A body fell from the top of the
bookcase. He looked up. He saw ten more bodies stuck to
the ceiling.

The tractor outside stopped its engine.
The clock struck three.
At this point a door opened.
A tall and exceptionally beautiful girl entered the room.
She was wearing a low-cut and very tight dress.

(There was actually no need to delete the tractor line and re-insert it again. We could have used a more advanced **ed** command that moves lines from one place to another.)

We have thus escaped fairly lightly from our crime of omitting the dot at the end of inserted text. You will not always be so fortunate. If you have been typing away happily for half an hour to **ed** without any response, the chances are there was a missing dot somewhere. Hence a good rule for **ed** is: a dot removes doubt. If you are already in command mode a dot will simply print the current line, and thus reassure you that all is well. If you are not in command mode a dot will get you there.

Having reached the stage where you can now do simple edits, we shall suspend our editing session for a while and explain some general properties of **ed**.

THE GENERAL FORM OF A COMMAND

We have so far separated the setting of the current line from the commands, such as **i**, which change the buffer. You can, once you have gained a little confidence with **ed**, combine the two.

In general the form of an **ed** command is

[address [,address]] command-name [argument]

where the *address* is a specification of a line — like the ones we have used to set the current line. As you can see, a command-name is preceded by zero, one or two addresses. Most commands, as examples below will show, permit any of these three possibilities. If no addresses are supplied a default assumption, normally the address of the current line, is made. A pair of addresses constitutes an *address range*, and means that the command is to be applied to every line from the beginning of the address range up to and including its end.

We shall illustrate the form of commands by showing a sequence of examples of the **d** command, which deletes lines.

d	delete the current line
.+2d	advance the current line by two, and then delete the new current line
/Daimler/d	advance the current line to the next line containing **Daimler** and delete this
3,5d	delete lines 3 to 5 inclusive
.,/Daimler/d	delete all the lines from the current line to the next line containing **Daimler**
1,$d	delete the entire buffer

Two points about these examples:

- you can, if you wish, add spaces before the **d**, e.g. **3,5 d**

99

- although all our examples show the **d** command, most other **ed** commands have the same alternative forms, and we could equally well have used, say, the **c** command. One command that is particularly useful with a pair of addresses is the command **p** which prints lines. In particular **1,$p** prints the whole buffer — an operation we assumed in our earlier example, and **3,5p** prints lines 3 to 5 inclusive.

WRITING TO A FILE

Many **ed** users, mindful that disaster may strike at any time, periodically write the buffer to the current file. Their work will then be saved, and if they have a subsequent appalling disaster with the buffer, they can simply abandon it, confident that at least some of their work has been salvaged. You write the buffer by using the **w** command.

If you simply type the command

w

this writes the entire buffer to the current file. The current file is normally the filename you typed on the original **ed** command, e.g.

ed chapter2

(There are ways of changing the name of the current file, but these are beyond the scope of this book.)

The **w** command is an exceptional command: it actually makes a gratuitous remark. When it has written the file — which may take a while if the buffer is long — it tells you, quite voluntarily, the number of characters (or, on some versions of **ed**, the number of lines) that it has written.

The **w** command is also different in a second way: if you do not specify any addresses, then the **w** is assumed to apply to the whole buffer. This happened, for instance, in our example above. For most **ed** commands, on the other hand, the default assumption is the current line. Thus, fortunately, typing **d** alone does not delete the entire buffer, but just the current line.

Given hrmt's role in the design of **ed**, the default assumption is the most frequent situation. Only **w**, and a handful of other **ed** commands, are most frequently applied to the whole buffer.

You can always override the default address range by giving one or two explicit addresses before a command. Thus

. − 1w

sets the current line back one and writes this line, and nothing else, to the current file. (This is likely to be a disaster, unless the rest of the buffer is written separately, as everything else would be lost.)

The command

1,/Daimler/w

shows the use of the **w** command over a range of lines. This writes from the start of the buffer up to and including the first line containing **Daimler**. This **/Daimler/** line then becomes the current line.

The **w** command also has an optional argument. If you want to leave the current file intact, and write to a different file you can use commands such as

w newcopy
6w line6
1,/Daimler/w uptoDaimler

The first of these writes the whole buffer to a file **newcopy**; the second writes the sixth line of the buffer to a file **line6**; the third writes a range of lines to a file **uptoDaimler**. (Note that you need to put at least one space between the **w** and the filename that follows it — one of the few places in **ed** where a space is necessary.) The **w** command is quite ruthless: if a file already exists with the given name, then **w** overwrites the previous contents, destroying it forever.

As an alternative to **w** it is often useful to use **W**, which appends on the end of a file, rather than overwrites it. (On some implementations, **wa** is used rather than **W**.)

CHANGES WITHIN THE CURRENT LINE

We said earlier that there were two kinds of changes you could make to a file: inserting or deleting complete lines, and making alterations within a line. So far we have only covered the former, which is achieved by commands such as **i** and **d**. This sort of editing is most frequently used when the material being edited is a program. When you are editing textual material, particularly when you are making changes to an existing document, it is much more usual to change the odd word or phrase within a line, rather than to slaughter or create complete lines. It is therefore high time we explained how to make changes within a line.

The command to do this is the **s** command, which has the general form

s/*pattern*/*replacement*/**p**

For the time being we shall take both the *pattern* and the *replacement* to be simple strings of characters. The action of **s** is to replace the first occurrence, within the current line, of the *pattern* by the *replacement*. The **p** on the end, which is optional, causes the current line to be printed after the substitution has been made. (It is an instance of a more general facility: you can append the **p** command, which prints the current line, to several of the **ed** commands. You then get two commands for the price of one.)

We shall now return to our editing session and use the **s** command.

☛ The tractor outside stopped its engine.

    1
    Greg Daimler entered the room. There were seven bodies on
    s/seven/18/p
    Greg Daimler entered the room. There were 18 bodies on

Here we set the current line to the first line of the buffer, and change **seven** into **18**.

For many people the **s** command is the most popular **ed** command, so we shall show several more examples of its use.

☛ Greg Daimler entered the room. There were 18 bodies on

s/18//p
Greg Daimler entered the room. There were   bodies on

Here we apply **s** to the current line, and replace **18** by nothing, i.e. we delete it. We now notice that there are two spaces before **bodies**. To turn these into one we type

s/ / /

This replaces the (first) pair of spaces on the line by a single space. We omitted the **p** on the end because we were confident this would work. (Note that here, as everywhere else in **ed**, a space is treated just like any other character.)

You can add to the **s** command a **g** suffix (as well as, or instead of, the **p** suffix) if you want all occurrences of the pattern to be replaced, though this still applies only within the current line.

☛ Greg Daimler entered the room. There were bodies on

s/e/E/gp
GrEg DaimlEr EntErEd thE room. ThErE wErE bodiEs on

Here we replace every **e** in the current line by **E**. This is a bizarrE thing to do, but it gives us a chance to show a command that acts as a valuable counterweight to the **s** command. If you type **u** (for undo) this cancels the previous **s**.

☛ GrEg DaimlEr EntErEd thE room. ThErE wErE bodiEs on

u

.

Greg Daimler entered the room. There were bodies on

Here we undo our substitution of **E** for **e**, and print the current line to make sure that the previous substitution has, indeed, been undone.

Unfortunately the **u** command works only with the most recent substitution, and applies only to the current line. You cannot (unless you have a super extended **ed**) undo other commands, such as a tragic

1,$d

where, by typing **d** when you mean to type **p** you delete the whole of the buffer rather than print it.

Finally, there is a special way of combining **s** with a context search. The pair of commands

/green/
s/green/blue/

which finds the next occurrence of **green** and then replaces it by **blue**, can be abbreviated as

/green/
s//blue/

The general rule is that a null pattern means the pattern you most recently used. Another application of this, where **ed** is being applied to a file of nursery rhymes, is

/piggy/
This little piggy went to market.

//

This little piggy stayed at home.

Here, having found one **piggy**, we want to find the next. All we need to type is '*//*'.

QUITTING

The command that beginners to **ed** most yearn to type is **q**, which means that the editing session is complete, and it is time to quit the editor. Having quit the editor you are then returned to the normal command status in the shell. Thus you get the '$' prompt, and you can type ordinary UNIX commands again, rather than **ed** commands.

(More generally, the letter **q** is often a good thing to type to UNIX when matters are getting out of hand. The convention that **q** means quit applies to a lot of other UNIX programs as well as the editor.)

The normal way of leaving the editor is to type

w

q

in order to write the buffer back to the current file and then quit. In some implementations this can be written as one command: **wq**.

If you try to quit, having made changes in the buffer since the last **w**, then these changes will be lost. There are two cases where this occurs

- *the Great Pest's quit* when you have spent two hours editing your buffer and then forget to write these changes back to the current file
- *the ignominious quit* where you have made such a mess of your editing that you want to escape without changing your original file.

In either case **ed** questions the quit. (It has, of course, no means of distinguishing the two cases.) On friendly implementations it types a message such as 'sure?' and you have to type an explicit **y** if you are in the ignominious state of really wanting to quit. On less friendly implementations, hrmt simply gives his normal '?' error message to the first attempt to quit, but if you try again the quit will work.

BROWSING AND BREAKING

When you are editing a file you may sometimes be only dimly aware of its contents. This may apply, for example, to an old file, a very long file, or to a file created by someone else. It is often useful, therefore, to use **ed** to browse through the buffer to get an impression of what is there. You can, for instance, use a context search to look for certain words.

Sometimes you want to go through part of a file line by line. You can do this by successively typing

.+1

However, hrmt finds this verbose, and he has provided an alternative form that is shortened by the maximum amount: if you type a null line, i.e. you just type the RETURN key, then hrmt interprets it as **.+1**. Thus to browse through the buffer

103

line by line you just keep pressing the RETURN key. If you reach the end of the buffer, hrmt will reply with a question mark if you try to proceed further.

If you want to look at a sequence of lines surrounding the current line — the sort of image you see on a screen editor — you can type a command such as

.−10,.+10p

Because this is such a common operation some versions of **ed** have a special command to achieve this effect — indeed the special command has a better effect since, unlike the above use of **p**, it leaves the current line positioned at its original place.

Sometimes, during your browsing, you may want to note the number of the current line; you may for example want to refer to the line in a subsequent **d** command. To do this, you can type

.=

The reply is the line number.

Occasionally you can get characters into your buffer that you cannot see. Examples are tab and backspace characters. Beginners are especially likely to be puzzled by such unseen hazards. If you want to be sure of what is really in your lines you can type **l**, instead for **p**, to display the lines. The **l** command displays something visible for every character, though the exact way it represents the unseen characters depends on your version of **ed**. A typical convention is

a tab comes out as >
a backspace comes out as <

Other non-printing characters come out as a backslash followed by the internal code of the character. In general, however, the beginner is not interested in the details, it is enough to know that some funny characters have got into the line and need replacing.

The ultimate in browsing is to type

1,$p

but if your file contains 10,000 lines you may regret doing this — the display will take a long time. Fortunately, while using **ed**, you can type a break-in without a catastrophic effect. Such a break-in simply returns you to command mode in **ed**. The current command is abandoned and the buffer remains in the state it was when you typed the break-in. Break-ins can therefore be used to terminate tedious and unwanted printing that you have set in motion.

This use of break-in contrasts with some other UNIX programs, where a break-in abandons everything and returns you to the shell.

COMPLETE EXAMPLES

Since our descriptions of **ed** commands have been scattered over several pages, it might be helpful to examine some complete sample sessions in order to see how the commands fit together. We show five sample sessions below. The first one illustrates the use of **ed** to create a new file.

104

```
$ ed
a
When Greg Daimler regained consciousness he
found himself in a dark room. He smelled gas:
a horrific new nerve gas that could wipe out
a million people in a second. No worry here.
The gas might wipe out a million ordinary
people, but ordinary people did not have nerves
like Greg Daimler. Daimler simply smiled.
The gas had killed all the poisonous snakes
and scorpions that were surrounding him.
.
/dark/
found himself in a dark room. He smelled gas:
s/dark/small dark/p
found himself in a small dark room. He smelled gas:
w chapter2
405
q
$
```

Here we start **chapter2** of the book. Since we have no existing file we supply no
argument to **ed**. When we come to do the **w** at the end, we name the file we want to
write to. When you create a new file your first command is invariably **a** since there
is nothing else to do but to append to the null buffer that is already there. In our
session above, we noticed an error after we had typed in the new material. The
dark room should have been a small dark room. We therefore used the **s** command
to make this change before writing our file. In this case **s** was used to insert a new
word, rather than to replace anything, but this manner of use is not fundamentally
different from a replacement. (The above use of **s** could, incidCL####y, have been
abbreviated as **s//small dark/p** since the word **dark** had just been found on a
context search.)

The advantage of using **ed**, rather than **cat**, to create a new file is that you can
make changes like this as you go along.

Sample session 2

The above session would have been identical if the first line had been

```
$ ed chapter2
```

and the penultimate **ed** command had been **w** instead of

```
w chapter2
```

The reason is that if **ed** is called with a non-existent file, as we are assuming **chapter2**
is, it simply gives its favourite error message, the question mark, and proceeds
exactly as if it was editing a null file. However the filename is remembered, and
treated as the current file; thus the **w** in our example writes to **chapter2**.

Although this way of creating a new file is only trivially different from

Session 1, some people prefer it. If you use the Session 1 method there is a small danger that, after a harrowing **ed** session, you will forget which file you are supposed to be creating.

Sample session 3

```
$ ed chapter2
405
1i
DAIMLER BREAKS OUT


.
w
425
q
$
```

Here we add a title line at the start of the file. The title is followed by a blank line. We then write the buffer back on top of the original file. (The difference between 425 and 405 tells us that the file is now 20 characters longer.)

Sample session 4

```
$ ed chapter2
425
/wipe/
a horrific new nerve gas that could wipe out
/wipe/
The gas might wipe out a million ordinary
s//knock/p
The gas might knock out a million ordinary
/wipe/
a horrific new nerve gas that could wipe out
w
426
q
$
```

Here we are a little worried about the repeated use of the word **wipe**. We find two occurrences and change the second to **knock**. We then search for the next **wipe** and find we get round to the first one again. There are therefore no other occurrences of **wipe**. Happy, we write the file and quit.

Sample session 5

```
$ ed chapter2
426
1
DAIMLER BREAKS OUT
```
      ↰ *null line typed here*

    ↰

    ↰ *null line typed here*

When Greg Daimler regained consciousness he
```
.+1,$c
```
... IF YOU WANT TO READ THE REST OF THIS, PLEASE
BUY ME AN I-LOVE-UNIX T-SHIRT.
```
.
```
1,$p
DAIMLER BREAKS OUT

When Greg Daimler regained consciousness he
... IF YOU WANT TO READ THE REST OF THIS, PLEASE
BUY ME AN I-LOVE-UNIX T-SHIRT.
w /usr/friend/thrills
145
q
$

Here we start by printing line 1. We then browse through the buffer by typing two
null lines. (Since the second line of the buffer is a blank line, the reply to the first
null command is a blank line. Thus the above display shows three blank lines in
succession.) When we reach the first line of the story we replace all the lines
beyond it by an offer that no-one could refuse, and write the buffer to a **friend**
(who has given us write permission to his home directory). We do *not* write this
buffer back on top of our current **chapter2** file, as we do not want to destroy the
original.

REGULAR EXPRESSIONS

The second banana skin in **ed** is the *metacharacter*: a character that is not what it
seems.

The banana skin arises from one of the most common phenomena in
computing: a simple facility is made much more general and powerful; the gains
are immense, and the designer of the new facility glows with pride; there is,
however, one small problem: the simple facility is not simple any more.

In this case the phenomenon arises with the context searching facility. When
you use this you actually search for a *pattern*. In our simple examples so far this
pattern has consisted only of fixed characters, such as **/dark/**. It can, however,
contain variable elements. The variable elements are indicated by so-called
metacharacters, which are characters with special meanings. We have already seen
the use of metacharacters in the shell. The characters that we called *wildcards*, such
as * and ? are actually examples of metacharacters. The **ed** metacharacters are,
however, generally different from the wildcard characters. The following is a list of
some of them

.   means any character. (A dot, as we know, is always **ed**'s first choice as
                    a character with a special meaning.) Thus **/c.t/** matches **cat**, **czt**, **c + t**,
                    etc.

x∗   where *x* is any character, means any number of *x*'s, including none at
                    all. Thus **/ab∗d/** matches any of **ad**, **abd**, **abbd**, etc. Similarly **/a.∗d/**
                    matches any string starting with an **a** and ending with a **d**. (The **a** and

d must, however, be on the same line, since **ed** works line by line. If there is more than one **a** or **d** on a line, **/a.*d/** matches from the first **a** to the last **d**.)

$ means the end of the line. Thus **/d$/** matches a **d** at the end of a line. This use of '**$**' is somewhat analogous to the use of '**$**' to mean the last line of the buffer, e.g. **1,$p**

∧   means the start of the line. Thus **/∧T/** matches a **T** at the start of the line; **/∧$/** matches a blank line

[Aab]   means either **A** or **a** or **b**. (This is the one **ed** metacharacter facility which exactly mirrors a wildcard facility in the shell.)

[∧Aab]   means any character that is neither **A** nor **a** nor **b**. This use of '[∧' to mean 'none of' is entirely separate from our previous use of '∧' to mean the start of a line.

[,;]*   means any sequence (including a null one) made up of spaces and/or commas and/or semicolons.

The patterns you use in a context search are called *regular expressions*. (This is a term used in the mathematical analysis of syntax; it is not just a term coined by **ed** — otherwise it would have a shorter name.) You should remember the following points about regular expressions:

- a beginner's first acquaintance with metacharacters often arises when he uses them by accident and peculiar things happen. Thus he types /ing./ to find **ing** followed by a dot, and is surprised when **ed** finds a line containing **ings** instead. (The dot matches anything.)
- if you really want a character to mean itself you can precede it with a backslash — in a similar way to using a backslash in the shell. Thus the above **/ing./** should have been

    /ing\./

- the concept of regular expressions, and the use of metacharacters, is present in several UNIX programs. Some programs, such as **grep**, use identical metacharacters to **ed**. (We shall soon explain this extended use of **grep**.)
- all regular expressions are matched within the current line. You cannot match a string that straddles several lines.
- regular expressions can be used in the *pattern* of an **s** command, as well as in a context search.

EXAMPLES OF REGULAR EXPRESSIONS

The following are some examples of the use of regular expressions.

Example 1

    /[Hh]e/

finds the next occurrence of **He** or **he**. Note that **ed** treats upper case letters as different from lower case ones. Hence if you are searching for all occurrences of the pronoun 'he', don't forget to include 'He' in your search as well.

Example 2

s/:.*$/:/p

Here we see a regular expression on an **s** command. The regular expression matches the string from the first colon in the current line, right up to the end of the current line. This is replaced by a colon, so the net effect is to delete everything after the first colon in the line. (If the current line does not contain a colon, **ed** will give the '??' error message, which it always gives when it fails to find a string or pattern.)

Example 3

Note that '∧' does not stand for the first character on the line. Instead it can be thought of as an imaginary character preceding the first character on a line. The distinction is important when you do a substitution. Thus if our current line is

    Greg is afraid

then replacing '∧' works as follows

s/∧/'/p

'Greg is afraid

Here we replace the imaginary character at the start of the line by a quote. The rest of the line is unaffected. (Indeed the imaginary character is unaffected, because **ed** always assumes it is there.) On the other hand consider

☛ Greg is afraid

s/./'/p

'reg is afraid

Here the dot matches the first character on the line and this is replaced.

Example 4

The '$' on the end of the line is as imaginary as the '∧' at the start. It is often useful as the subject of substitution, e.g.

☛ Greg is afraid

s/$/ of nothing/p

Greg is afraid of nothing

Note the space before the **of** in the above substitution. If we had left it out the result would have been

    Greg is afraidof nothing

Example 5

s/∧ *//

deletes any spaces that occur at the start of the current line.

Example 6

s/ *//

might look like a command to delete the first sequence of spaces on the current line. Actually its effect is identical to Example 5. If the current line does not begin with a space the above pattern happily matches a null string at the start of the line. It replaces this by a null string, thus having no effect. Having done this onerous replacement it does no more; it therefore does not look for spaces later in the line. The moral is to beware the use of the asterisk metacharacter unless the beginning of the repetitions is clearly delimited — otherwise you need a twisted mind to work out what will happen. (The correct pattern for our replacement is *two* spaces followed by an asterisk — this means one space followed by zero or more further spaces.)

CONTEXT OF EDITING METACHARACTERS AND WILDCARDS

Note that **ed** metacharacters only apply to regular expressions enclosed within '/' signs. They do not apply elsewhere in **ed**, nor do they apply to shell commands. Similarly shell wildcards do not apply to **ed** commands. Thus

> **cat ve***

if used in the shell, might **cat** a file called **verylongname**. You could not use

> **w ve***

as an **ed** command to write to the same file. Instead you must write the name out in full.

USE OF AMPERSAND IN A REPLACEMENT

There is one other place in **ed** where a character is not what it seems: the character **&** in the replacement string of an **s** command means the pattern you have just matched. Thus

> **s/dark/small &/**

is the same as

> **s/dark/small dark/**

The use of **&** is of most benefit when the pattern is a regular expression. Thus

> **s/10*/(&)/**

matches a string consisting of a **1** followed by any number of **0**'s, and substitutes a pair of parentheses round whatever it matches. Thus

> **1**   becomes **(1)**
> **10** becomes **(10)**
> **100** becomes **(100)**

For beginners this marginal advantage is more than offset by the banana skin effect of the ampersand. For example

> **s/Jones/Jones & Sons/**

turns

> The name of Jones is known for accuracy.

into

> The name of Jones Jones Sons is known for accuracy.

(If you really want an ampersand in a replacement string you must put a backslash in front of it.)

There is one consolation: at least the pattern metacharacters do not apply in replacements — you can, for example, freely use dots. The ampersand together with the '/', which is taken to mark the end of the replacement, are the only two characters you need worry about.

REPEATED EDITS

One of the huge advantages of storing a document on the computer is that you can make systematic changes to it. Thus, with our novel on the computer, we can easily rename Greg Daimler as Cyril Daimler, if we want to. Likewise we can change every occurrence of 1984 into 1985, or every occurrence of 'at this moment in time' to 'now'.

The use of systematic changes is also common for files that are programs: programmers are always refining their programs by changing variable names, formats, and so on.

You can accomplish repeated substitutions in **ed** by preceding the **s** command by a pair of addresses to show the range in which the substitutions are to be made. For example

1,$s/Greg/Cyril/gp

replaces all occurrences of **Greg** by **Cyril** (since it is applied in the range from line 1 right up to the last line). Let us hope that there are no occurrences of **Gregory**, because these would be turned into **Cyrilory**. It is a quirk of **ed** that the **p** on the end of this substitute command only causes printing of the last line in which a substitution has been made — not every such line. The **g** before the **p** is important. It means that every **Greg** on each line within the address range is replaced; if we had omitted the **g**, only the first occurrence of **Greg** on each line in the address range would be replaced. Thus the line

> She looked at Greg.   Greg smiled.

would become

> She looked at Cyril.   Greg smiled.

As a second example of a systematic substitution, this time in a limited line range, the command

. − 10,. + 10s/he/she/

substitutes **she** for **he** in the ten lines before and after the current line (and also, of course, in the current line itself).

REGULAR EXPRESSIONS IN THE GREP COMMAND

You may remember that the shell command

grep *pattern file ...*

prints out all the lines of the *file*(s) that contain the given *pattern*. In our previous examples the pattern was always a fixed string. We mentioned earlier in this Chapter that the pattern could be any regular expression, written using metacharacters identical to **ed**.

An example of this extended use of **grep** is

grep '[,;].*[,;]' **chapter1**

Here we have an elaborate pattern that matches
a comma or a semicolon ([,;])
followed by any string of characters (.*)
followed by a comma or a semicolon ([,;])
This command therefore displays all lines of **chapter1** that contain a comma or semicolon, followed, later in the line, by another comma or semicolon, i.e. all the lines that contain two or more commas or semicolons (or one comma and one semicolon).

This usage of **grep** explains its curious name. The name stands for Globally find Regular Expressions and Print.

INCLUDING OTHER FILES

The **r** command in **ed** reads a file and inserts it into the buffer after a specified line. Hence

$r boast

adds the contents of the file **boast** at the end of the buffer (since '$' means the last line). When it has read the file, the **r** command prints the number of characters read, and sets the current line as the last line read.

It is common practice to keep popular pieces of text or program in separate files so that they can be included within other files you create. Thus **boast** might be a modest description of yourself, which you add at the end of every document you write.

LOOKING AT THE OUTSIDE WORLD

You can, while using **ed**, execute any shell command you like, and you can do this without leaving the editor or changing your buffer. All you do is put an exclamation mark on the front of the shell command you want to execute, e.g.

r boost
?boost
!ls
boast   boaster   boastest
!
r boast
7943

Here we try to read a file **boost** but find it does not exist. (The message '?boost' is one of hrmt's most verbose sayings.) We therefore use the shell command **ls** to give a listing of our files. This shell command produces its output in the normal way and then **ed** types another exclamation mark to indicate you are back in the editor again. You now know your filename is **boast** and can use it in the normal way.

Some versions of **ed** allow the contents of the buffer to be piped to a UNIX command, e.g.

1,$ | spell

sends the whole buffer to the **spell** command. Otherwise, if you want to use your buffer in a shell command, you have to write it first, e.g., assuming our current file is **chapter2**

w
1234
!spell chapter2

The advantage of using commands such as **spell** from within the editor is that, if there are any mistakes to correct, then you are still in the editor and can get straight down to doing the corrections.

FURTHER EDITING FACILITIES

Unfortunately Dudley Detail is still battling with the dreaded file-moth that struck him during the last Chapter. He is thus not available to give us the benefit of his detailed knowledge of **ed**. His brother is, however, happy to oblige. This man is a vicar but, sadly, suffers from poor health. The Ill-Reverent Detail, as he is called, is writing the standard work on **ed**; he is currently working on Volume 14: *Edits with more than twenty metacharacters.*

His comments on our introduction to **ed** are not re-assuring. "Your description is much too superficial," he said. "You have not mentioned marking lines, moving blocks of text about, encrypting the buffer to gain security, joining lines together, the **g** on the front to make commands apply to the whole buffer, splitting regular expressions into separate parts, specifying newline characters in replacements, doing a context search backwards, using an alternative to the '/' on **s**, ... ".

REFERENCE EXAMPLES

In spite of these appalling omissions, we shall conclude our description of **ed** here. In order to help you remember the features of **ed** that we have covered, we show in this Section a simple example of each.

Addresses
    These specify a line in the buffer.

12	twelfth line
.	current line
$	last line

.+3	three after the current line
$-6	six before the last line
/pig/	the next line that contains **pig**
//	same as previous pattern

Metacharacters

These apply in patterns between '/' and '/'. Each of the following advances the current line to the next line containing the stated pattern.

/∧x/	**x** at start of line
/x$/	**x** at end of line
/x.y/	**x**, then any character, then **y**
/x.*y/	**x**, then any sequence of characters, then **y**
/[xy]/	**x** or **y**
/[∧xy]/	any character that is neither **x** nor **y**
/\./	a dot
/\//	/

Commands

(null)	advance current line and print it
/pig/	advance current line to next line containing **pig** and print it
a **extra line 1** **extra line 2** **.**	append lines after current line
c **replacement** **.**	change (i.e. replace) current line
d	delete current line
1,/pig/d	delete from line 1 to first line containing **pig**
i **precedent 1** **precedent 2** **.**	insert extra lines before current line
l	print current line, including invisible characters
p	print current line
1,$p	print the whole buffer
q	quit
/Author/r boast	insert the file **boast** after the next line containing **Author**
r /usr/him/x	insert the file **usr/him/x** after the current line
s/new/fresh/p	replace first **new** in current line by **fresh**, and print the line
s/new/fresh/gp	replace every **new** in current line by **fresh**, and print the line
s/very //p	delete the first occurrence of **very** (followed by a space) in the current line, and print the line
1,$s/new/fresh/gp	replace every **new** in the buffer by **fresh**, and print the (last) replaced line
s/xx*/(&)/	replace, within the current line, the first sequence of **x**'s by the same sequence in parentheses
u	undo last substitution

w	write the buffer to the current file
w mycopy	write the buffer to the file **mycopy**
.w bestline	write the current line to the file **bestline**
W xxx	append the buffer to the file **xxx**
.=	print line number of current line
!ls	execute the shell command **ls**

Error messages

?	unrecognized editing command
??	pattern could not be found
?xxx	something is wrong with file xxx
?TMP	an internal file has overflowed — something is too big

Banana skins

Missing dot after inserted text

Unintentional use of metacharacters

SCREEN EDITING

UNIX has a screen editor called **vi**. If **ed** is an editor for smart people on dumb terminals, then **vi** is an editor for even smarter people on less dumb terminals. Though you, the current reader, are definitely extremely smart, we must allow for other readers who are less gifted; we shall therefore not plunge into the details of **vi** here. It may even be that your UNIX has an alternative screen editor, which might be more suitable for beginners, so there is no immediate need to learn **vi**. All we shall do here is mention some principles of screen editors.

Screen editors work with a buffer, just like **ed**. Unlike **ed**, the buffer is always displayed on the screen. A typical terminal will display 24 lines of text, and we shall assume that our screen editor devotes 22 lines of the screen to displaying the buffer — the remaining two lines being used for showing the current state of play and, on occasion, for echoing characters typed at the terminal. Obviously the buffer will generally be larger than 22 lines; the screen can be thought of as a 22-line 'window' that can look at any part of the buffer. Thus a screen editor has commands which allow the user to move the window to any desired part of the buffer.

To locate a character that is in the window, the user moves a cursor left or right, up or down, until it reaches the desired point. Thus instead of the concept of a current line, you have the concept of a current character. (Some screen editors have subsidiary concepts of the current word and the current line, as well as the current character, but we shall not worry about these here.) All edits are done at the current character position. Thus you can delete the current character or insert in front of it. The great advantage of a screen editor is that you can *see what you are doing*: as you make each change the screen editor will redisplay the window so that you can see the effect of the alteration.

To bring out the difference between screen editing and line editing we shall consider the **ed** command

s/he/Ron/p

With a screen editor you do not need a pattern to find the **he**. You just point a cursor at it — you may need to move the window first. You then twice type the *delete command* (a single key on almost every screen editor) to delete the **h** and **e**. The screen changes as you make the deletions. To finish the edit you type the *insert command* followed by the text **Ron**. Lastly you type a terminator to indicate the end of the insertion.

Some implementations of **ed** have a limited form of screen editing, in that you can move a cursor along the current line, and change the character pointed at by the cursor.

CHAPTER 9

Documentation and communication

With all his honours on, he sighed for one
Who, say astonished critics, lived at home;
Did little jobs about the house with skill
And nothing else; could whistle; would sit still
Or potter around the garden; answered some
Of his long marvellous letters but kept none.
AUDEN

In this Chapter we explain how to extract information about your UNIX system, and how to communicate with other users.

The ideal operating system has an interactive information service. Whenever you have a query such as

- how does the *xxx* command work?
- what commands manipulate directories?
- why does this line not do what I intended?

you simply type the query on your terminal, and the operating system immediately provides a helpful and friendly answer. This ideal information service is even better than a human adviser standing by your side, since the information service will not laugh at your ignorance and stupidity.

The nadir of operating systems have no information service. Instead you have to buy a printed manual, and search through it whenever you want information.

No operating system in existence today even gets close to our ideal. There are plenty of systems close to the nadir — some even seem to be inferior to the worst one could imagine: the printed manuals run to several fat volumes; each volume is in a loose-leaf binder where pages have been constantly changed, and several pages have pencilled corrections.

UNIX implementations vary in their point on the spectrum between the ideal and the nadir. Most are at least some way on the road to the ideal, since the documentation is available on the computer and can be consulted from a terminal.

UNIX DOCUMENTATION

The authoritative definition of UNIX is the *UNIX Programmer's Manual*. There are several different versions of this manual, depending on date, machine, and local variations.

The *UNIX Programmer's Manual* is (normally) divided into two volumes. The most important is Volume 1, which gives a fairly complete definition. This is written as concisely as possible — though it is still a bulky work — and assumes a reasonably sophisticated reader.

Volume 1 is supplemented by Volume 2, which is even bigger than Volume 1, and may be divided into several sub-volumes. Volume 2 is a comparatively unstructured work, containing a collection of papers on different aspects of UNIX. Some of these papers are tutorial and good for beginners; some are for experts and are concerned with management or implementation; some give fuller details of specialized UNIX programs, such as compilers and text preparation systems; some describe local variations of UNIX. Most of the papers are self-contained.

Some tutorial material, together with some excellent technical papers, can be found in the special issue of *The Bell System Technical Journal* that was devoted to UNIX. This is Volume 57, Number 6, Part 2 and is dated July-August 1978.

A typical UNIX implementation will have Volume 1 stored on the computer, and available interactively. We shall assume in this Chapter that your UNIX is one of these. The advantages of storing documentation on the computer are great:

- it can be consulted from any terminal
- it is cheaper than printing lots of manuals

- it can be updated quickly
- it can be processed by software tools, for example tools to search it for given words, tools to display parts of it, tools to edit it, and so on.

The only real disadvantage is that vast quantities of interactive documentation occupy a lot of file storage, and this may necessitate some pruning to fit on small systems.

UNIX documentation, such as Volume 1 of the *UNIX Programmer's Manual*, is normally stored in the computer in an encoded form. (Specifically it is the input format for **nroff/troff**, which we shall describe later.) When a user asks for a part of the documentation to be displayed on his terminal, the encoded form is converted to a printable form. This has the disadvantage that displaying of documentation can be slowish, but the great advantage that the form of the display can be adapted according to the type of terminal (e.g. width of lines, use of bold face characters, etc.). There may also be a secondary advantage that the encoded form occupies less file space than the printable form.

If you are going to access the *UNIX Programmer's Manual*, it is useful to know a little about its organization. Volume 1 is divided into eight Sections.

Section 1, which is by far the most important one, contains descriptions of all the UNIX commands. The shell itself, which corresponds to the **sh** command, is described in this Section, though the description is certainly not written for novices. There is a sub-classification used for the commands within Section 1, which normally works as follows

1C commands for communication with other systems
1G commands for graphics
1M commands for system maintenance (see also Section 8 below)
1   commands for general use

Sections 2 and 3 are of interest to programmers, particularly to those writing in the C language. They describe libraries and ways of using, from within a program, certain facilities built into UNIX.

Section 4 gives information about the control of input/output devices.

Section 5, also for programmers, contains information about files built into, or created by, the UNIX system.

Section 6 is the next Section, after Section 1, that is likely to concern beginners. It contains descriptions of the game-playing programs that are available.

Section 7 contains miscellaneous useful information, such as a definition of the ASCII character set, and some material useful in document preparation.

Section 8 is for people who look after UNIX systems.

Some local variants of Volume 1 contain further Sections, over and above these eight.

Each Section consists of a number of 'manual pages', one page for each item. In Section 1, for example, there is one page for each command name. Some of these manual 'pages' actually occupy several real pages. In particular the page about **sh**, the shell, takes half a dozen or so real pages. The pages in a Section are arranged in alphabetical order.

It is common to refer to pages by a name such as

ls(1)
graph(1G)
chess(6)

The number in parentheses gives the Section number where the manual page about the given command can be found. Thus **chess**, the chess playing program, is among the games in Section 6.

EXTRACTING INFORMATION FROM THE MANUAL

Assuming Volume 1 of the *UNIX Programmer's Manual* is available interactively on your implementation, you use the **man** command to access it. For example

    man ls

gives you the manual page for the **ls** command. The argument to **man** must be the name of a manual page; normally the argument is the name of a command that you want to find out about.

    Generally **man** will search every Section of the manual and print out each page it finds with the given name. (There might even happen to be a file called **ls** in Section 3 of the manual as well as in Section 1, and if there were, you would be told about this too.) You can limit the search by specifying the Section you want, as in

    man 6 chess

This can speed up the search, particularly for names outside Section 1, which is scanned first.

REDIRECTING OUTPUT

Since **man** is an ordinary UNIX command its output can be redirected or put into a pipe, e.g.

    man ls > myfile
    man chess | lpr
    man ls | grep group

In the first example above, the output from **man** is put into **myfile**. (This is not generally a good thing to do, as if each user kept their own copy of the documentation, file space would soon become exhausted.) The second example pipes the manual page for **chess** to **lpr**, so that a hard copy is printed. The third example also uses a pipe, this time to find all the lines of the manual page for **ls** which contain the string 'group'.

FORMAT OF MANUAL PAGES

Manual pages have a standard format to make it easy for people to find the information they want.

    Each page starts with the heading 'NAME' followed by the name of the command (or whatever) described in the page. The name is in turn followed, on the same line, by a one-line description. For example

```
$ man ls
NAME
ls   list contents of directory
.

.

.
```

The page then continues with five more headings:

SYNOPSIS
DESCRIPTION
FILES
SEE ALSO
BUGS

For some pages one or more of these headings may be omitted.

The SYNOPSIS gives a syntactic definition of the command, and the DESCRIPTION gives a verbal definition — this is normally the longest part of the manual page. The FILES Section describes any files, usually built-in UNIX files, used by the command. Thus the **spell** program might use a system file with an odd name like **/usr/dict/hlistb**, which contains its dictionary of words. The SEE ALSO heading covers related commands, and finally the BUGS heading covers problems. These 'bugs' tend to be descriptions of peculiar behaviour ("If you do this unusual thing then the result will be ... ") rather than catastrophic problems that really need to be corrected immediately.

We hope the time will come when you implement your own UNIX commands, which are so useful that they are made available as part of your local UNIX system. If so, your commands must be properly documented or they are useless; it is obviously sensible if your own documentation follows general UNIX conventions. Thus one day you might yourself write a UNIX manual page.

OTHER FORMS OF HELP

The **man** system is only useful if you know the name of the command that does the job you want. If you do not know the name, guessing will not always get you there. How long would it take to guess that the name of the command which scans for a given string is **grep**?

To combat this problem, some implementations of UNIX provide a **help** command (sometimes called **apropos**), which tries to identify the name of the command to do a given job. Typically the **help** system works as follows.

The person who looks after your UNIX implementation creates a file containing a one-line description of all the commands available. (The lines after the NAME headings of manual pages can be used to build this file.) When the user wants help he simply types

> **help** *string*

and **help** searches the file for the *string* and prints all the lines it finds, e.g.

```
$ help scan
awk(1):   pattern scanning and processing language.
scanf(3s):   formatted input conversion.
```

If the user was really after the **grep** command, he has not found what he wants, but at least the **help** has revealed the existence of **awk**, which might be a useful language to learn. (**Scanf**, being in Section 3, is only of interest to specialists.) If the user tries a synonym for 'scan', e.g.

```
$ help search
grep(1):   search a file for a pattern.
```

he finds **grep**. He can then use

man grep

to get full information.

The user could also have tried another tack in his search for **grep**. He could have typed

help file

Here he would have received a long list in reply, since most UNIX commands deal with files, but **grep** would certainly have been somewhere in the list.

SUBSIDIARY HELP SYSTEMS

Those UNIX commands, such as **ed**, which have their own sub-commands may have their own help system. Typing **h** or a question mark often invokes the help system. In particular, some implementations of **ed** support an **h** command, which gives a list of all available editing commands.

CRITIQUE

The **man** and **help** commands, if you have them, are certainly valuable but they are some way from the ideal information service. In particular

- neither helps directly with specific problems of the "What on earth have I done here?" variety.
- there is a gap between **help**, which provides one line of information about each item, and **man**, which often provides material of too much detail and sophistication. On our local system this gap is bridged by the command **how**, which supplements **help** by listing all the options available on any given command; it provides a one-line description of each option, plus certain other vital information where needed. This command, or its equivalent, is now becoming more widespread.

Those of us who design and implement programs to be used by others are only just beginning to realize that it is no good providing advanced facilities unless you give ordinary people help in using them. The huge research and development effort in producing ever more advanced systems needs to be matched by an equal effort spent on the even more daunting task of providing interactive guidance when these advanced systems go berserk in the hands of inexperienced users.

The wider availability of high-quality graphics terminals will help make such guidance easier to provide. One aid, now commonly used in software written for such terminals, is the *pop-up menu*. Here the user, when puzzled, presses a special

HELP key on his terminal, and a 'menu' pops up on part of the screen; this menu explains what commands can be typed in the current state. For example, a user who had slipped on the **ed** banana skin of omitting a dot would be told, in the menu, that a dot would return him to command mode.

It will take some time for such aids to be universally available. In the meantime you must be content with the thought that the UNIX **man** and **help** system, imperfect as it is, is much better than most operating systems provide.

COMPUTER-AIDED INSTRUCTION

Some implementations of UNIX have computer-aided instruction programs to help you learn certain aspects of the system. These programs typically present you with a description of how to perform some action, for example to edit a file, and then ask you to do a simple exercise to test whether you have understood the material.

Opinions differ on the use of such programs, but if you are interested in trying you may well find a command called **learn** on your UNIX.

MAIL

We have now completed our discussion of the passive side of communication: extracting information from UNIX. In the remainder of this Chapter we discuss active communication: exchanging messages with other people by electronic mail.

Electronic mail is used both locally, between users on the same computer, and globally between users on different computers connected together on networks. Computer networks are growing rapidly; they vary between networks covering the computers in one building to international networks. Such networks are increasingly used by businesses and by individuals to exchange information.

We shall concentrate here on local mail. If your computer is connected to some network that supports global mail, the chances are that the global facilities will be an extension of the local ones.

FINDING THE CURRENT USERS

As a prelude to sending mail, it is often valuable to find out who is currently logged in to your computer. To do this you simply type the command

who

UNIX will reply with something of the following form

bill	tty01	Jul 1	12:45
aper	tty03	Jul 1	13:16
me	tty11	Jul 1	13:50
anne	tty13	Jul 1	13:20
dudley	tty15	Jul 1	04:20

This is a list of the login names of all the people currently logged in to the system. You yourself must be somewhere on this list. Against each login name is an identification of the terminal that they are using, and the date and time at which they logged in. Terminals are usually identified by **tty** (which was originally an abbreviation for 'Teletype') followed by an arbitrary number.

If your UNIX system has all its terminals in the same room, you may think the **who** command is useless. It is easier to find out who is logged in by looking round the room. However this is not necessarily so. Some users have several possible login names, and the **who** command tells you which one they are using.

As an extension of this, you can solve an identity crisis by typing

who am I

UNIX then solves at a stroke one of the deepest problems of philosophy by replying

        me   tty11   Jul 1 13:50

The output from **who**, like any other UNIX command, can be fed into a pipe. Thus

who | grep bill

finds all occurrences of **bill** in the output from **who**. Thus if **bill** is not logged in, the reply will be null (unless there is another user called **spoonbill** or the like); if **bill** is logged in, the reply will be the corresponding line from **who**.

BEING INQUISITIVE

If you are nosy by nature, UNIX provides a number of tools to help satisfy your curiosity. Some implementations allow you to enquire about the personal details of a particular user. The command to do this varies, but one possibility is

finger anne

The name **finger** implies a close personal relationship, but all you are told is **anne**'s full name, the time at which she last logged in, and perhaps her status and location within the organization that owns your UNIX.

Not only may you be able to find out who people are, but you can also find out what they are doing by typing the command

ps −a

This tells you all the processes that are currently running. Part of the information given against each process is the terminal that controls it, and from this you can deduce the user. (On some implementations you can type −**au** instead of −**a**, and get users' login names against each terminal, so there is no need to tax your deductive powers.)

COMMUNICATING

There are two commands for sending messages to other people: **write** and **mail**. The former is a brusque way of interrupting what they are doing and displaying your message. The latter is a more civilized form of communication. We shall start by being brusque, and then go on to reform ourselves.

Because **write** is an immediate form of communication you can only write to someone who is currently logged in. Hence typing **who** is often a prelude to using **write**. The argument to the **write** command is the login name of the person you want to address.

If we type the command

write anne

then the effect as we see it is not dramatic: our terminal appears to go dead. The reason is that UNIX is waiting for some input — our message — in exactly the same way as if it wanted input to, say, the **cat** command. The action happens at **anne**'s terminal. What she is doing is interrupted by the message

Message from me tty11...

Thereafter each line of input that we type is displayed on **anne**'s terminal. This continues until we terminate our input by typing ∧ **d**. Thus our use of **write** might be

```
$ write anne
I am sorry to interrupt you, but I have just found out
about the write command.
∧ d
$
```

It is possible to carry out a two-way conversation using **write**. **Anne**, when she finds that **me** is writing to her, can decide to write back by typing the command

write me

After she has done this, not only are the lines of input that we type reproduced on **anne**'s terminal, but the lines of input typed by **anne** are reproduced on our terminal. This is a fine recipe for a chaotic conversation, so some UNIX users have developed informal rules for saying when they want their correspondent to type. A common rule is that

(O)

meaning 'over' is a signal for the other to proceed; using this convention, our conversation with **anne** might proceed as follows.

```
$ write anne
I have got a new UNIX game I want to play with you.
Are you free tonight?
(O)
Message from anne tty13...
NO. (O)
Are you free tomorrow night? (O)
NO.
EOF
Then I will come round now.
∧ d
$
```

When **anne** received our message ending in '(O)' she decided to write to us. We therefore received the line

```
Message from anne tty13...
```

followed by her brief message. We then asked if she was free the following night, and, having said no, she must have inadvertently typed the ∧**d** key thus terminating her **write**. The recipient always gets a line containing the word EOF (meaning end-of-file) at the end of a **write**. Undeterred by her error, we type the final line of our message followed by ∧**d** to terminate our side of the conversation.

The way **anne** sees the conversation is as follows.

```
Message from me tty11...
I have got a new UNIX game I want to play with you.
Are you free tonight?
(O)
$ write me
NO. (O)
Are you free tomorrow night? (O)
NO
∧d
$ Then I will come round now.
EOF
```

SENDING MAIL

More civilized communication uses **mail** rather than **write**. The mail system varies between implementations but it generally has the following properties

- recipients of messages do not need to be logged in when a message is sent
- mail is automatically stored, perhaps for several weeks, until the recipient logs in and opts to look at it
- the same message can, if desired, be sent to more than one person (On certain implementations some or all of these people may be on other computers, interconnected with the sender by a network.)
- there is a system for saving messages that you receive.

Sending a message using **mail** is almost identical to using **write**. The main difference is that the message can be terminated with a line consisting of a single dot, as an alternative to ∧**d**. For example

```
$ mail anne
You cannot have recieved the message that I was
coming over, because when I got there you had gone.
Please mail me as soon as possible.
.
```

If you want to send the same message to several people, you write all their login names as arguments to **mail**, e.g.

mail anne yvonne mary

126

You can, if you wish, send mail to yourself, e.g.

mail me

This may be used to remind yourself of something you should do when you next log in.

On systems that allow mail to be sent to remote users on other machines, the name of the recipient is often written in the form

xmachine!him

where **xmachine** identifies the computer and **him** the person. Conventions vary, however, so you will need to consult your local documentation.

If you have a long message to send to somebody, you can prepare it in a file and make **mail** take its input from this file, e.g.

mail anne < message

It is usually good practice to do this. When we noticed the spelling error in 'received' in our last message to **anne**, the line had been sent and there was no correcting it.

RECEIVING MAIL

When you log in to UNIX, you are told if there is any mail waiting for you (e.g. 'You have mail'). On some implementations you are also told if new mail arrives while you are logged in (e.g. 'You have new mail'). In either case, if you wish to examine your mail you simply type

mail

There may, in general, be a number of items of mail waiting to be read. These are stored in your 'mailbox', which is a file deep in the UNIX filing system (often in the directory **usr/spool/mail**). When you ask for **mail**, the first message in your mailbox is printed and then a question mark is displayed, asking you what to do next. There are several possible actions, of which the following are the most popular.

- typing a RETURN goes on to the next message, if any
- typing **d** deletes the message and then goes on to the next one
- typing

     s *filename*

  saves the message in the given *filename* and goes on to the next message (or, on some implementations, exits from the mail system). If you omit the filename the message is saved in a default file called **mbox**. Many users, after they have been using UNIX for a while, build up an **mbox** file containing valuable messages they have saved. Note that this **mbox** file is your own file, controlled by you, and is separate from the mailbox that accumulates your incoming messages. Saved messages are appended to the end of files, so that the previous contents remains intact.
- typing **q** quits from the mail system and returns to the shell
- typing a question mark summarizes the available commands in the mail system.

Note that, on many implementations of UNIX mail, if you just read your messages and do not save them or delete them, they remain in your mailbox and are re-displayed next time you type **mail**. It is like saying to the postman: "That letter is very interesting. Bring it again at the next delivery and I will have another look at it."

As an example of the receipt of mail, we assume that when **anne** next logs in she has two messages waiting, one from Dudley and one from us. What she types is as follows

```
$ mail
From dudley Tue Jul 1 13:00:59
I love you.  Meet me tonight as usual, after I have
finished my UNIX session.

? s treasure
From me Tue Jul 1 12:10:21
You cannot have recieved the message that I was
coming over, because when I got there you had gone.
Please mail me as soon as possible.

? d
? q
$ mail dudley
   .
   .
   .
```

Here **mail** displays the first message and prompts with a question mark. Note that all mail messages are prefixed with the sender's name, and a *postmark*, which gives the date and time of sending (accurate to the nearest second). Do not therefore try using UNIX mail for your anonymous poisoned pen letters to the superuser.

Anne saves **dudley**'s message in a file called **treasure**, and then the mail system displays the next message, which is ours. Unfortunately **anne** mistakenly types the **d** key to destroy this message. Distraught at her error, she quits the mail system. She then prepares to send some mail to **dudley** to reply to his ridiculous message.

CONTROLLING MAIL

Junk mail is a problem with conventional mail systems. With electronic mail the problem is worse, because mail is so easy to send. Unfortunately it is not possible to filter out junk mail automatically, but UNIX does offer some controls over **mail** and **write**. In particular you can totally inhibit the latter by typing

mesg n

Thereafter no-one can write to you until you type

mesg y

to allow writing again. It is particularly valuable to inhibit writing if your terminal is a printing terminal used for document preparation. In fact some UNIX document preparation programs automatically inhibit writing, so that an inane message from a friend does not come out in the middle of the final copy of your best-selling novel.

Although you can control **write** you cannot control **mail**, unless your implementation has special extensions to do this. If it does you may be able to summarize the list of people who have sent mail to you, and then to delete messages from well-known bores. If you wish to automate the receiving of mail when you log in, you can put some appropriate commands in your user profile. Again the details are heavily dependent on your particular implementation of the mail system.

ACCESSING REMOTE MACHINES

The use of computers over networks is still in its infancy, and most implementations have their own *ad hoc* procedures and conventions for communication. In general it is not possible for users running a program on one machine to access files on another. Instead an explicit copy of the file has to be made for the machine that wants to use it. To help this procedure, some implementations of UNIX provide a version of the **cp** command called **uucp**. This stands for *U*NIX to *U*NIX **cp**, and it is assumed that both the donor machine and the receiver machine are running UNIX. You use **uucp** by typing a line of form

    uucp *file xmachine!newfile*

Your *file* is then copied to the *newfile* on *xmachine*. You can also, if there is permission, use **uucp** to copy files from other machines to yours.

Do not expect too much of **uucp**, however. To management, the free transfer of files between machines presents severe security problems, so you may well find that your use of **uucp** is limited to a few directories.

SUMMARY OF COMMUNICATION MECHANISMS

To summarize what we have said in this Chapter:

- use **help** and **man** to find out how to use your UNIX
- use **who** and **ps** to find out what is going on in your machine
- use **mail**, and perhaps occasionally **write**, to communicate with your fellow users
- if your computer is part of a network you may be able to use **mail** and **uucp** to communicate with people on other computers.

CHAPTER 10

Errors

To err is human
To forgive is divine
To give decent error messages is heavenly.
OLD PROVERB

In this Chapter we try to give a few useful suggestions on what to do when things go wrong. Unfortunately the number of possible errors and misconceptions in using UNIX, as with any other operating system, is so great that we can only scratch the surface.

UP AND DOWN

A computer system is said to be *up* when it is working and *down* when it is not. You can therefore think of your system as an aeroplane, particularly as a sudden transition from being up to being down is called a *crash*.

When your UNIX system is down, it may be because of hardware or software malfunctions or for scheduled maintenance. In many cases you are not interested in the reason for the failure — someone else has to put things right. All you want to know is when the system will come up again. If this is so, spare a thought for the poor devil who has to look after your UNIX; remember that the more you interrupt him with questions about when he will have finished, the longer this time will be delayed.

Fortunately crashes are rare on most UNIX systems. When they do occur there are two common phenomena. One is that each user thinks he caused the crash. ("I typed an **ls** command and the system crashed.") Remember that there are normally several processes running inside the computer — even if you are the only user — and it is unlikely that what you typed on your terminal directly caused the crash.

The second phenomenon is that crashes always occur at the worst possible time — half an hour before your deadline or when you have just typed 1,000 lines of text into the editor's buffer and have not yet saved it in a file. Experienced computer users solve the first of these problems by pretending their deadline is a day earlier than the real one — and keeping to the pretence. The loss of the buffer is, happily, sometimes solved by UNIX itself. If there is a crash while using **ed**, UNIX tries to preserve the **ed** buffer in a file called **ed.hup** (the **hup** means hiccup). Hence before you jump off a skyscraper because you have lost everything in an editor crash, log in again, when the system comes up, and see if you have an **ed.hup** file.

INITIAL PROBLEMS

If when you come to use your terminal you cannot get any sense out of it, it is not always easy to tell if this is because your UNIX is down, or because there is some problem with the terminal. Your best action may be to look at other users, if there are any at hand, and see if they are smiling. If they are, then there is something amiss with your terminal, or more likely, UNIX's view of it. Expert help is usually needed, though you could experiment with changing line-speeds, or with pressing keys such as FULL-DUPLEX or BREAK.

If you can communicate with UNIX but your attempts to log in are invariably rejected, then you need help from the superuser. Either she does not regard you as a proper user or your password is wrong — perhaps because a kind friend has changed it.

Once you have successfully logged in your real problems start, because there is usually only one person to help you: yourself.

HUNG TERMINALS

A common problem is for a terminal to go into an apparently frozen state. This is called a *hung* terminal. There are three possible reasons for this

(1) UNIX is down
(2) you are executing a command that takes a long time to finish. Indeed you could be running a program that is in an endless loop.
(3) UNIX is waiting for you to type.

Of these, case (3) is by far the most common. Beginners often forget to type the RETURN key at the end of a line, with the result that they are waiting for UNIX to do something, but UNIX is waiting for them to finish their input line. A second possibility is that the frozen terminal may be caused by scrolling: perhaps UNIX is waiting for you to type a character to request the next screenful, or perhaps you have, intentionally or otherwise, typed ∧ s to freeze the screen — you may then need to type ∧ q to unfreeze it. A third possibility is that you ought to have typed ∧ d at the end of some data and you forgot to do so. You may then think that your data is complete and that UNIX is processing it, but the reality is otherwise. A fourth possibility is that UNIX has prompted you for a reply to some question, and is awaiting a reply. Such prompts should, however, be obvious to see (except in hrmt's **ed** and the like): even if the prompt is only a question mark, it should be evident that you need to type something.

Because of these four possibilities, the first thing to do with a frozen terminal is to *type something*. A RETURN is a good start, and ∧ **d** or ∧ **q** are other excellent choices.

If this does not help, then case (1) or (2) may apply. If the characters you type are echoed on the screen, then the chances are that UNIX is not down but is executing a long command. In this case if you want to terminate your long-drawn out process, the break-in key will normally do the trick.

THE INSATIABLE APPETITE

An alternative to the frozen terminal is the terminal with the insatiable appetite: every line you type is gobbled up by the terminal without any reply. This problem is almost always caused by a missing terminator for data. Hence consider typing ∧ **d**, or, if in **ed**, a dot. If all else fails type the break-in key.

THE INESCAPABLE PROGRAM

A common problem with badly designed computer-aided instruction programs is as follows.

An innocent user enters the program by typing the appropriate UNIX command, and plays with it for a while. He then gets bored, and decides to quit. The program has displayed

What is the capital of Bulgaria?

The user tries **q**, ∧ **d**, a dot, a RETURN, the break-in key, and many other desperate replies to the question, but the reply is always something like

```
q is not the capital of Bulgaria.
Try again.
What is the capital of Bulgaria?
```

There is, unfortunately no infallible way of escaping from such programs — and they arise in many fields as well as computer-aided instruction. All we can say is that the vain attempts tried above are often the best ones. In addition it is worth trying **h** or **?**; these may enter a help system, if there is one, which tells you how to escape.

If you get really distraught the only way out is to abandon your terminal, and hope that the next person to come along knows what the capital of Bulgaria is, and, more to the point, knows how to escape from the program that you are using.

THE SCREENFUL OF GARBAGE

If your terminal displays an incomprehensible collection of apparently random characters then you have probably tried to display a binary file (or a file encrypted by **ed**). Such a display can cause a secondary problem in that one of the random characters that is output may cause your terminal to go into some special mode. You will then need to find what to you is an equally random character in order to get back to normal again. If all else fails, switching the terminal off and on again might help.

ERROR MESSAGES

Having covered general problems, we shall now go on to introduce more specific troubles.

When you make a mistake in a UNIX command, one of the following will happen

- UNIX will be unable to execute the command and will give an error message
- UNIX will execute the command in a way that you did not intend

The latter is the more troublesome case, but, when you become a comparative expert with UNIX, it will enable you to make some money. There is a large class of people who, when UNIX starts behaving oddly, assume the fault lies with UNIX and not with them. "It can't be my fault: all I typed was ... , and this bug-ridden UNIX system treated it as ... ". This is where you make your money. Ninety-nine percent of the time, the mistake turns out to be the user's; you therefore have a standing bet that you will give any user ten shares in IBM for each UNIX bug they find, provided that they give you one share if the mistake turns out to be theirs. Within a year you will control IBM.

To return to the former case, that of the error message from a UNIX command, you will find that messages vary considerably between UNIX implementations, and the messages shown in this book will not necessarily be the ones that appear on your terminal. In general, however, UNIX error messages though terse are generally accurate and helpful. They are, nevertheless, some way from being heavenly. (We are talking here of error messages from shell commands.

When you get deep inside programs such as the editor, you get the program's own style of messages. As we have seen from **ed**, these can be even less heavenly than the normal messages.)

Sometimes a message will tell you what went wrong, e.g.

$ **poetry**
poetry: Command not found.

Sometimes the message will tell you what you should have done, e.g.

$ **cp xxx**
Usage: cp f1 f2; or cp f1 ... fn d2

Here you only gave one argument to the **cp** command, and are told that the way to use it is to type

cp *f1 f2*

(i.e. **cp** one file to another) or

cp *f1 ... fn d2*

which means copy a set of *n* files to a directory. (We have not, in fact, covered this extended form in the book.)

Often messages are prefixed by the name of the command or file in which the error arose, e.g., if **xxx** is a non-existent file

$ **cat xxx**
cat: can't open xxx.
$ **ls xxx**
xxx not found

These examples also show that there are a few inconsistencies between error messages from different commands — at least on our UNIX implementation. The error message from **cat** is prefixed by 'cat:' but **ls** produces a different message (though the error, to you the user, is the same as the error on the **cat**) and does not prefix it with 'ls:'.

In the above examples the prefix, when it does occur, is not specially useful as you know what command you are executing. However the prefix is valuable when you are executing a command file, when you are running background processes, or when you have typed ahead and are executing a command that you typed perhaps three lines earlier.

ERRORS WITH FILES

The error message

Can't open xxx.

is probably the most common error message in UNIX. It means that your file **xxx** cannot be accessed, either because it does not exist, or because you do not have permission to read it. If the message puzzles you, because you think **xxx** does exist and you have permission to read it, a common reason for your confusion is that you are in the wrong directory. Thus it well worth using the **pwd** command to find

135

out what your current directory is. The **pwd** command is actually useful in a much wider context than when you are puzzled by errors. Observers of university UNIX systems have said that **pwd** is one of the most commonly-used commands; it is invaluable to inquisitive students who explore their UNIX file structure and get lost.

If typing **pwd** does not reveal your problem, it is worth trying **ls** to get a listing of the directory in which you think **xxx** is. The command

ls −l

is valuable if you want to look at the permissions attached to files.

If your file is accessed via a pathname such as

a/b/c

It may help to explore the path step by step, e.g.

cd a
cd b
cat c

The error should be revealed on one of the steps.

If you have built a complex hierarchy of directories, and you know that the file **xxx** is somewhere but you are not sure where, then you can be intrepid and use the **find** command. This command is only for the brave, and we shall not describe it in this book save to say that

find . −name xxx −print

will search for **xxx** in the current directory and all its sub-directories, and will display the pathname of any occurrence(s) it finds. Thus if you set the current directory to your home directory, the magic **find** command shown above should locate your file. More dramatically, you can set the current directory to the root directory (/), and the **find** then searches the whole file system to locate the required file. It may, however, take a long time to do so. The only possible stumbling block is that you might not have read or execute permission for some directory which is between the **find**'s starting directory and **xxx**.

Errors in writing files are less frequent than errors in reading them. However messages such as

xxx: Cannot create
xxx: Permission denied
xxx: File exists

are still quite common. Two likely causes are

- a file **xxx** already exists and has not got write permission
- the directory containing **xxx** does not have write permission and hence you cannot create any new files within it

The latter frequently occurs when you are exploring other people's directories.

With some UNIX shells (e.g. **csh**) it is possible to prevent the disaster where the Great Pest destroys a file when he types

cat > randomname

and **randomname** happens to be a valuable file that already exists. You may be able to prevent this by **set**ting a variable called **noclobber**. The Great Pest is then thwarted by the "File exists" message.

Your worst problem with writing files arises when the file space of your UNIX system becomes full up, and either you or some other users must delete old files to make way for new ones.

EXECUTING COMMANDS

If you try to execute a command

   x

and get a message like "Command not found" or simply "not found", then the reason is that there is no file called **x** in any of the directories in your search path. (If you are worried about your search path, type **set**; this may also have the benefit of revealing other potential problems in your environment.)

If the response to your command is

   x: permission denied

or

   x: cannot execute

then **x** does exist, but you do not have permission to execute it.

MISUSE OF SPACES IN SHELL COMMANDS

The rule for spacing in shell commands is simple: you just type one or more spaces before each argument. Although the rule is simple, it is still easy for beginners to omit necessary spaces or to put in wrong ones. In both cases the punishment is that your command will be interpreted in entirely the wrong way — a severe penalty for an apparently harmless crime.

For example the following are the effects of bad spacing in the command

ls −l

Error 1: missing space

   $ **ls−l**
   ls−l: Command not found.

Here **ls−l** is taken as the command name, and UNIX can find no such command.

Error 2: extra space

   $ **ls − l**
   l not found

This is taken as a use of the **ls** command with a null option (a minus sign on its own). Since the **l** that follows the minus is preceded by a space it is taken as the second argument. In the case of **ls** the second argument is the name of the file — usually a directory — that is to be listed. The file **l** cannot be found, and hence the above error message is given. (If you did happen to have a file called **l** it would indeed be listed, and you would be somewhat surprised at the effect of your command.)

UNINTENDED WILDCARDS

We have emphasized the problems caused by metacharacters in **ed** and, to a lesser extent, by wildcards in the shell. Remember that

grep * xxx

does not search for all lines of the file **xxx** that contain asterisks. Instead the shell replaces the asterisk by the list of all the filenames in the current directory, so you get a peculiar command indeed.

In general, therefore, if a command seems to be behaving in a particularly perverse way, check to see if it contains any wildcards. If you want to be sure, try the command as an argument to **echo**. For example

echo grep * xxx

would have told us what the shell turned our **grep** command into.

SOME SPECIFIC MESSAGES

The following is a list of some specific error messages which occur frequently and sometimes cause bewilderment.

Bad directory

You have tried to use as a directory a file that is not in the proper format for a directory. The error normally arises when you mistakenly specify an ordinary character file where you should have written a directory file.

Broken pipe

One of the commands in a pipeline has failed, and has thus not relayed information to the next command in the pipe (or has not accepted information from the previous command in the pipe).

Can't access xxx

This is similar to being unable to open a file: the file **xxx** does not exist or you do not have permission to look at it.

xxx: cannot unlink

This normally arises when you try to **rm** a file that you do not have permission to delete (either because of the permissions on the file itself or permissions on the containing directory). The message can arise on an **mv** command, which tries to delete the old file after making a new one.

Core dumped

If you get this message it is both good and bad news. The bad news is that there is something wrong with the program you are using. The good news is that it is not your fault; it is the fault of the person who wrote the program. (If this is also you, the news is doubly bad.) The message arises when a program tries to do something impossible, such as to divide by zero, or to refer to some storage that does not exist. When you get the "Core dumped" message, a file called **core** is gratuitously created in your current directory. This is an image of the store of the computer at the time the fault occurred; it can be examined by programmers with suitable tools. The "Core dumped" message is often preceded by a message to pinpoint the cause of the trouble; one such message is the puzzling "Bus error".

No such tty

This means that you tried to refer to a terminal that does not exist.

xxx: 400 mode

The permissions for the file **xxx** do not allow the current operation. The 400 (or whatever number you get) has the same meaning as the first argument to the **chmod** command.

MEAN TRICKS

Finally, the most baffling errors of all arise when your kind friends play mean tricks on you by changing your user profile, by altering some of your files or by creating new ones. Every UNIX user can be a Machiavelli: a sly observation of a password and a new career begins.

An example is the file-moth trick we played on Dudley. This was, of course, an extremely funny joke, but a joke is never funny a second time. If someone did it to us it would be childish and time-wasting.

The essence of a successful trick is that the subject is taken in. Nevertheless if, when you log in to your UNIX and get a message that you are connected to the bank's computer and can edit the file containing the amount of money in your account, try to remember to do a few UNIX checks before ordering the new Rolls-Royce. Good checks to try are pressing the break-in key, typing commands such as

ls −**al**	to list all files, with their owners, etc.
set	to show your environment
pwd	to show your current directory

If you understand such things, you should also display your user profile.

Don't be too hasty, though; you might as well savour for a while the sense of infinite richness, even if the illusion is inevitably bound to be shattered.

CHAPTER 11

Document preparation

A sweet attractive kind of grace,
A full assurance given by looks,
MATTHEW ROYDEN

If a document is to serve its purpose, whether it is a technical manual or a letter seeking a job, it must look good and read well. UNIX helps you achieve both these goals, though it cannot go as far as turning each of us into a Brian Kernighan.

A document initially attracts the reader if it is well laid out in terms of headings, indentation, and so on. The bulk of this Chapter is devoted to explaining UNIX's text formatters, which help you lay out your documents. At the end of the Chapter we give a brief introduction to some of UNIX's aids to good writing.

TEXT FORMATTERS

To understand the need for a text formatter we shall assume a world without one.

Working in this world, you use UNIX to prepare a complete chapter of a book. You carefully keep the lines of similar length, so that the book looks good when displayed (using **cat**, for example). When doing a final check of the chapter you notice that you have omitted three vital words in the first line of a paragraph. This is a minor disaster: by adding these three words you make the first line much longer than the rest — perhaps even too long to fit on the paper you print on. You therefore need to retype the whole paragraph to get the lines equal again.

Such time-wasting procedures are common with traditional typewriting and printing. To quote an instruction to proof checkers: "If you substitute a word or phrase, make the new material the same number of letters as the old. If this is not done, the balance of a paragraph must be redone".

With UNIX's text formatting aids such problems vanish. Indeed it would be a disgrace if they did not, as even the humblest of word processors can eliminate these problems. UNIX has programs that will automatically divide text into lines of any desired size. The main programs available are

- **troff**, which prepares text for a computer controlled typesetter
- **nroff**, which prepares text for devices where all characters have the same width: this covers most matrix printers, daisy-wheel printers, line-printers and display terminals; thus **nroff** caters for the majority of output devices that are likely to be available on your computer.

Nroff and **troff** are closely related, and the facilities of the former are (almost) a sub-set of the latter. Your UNIX implementation may also have further programs in the 'roff' family.

In this book we shall describe **nroff**. We do this for two reasons

- once you know **nroff** you can easily adapt to other members of the family
- most computer systems support devices for which **nroff** is suitable, but few support typesetting devices.

Although **nroff** is simpler than **troff**, we would still need to devote the best part of a book to it if we wanted to give tutorial explanations of every feature. In this book our aim is more modest: we shall give a simplified introduction to **nroff**'s most valuable facilities, so that you will know enough to use it for many tasks. If, however, you want anything unusual or fancy you will need to consult the full **nroff** documentation, as given in the *NROFF/TROFF User's Manual*. You can find this in Volume 2 of the *UNIX Programmer's Manual*.

FACILITIES AVAILABLE

To introduce **nroff** we shall first outline its main facilities. These are as follows.

Nroff will divide documents into pages with a heading and page number on each page, if required. It will also deal with so-called *footers* at the bottoms of pages. Some documents, for example, have their date as a footer at the bottom of each page. (**Nroff** will also, incidentally, deal with *footnotes*, which are a separate concept from footers.)

Nroff will automatically *fill* and *justify* text. These are complementary processes, and we shall start by explaining the former. Filling consists of adding words to each line of output until no more words will fit. This ensures that all the lines are of similar length, but does not make them of *identical* length. Some lines will be shorter than the maximum line length. For example if an output line has been filled to a position three characters from the right-hand margin, and the next word consists of four characters, then it is necessary to start a new line. Thus the original line will be three characters short of the maximum. In general the output will have some lines of the full length, some one character short, some two characters short, and so on. It therefore has a *ragged* right-hand margin. Most letters produced on ordinary typewriters have this appearance. The process of justification (or, as the **nroff** documentation calls it, *adjusting the margins*) straightens ragged margins. This is done by putting extra spaces *between* the words in a line in order to pad the line out to the full length. If a line is three characters short, therefore, three extra spaces (or, on some fancy printers, six extra half-spaces) will be added. The text in almost every book is justified in this way, in order to give a more pleasing effect. The following example shows a piece of text that has a very ragged margin — it has neither been properly filled nor justified.

> **The use of nroff to format text is an invaluable**
> **aid to any writer, whether he be producing**
> **a book or a letter.**
> **A good property of nroff is that you can gradually**
> **learn new features so that your documents get**
> **better and better.**

If you feed this text to **nroff** it comes out in filled and justified form as follows — we show the output as it would appear on a 'letter-quality' printer with a line length of 42 characters

```
The use of nroff to format text is an  in-
valuable  aid to any writer, whether he be
producing a book or a letter.  A good pro-
perty of  nroff is that you can gradually
learn new features so that your  documents
get better and better.
```

Notice the extra spacing in the first two lines. It has been inserted in the second half of the first line, but in the first half of the second line. Such alternation is a characteristic of a good text formatter; it gives the output a balanced appearance.

As an adjunct to the processes of filling and justification, **nroff** will automatically hyphenate words in order to split them across lines. It does this gracefully, rather than by splitting words at arbitrary points. You can see that the words 'invaluable' and 'property' have been hyphenated in the above output text, thus avoiding excessive extra spacing. If, however, you do not like **nroff**'s hyphenation you can switch it off.

Nroff caters for separate *fonts*. Broadly speaking a font is a set of characters in a single style of type. A font might include all the letters of the alphabet, both upper case and lower case, the digits 0 to 9, plus all the popular punctuation signs. Typesetters offer all kinds of sizes and styles of characters. You only have to compare two different books, or a book and a magazine, to get an impression of the variety available. The devices that **nroff** caters for are, however, much more limited. They typically only offer three fonts, which are all of the same size and all related to the same type style. The fonts are:

- Roman, which is the normal style
- **Bold, which makes characters stand out**. The effect of bold type is often achieved on printing devices by striking the same character more than once, perhaps with the strokes slightly offset from one another.
- *Italic, where characters are slanted.* Few computer output devices offer true italics. Instead characters that should be in italics are underlined; this achieves the desired effect of showing that the characters are something special.

Finally **nroff** helps with the layout within pages. It covers such matters as paragraphs, indentation, and section headings.

In subsequent Sections we shall explain how you use some of these facilities. However, as we warned earlier, we confine ourselves to the mainstream; if you are interested in special footers or footnotes, for example, you need to consult the **nroff** documentation yourself.

SOME ADVICE

There are two common mistakes made by beginners preparing documents. The first is to think only in terms of one printing device or display. If you do this you will pay the price when your beloved printer is replaced by a 'superior' one, or when there is a need to transfer your document to another computer system. Different output devices can produce very different images of a document. Problems can be avoided if you think in terms of the underlying nature of your document rather than a particular image of it. Thus think of paragraphs and sections, rather than of the blank lines and spaces used to lay these out. Moreover think of italics rather than of the underlining that some devices use instead of italics.

The second mistake is to become crazed with the power available in a formatter. Fortunately this book does not cover some of the really suicidal devices available in **nroff** and **troff**. However even a simple facility such as justification may be over-exploited. Remember that although a justified document can look professional, the extra spaces introduced by the justification may make the document *less* easy to read.

METHOD OF USE

Some text formatters can be used interactively, i.e. you type unformatted text in and immediately see beautifully formatted text come out. You do not use **nroff** in this way. Instead you prepare your input text in a file, and then feed the file to **nroff**; if, for example, your input is in the file **mybook** you use the command

nroff *options* **mybook**

We shall suggest suitable *options* later. When you first see the output from **nroff** you will doubtless notice errors — perhaps all the indentation will be wrong. You then correct the errors by editing the input file and feeding it to **nroff** again.

For beginners this non-interactive method of working is tedious and generally unattractive. Nevertheless some professionals are happy to forego the advantages of interaction because of compensating advantages that non-interactive text formatters can provide. These advantages are not obvious to beginners, but broadly speaking, they derive from the flexibility of having an **nroff** 'program' to generate your output text; you can make systematic changes to this program in order to cater for different environments. A similar situation arises with programming languages: a beginner may like interactive BASIC while a professional may prefer non-interactive Pascal.

OUTPUT ON A TERMINAL

Even when the final product of **nroff** is to be printed, you can still examine the results at a display terminal. However, display terminals do not normally have bold and italic fonts, so you lose this dimension.

People who want to impress prepare their electronic mail using **nroff**, e.g.

nroff myletter | mail anne

More typically **nroff** output is redirected to a file, e.g.

nroff myletter >myfile

Then you can examine the **myfile** output file at a terminal before printing (or mailing) it. If you examine the output file using **ed** and list lines using the **l** command, you will see how bold and italic characters are done (assuming there are some of these in your file). As we have said, bold face is effected by backspacing and printing the same character over again — an effect you cannot observe if the characters are displayed on a display terminal unless your eyes are exceptionally fast.

Nroff output tends to have a lot of blank lines on the end, in order to fill out the last page. These can be somewhat annoying when the output is displayed, since the screen size of display terminals is normally smaller than a page size geared for printers.

PREPARING INPUT

If you feed to **nroff** a file containing some ordinary text that you prepared before you knew **nroff** existed — we call this *raw text* — then **nroff** will do its best.

145

However if you wish to exploit **nroff** properly you must prepare your document with its capabilities in mind. In particular you need to insert **nroff** *requests* into your document, in order to indicate what lines are to be indented, where the section headings come, and which characters are to be in italic or bold fonts. (The **nroff** user is humbler than most: he issues 'requests' rather than 'commands'.) Most requests begin with a dot and occupy a line by themselves.

The following is a sample of some **nroff** input that has requests embedded in it

These people have been consulted and all agree
with my proposal

.in +10
.nf
Brian Jones
Joan Brown
Bert Smith
.fi
.in −10

I am therefore going ahead to implement my ideas;
I expect to finish by the Summer.

The above text contains four requests — the four lines that begin with a dot. The request

.in +10

causes everything that follows to be indented ten more spaces than the lines preceding it. The request

.in −10

has the opposite effect, and thus restores the original indentation. This pair of requests therefore acts as a kind of bracketing that delimits lines to be indented. Two further requests are used above: **nf** and **fi**. These mean *no fill* and *fill*, respectively. The **nf** request stops **nroff** from filling subsequent lines; instead the input lines are output without change. The **fi** request cancels the **nf** and causes **nroff** to resume its normal process of filling and justification. (You can, if you wish, switch off justification independently of filling. You do this if you want a ragged margin.)

In our example we want the three names Brian Jones, Joan Brown and Bert Smith to come out on separate lines, exactly as in the input. We use the **nf** request to achieve this. If this request had been omitted then all the names would have come out on the same line, thus

```
Brian Jones Joan Brown Bert Smith
```

At the end of the list of names we restore filling by using the **fi** request. Subsequent text is therefore filled.

The output corresponding to our input is as follows

```
These  people  have  been  consulted  and  all
agree with my proposal

                    Brian Jones
                    Joan Brown
                    Bert Smith

I  am  therefore  going  ahead  to  implement  my
ideas;  I  expect  to  finish  by  the  Summer.
```

Note that blank lines in the input are carried over to the output. Our input had a blank line before the first name and after the last name, in order to improve the layout.

COMMENTS

Nroff has a huge number of possible requests, of which only a small fraction are described in this book. The names of requests consist of a two-character abbreviation of the function performed (such as **in** for indent). In order to make your **nroff** input easier to understand and change, it is highly desirable to put comments after requests. These are written in the following way

.in +10 \" indent ten more

As you see the comment follows a request and is prefixed by a backslash and a double quote.

PAGE AND LINE BREAKS

The general philosophy of **nroff** is this: there are a number of automatic mechanisms that are designed to give the form of document that most people need; people who want to change the automatic behaviour can use special requests to achieve their aim.

As an example, **nroff** automatically divides text into pages. Normally it fills each page with text, but if you want to force it to abandon the current page and start a new one you can issue the request

.bp

As a second example, we have already seen that although **nroff** normally fills (and justifies) text, you can switch this off using **nf**. Moreover if you are filling text, you can still force a new line to begin (i.e. a line *br*eak) by issuing a **br** request. As an example of this, our previous list of names could have been written

Brian Jones
.br \" start a new line
Joan Brown
.br \" start another new line
Bert Smith

This is an alternative to using **nf** and **fi**.

When you first use **nroff** you may have surprises with line breaks, but you soon become accustomed to controlling the way your output lines are to be broken up.

MACROS

The requests you can issue to **nroff** tend to be at a low level of detail, and you will soon find them tedious and error-prone. To alleviate this problem **nroff** has some files of *macros*. These macros have the effect of extending the built-in repertoire of **nroff** requests by providing some extra requests which are more powerful and easier to use. There are a number of alternative macro files available on most **nroff** implementations; each contains a coherent collection of macros designed for a certain style of document. These macro files are called *macro libraries*. One of the most popular is the **ms** macro library developed at Bell Laboratories. This is suitable for a wide range of documents.

The macro mechanism is so easy and natural that

- the average **nroff** user does not need to know what a macro is
- the new requests provided by macros can, with some provisos, be inter-mixed with the built-in requests we have covered already.

All you need to do to make the **ms** macros available is to include the − **ms** option on your **nroff** command, e.g.

nroff − **ms** *inputfile* > *outputfile*

You then have an additional armoury of requests. These new **ms** requests are represented by upper case letters, e.g. **PP**, whereas the built-in **nroff** requests are represented by lower case letters.

Most of the rest of this Chapter is devoted to explaining the **ms** macros. We recommend that you use the **ms** macros when preparing your documents. Perhaps because of their success, the ideas in the **ms** macro library have been used and extended in other macro libraries. You will not necessarily find the **ms** macros on your UNIX system but you should find something similar. One derivative of the **ms** macros is the **mm** macros; these use similar concepts to the **ms** macros, though unfortunately they employ rather different names for requests.

There are just two exceptions to our recommendation to use the **ms** macros (or one of their derivatives)

- short documents, say of one or two pages. When you use the **ms** macros **nroff** takes several seconds to get started, and such delays may be annoying for short documents
- documents with special needs. Later we shall discuss preprocessors and macro libraries to meet such needs.

Given our keep-to-the-mainstream approach, we shall not explain every single request available in the **ms** macros. Readers who require full details should consult the document *Typing Documents on the UNIX System: Using the − ms Macros with Troff and Nroff*; it comes in Volume 2 of the *UNIX Programmer's Manual*. A brief summary of the **ms** requests can be obtained by typing the command

man 7 ms

PARAGRAPHS AND SECTIONS

One valuable service provided by the **ms** macros is a simple set of requests to lay out the paragraphs and sections of your document.

Almost every document is divided into paragraphs. In works of a tutorial nature, like this book, paragraphs are grouped into sections where each section has a heading. The heading for the section you are just reading is '**PARAGRAPHS AND SECTIONS**'. In some works section headings are numbered, e.g. '**1. Intro-duction**'.

The requests for controlling paragraphs and sections are as follows.

PP means start a paragraph, with the first line indented

LP means start a paragraph with the first line not indented

SH means a section heading

NH means the same as **SH**, but headings are automatically numbered in sequence

IP means start an indented paragraph; the whole text of the paragraph is indented.

We call these the *paragraph/heading requests*. All the paragraph/heading requests are written on a line by themselves and are then followed by the text of the paragraph or heading. The text (even of the headings) can be as long as you wish. The end of the paragraph or heading is indicated by the next paragraph/heading request. Such a request not only terminates one paragraph or heading, but also serves to introduce the next one. The only exception is that the very last paragraph in the document has nothing to indicate its end — it simply ends when the input runs out.

Part of a document using these requests might take the form

```
.SH
An example of a section heading
.LP
This is the text of the first paragraph.
Its first line is not indented because we used LP
rather than PP.
.PP
This is the text of another paragraph.
Its first line is indented because we used PP,
but subsequent lines of this paragraph are not indented.
.SH
A further example of a section heading
.LP
The one and only paragraph in this section.
The end of this paragraph is the end of the text.
```

Each of the requests to start a paragraph or heading automatically causes an extra blank line to be output, in order to improve the layout. Section headings are automatically converted to bold.

Thus the above input comes out as shown in Figure 11.1.

```
An example of a section heading

This is the text of the  first   paragraph.
Its  first line is not indented because we
used LP rather than PP.

     This is the  text  of  another  para-
graph.  Its first line is indented because
we used PP, but subsequent lines  of  this
paragraph are not indented.
lines of this paragraph are not indented.

A further example of a section heading

The one and only paragraph  in  this  sec-
tion.   The  end  of this paragraph is the
end of the text.
```

Figure 11.1 Output from paragraph and heading requests

ARGUMENTS

Some requests have arguments — we have already seen examples of this with the **in** request, where the argument gave the indentation required. Arguments to **nroff** requests, like the arguments to shell commands, are written immediately after the request and are separated from one another by spaces. If an argument itself includes spaces, the whole argument must be enclosed within a pair of double quotes, e.g.

.xx ″An argument containing spaces″ two three

The above hypothetical request has three arguments. Note that the use of double quotes is different from the shell, where single quotes are used for this same purpose.

INDENTED PARAGRAPHS

The **IP** request frequently has one argument, and sometimes has a second one. The first argument is a *label* to put on the indented paragraph. The second argument gives the desired indentation. If this second argument is omitted then the standard indentation, which is the same as the indentation of the first line of a **PP** paragraph, is used. As an example, consider the input

.PP
There are three ways of getting there
.IP (1) \″ no second argument
by bus from Victoria coach station
.IP (2) \″ again no second argument
by train:
.IP ″(2 A)″ 10 \″ indented 10 characters

```
from Victoria
.IP "(2 B)" 10
from Charing Cross
.LP
I prefer the last, since it travels through
pleasant countryside.
```

Notice how the argument '(2 A)' has been placed within double quotes because it contains a space. The above input produces the output

```
There are three ways of getting there

(1)   by bus from Victoria coach station

(2)   by train:

(2 A)     from Victoria

(2 B)     from Charing Cross

I  prefer  the  last,  since  it   travels
through pleasant countryside.
```

Note that the end of each indented paragraph is indicated in the normal way by another paragraph/heading request. In the above example each of the indented paragraphs is terminated by the next **IP** request, except for the last, which is terminated by an **LP** request, which returns to the original margin.

DISPLAYS

Documents often contain figures, tables or programs. The way you want these laid out is not, in general, covered by the rules of laying out ordinary English sentences and paragraphs, since concepts such as justification and filling are not applicable. Often the best way of dealing with such material is for you, not **nroff**, to do the laying out; you then supply the laid out material, enclosed within the bracketing requests **DS** and **DE**, as the input to **nroff**. An example of such *displayed text* is

```
.PP
Trains in mid-afternoon are:
.DS
15:00 from Charing Cross
15:23 from Victoria
15:30 from Charing Cross
15:53 from Victoria
.DE
If you take the three o'clock train you need
to change at Ashford.
```

The effect of the **DS** and **DE** brackets on the lines they enclose is as follows

- the lines are indented (slightly more than the standard indentation of the first line of a paragraph)
- the lines are not filled — they are left exactly as supplied in the input
- a blank line is put in place of both the **DS** and the **DE**
- the lines are kept together, if possible, so that they are all on the same page. Thus if **nroff** is two lines from the bottom of a page when it comes upon our displayed text, which occupies four lines, it starts a new page. This feature is especially vital for tables, which look appalling if split across two pages.

The **DS** and **DE** mechanism is separate from the paragraph mechanisms. After a **DE** the previous paragraph resumes. Thus in our example all the material belongs to the same paragraph. If we had wanted to start a new paragraph after the **DE**, we should have placed a **PP** request there. The sentence "If you take ..." would then have been indented. As it stands our input produces the following output

```
    Trains in mid-afternoon are:

        15:00 from Charing Cross
        15:23 from Victoria
        15:30 from Charing Cross
        15:53 from Victoria


If you take the three  o´clock  train  you
need to change at Ashford.
```

This book was prepared using **nroff** (and, later, **troff**), and **DS** and **DE** were two of the most heavily used requests. They are even useful when a single line needs to be displayed, as in

```
The message printed is
.DS
Command not found.
.DE
This means that ...
```

The above comes out as

```
The message printed is

        Command not found.

This means that ...
```

When preparing tabular material it is helpful to use tab characters, like those available on typewriters. You can set tab stops in **nroff** by the request **ta**. For example

   .ta 8 16 30 48 60

sets tab stops at indentations of 8, 16, 30, 48 and 60 character positions. An occurrence of the tab character (∧**i** on some keyboards that do not have an explicit tab key) then advances to the next tab stop. A tab always causes at least one space to be output. Remember that the **ta** request only controls the output of **nroff**. When you type the tab character into the input file it may look different, as the standard UNIX tab positions will be assumed at this stage. It should, however, all come out right in the end.

PREPROCESSORS

We have suggested that you lay out your own tables and other displayed text. If, however, you have elaborate tables or forms, it is well worth finding out about further help that UNIX can give you. Firstly you may discover that your UNIX has some macros specially geared to your needs; we discuss this later. Secondly you should explore the use of **nroff** *preprocessors*. Such preprocessors are conceptually like macros in that they have the effect of extending **nroff**, but they are used in a different way. Preprocessors automatically generate low-level **nroff** requests (i.e. they produce part of your **nroff** program for you) and are used as filters in a pipe.

One preprocessor is called **tbl** and is designed for generating tables. An example of a command to use **tbl** is

   tbl myfile | nroff −ms >outputfile

If you have problems with your tables, a look through the documentation of **tbl** should show you mechanisms for solving them.

A second valuable preprocessor is **neqn** (or, for **troff**, **eqn**), which deals with laying out mathematical equations. Without **neqn** it requires titanic skill to make complicated equations look reasonable.

You may find that your UNIX has other preprocessors, geared to local needs. In a research environment, for example, there may be a preprocessor for citations to papers in learned journals.

We shall not give details of any of these preprocessors here, since they are all geared to specialized rather than general needs.

FONTS

The three fonts available in **nroff** are represented by the following letters
R   Roman, the normal font
I   *Italic*
B   **Bold**

By default all text except for certain headings comes out in the Roman font. To change font you use the **ft** request, and supply as its argument the letter representing the font you desire, e.g.

```
The
.ft B
ft
.ft R
request changes font.
```

will produce the output

The ft request changes font.

In addition to the letters **R**, **I**, **B**, the letter **P** can be used. This means the previous font, i.e. the font in force before you last used **ft**.

You can change font within a line by typing \f followed by the letter indicating the font you want. Thus our above example could be rewritten

```
The \fBft\fP request changes font.
```

This is shorter, but rather more difficult to read than the previous form. The first and third occurrences of **f** above set fonts but the second is a real **f**. You may have noticed that we used the letter **P**, not the letter **R**, to reset the font back to Roman. This is held to be good **nroff** style. Its advantage is that if you decide later to change the above sentence from Roman to italics, then you do not need to change the sentence itself: all you do is to put extra **ft** requests either side of it, as follows

```
.ft I
The \fBft\fP request changes font.
.ft R
```

Our original sentence does not need changing because the **P** now sets the font back to italics rather than to Roman.

USE OF BACKSLASH

In the previous Section we saw that the backslash character was used to herald an **nroff** request — in our case a font change — within a line. A host of other **nroff** facilities can be invoked within an input line; each of these is heralded by a backslash. Many of them are highly esoteric but a feature of importance to ordinary users is the use of the backslash mechanism to introduce characters that do not normally appear on keyboards. An example is

```
\(bu
```

which means a *bullet*, i.e. the character '•'. A bullet is frequently used as an argument to the **IP** request in order to mark an indented paragraph. You can see numerous uses of bullets if you peruse this book.

Most printing devices do not have bullet characters, but **nroff** does its best by overprinting an **x** with an **o**.

There are about a hundred special characters in **nroff** represented by

```
\(xx
```

where *xx* is some unique pair of letters. You can get Greek letters, mathematical symbols, copyright symbols, and all kinds of other characters that will impress your friends. If you want to use such characters consult the *NROFF/TROFF User's Manual*, and you may strike gold. However to get the characters printed really accurately, you will need a superior printing device, if not a typesetter.

FORBIDDEN CHARACTERS

The use of backslash by **nroff** leads us back into the world of forbidden characters, which is already all too familiar to users of **ed** or the shell. If you really want a backslash to appear in your output, you need to type the pair of characters \e. You must also avoid putting dots or closing-quotes (acute accents) at the start of your input lines. This is because they both mark a line as an **nroff** request rather than a line of text. (In this book we begin all our requests with a dot; a closing-quote is similar but it avoids breaking the output.) If you really want to put dots or closing quotes at the start of a line, precede them with a backslash and an ampersand. An example is

```
Things that annoy me in \fBnroff\fP include
.DS
backslashes
dots at starts of lines
\&...
.DE
```

This comes out as

```
Things that annoy me in nroff include

        backslashes
        dots at starts of lines
        ...
```

ERRORS

It is in the error messages of **nroff** that hrmt has achieved his ideal of perfection: most of the error messages of **nroff** are totally empty. Thus if you make an error in an **nroff** request, for example by typing the **PP** request as

```
.pp
```

(which is not a legal request) then this wrong request is contemptuously ignored. The effect as the user sees it is that two paragraphs are run together, because one of his requests to start a new paragraph has been rejected. Worse still, if he forgets to put the −ms option on his **nroff** command, then all his macro requests will be ignored.

There is, however, a way of partly outwitting hrmt. Many UNIX implementations provide a command

checknr *file* ...

which can be used to check all the **nroff** requests in the given *file*(s). **Checknr** is not perfect, as it misses some requests that **nroff** itself will treat as errors, but it is much better than total silence. We therefore suggest you adopt the following sequence of shell commands when preparing a new document for **nroff**, or when changing an existing document.

(1) Use an editor to create and/or change the document. We assume the resultant document is put in the file **masterpiece**.

(2) Execute the command

    checknr masterpiece

(3) Execute one or other of the commands

    nroff − **ms masterpiece** > *afile*

or

    nroff − **ms masterpiece** | *aprogram*

where *aprogram* may be anything from **lpr**, which prints its input, to **mail**. When you use the first of the above **nroff** commands you can look at *afile* by displaying it on your terminal; if it is satisfactory, you can feed it to *aprogram*. If you are not using the **ms** macros you should omit the −**ms** option in the above commands.

HOUSE STYLE

Most publishers have evolved a 'house style': a set of rules for punctuation, spacing, layout, etc. that is designed to make books look attractive and uniform. In an office environment there are similar rules for typewritten documents. A document produced by a typist who follows the rules will look considerably better than one typed by a rank amateur.

In the next few Sections we look at some of **nroff**'s conventions for spacing, and see how they relate to one particular rule of style, which is a rule for the spacing between sentences.

Your first reaction may be to ignore such rules: you will doubtless be pleased to get anything looking remotely acceptable out of **nroff**, and pernickety rules of style will be a secondary matter.

Nevertheless we hope you eventually decide to develop a uniform house style of your own. This can turn a mediocre document into a good one. Sad to say, the success of a document is more often determined by what it looks like than what it says. If you get as far as typesetting documents, there is much fascination in learning a little of the craft of the compositor in making documents pleasing to the eye.

SPACING AND PUNCTUATION

The normal rule for sentence separation in typewritten documents is to leave two spaces after the full stop (period) at the end of each sentence. To assist in this convention, **nroff** has the *ad hoc* property that if a full stop comes at the end of an input line, then it automatically puts two spaces after the full stop. (This is not, of course, done if the full stop happens to come at the end of an output line — extra spaces are not needed in this case.) Strictly speaking we should have said that **nroff** puts *at least* two spaces after the full stop, as it sometimes adds extra spaces to justify the line.

Nroff does not take any special action for a full stop that occurs within an input line. In this case you yourself should put two spaces after the full stop. This makes use of **nroff**'s general property that each space in the input gives at least one space in the output. It therefore assumes that if you type extra spaces in the input, then you really mean them to be there. (Similarly if you put a space at the start of a line, it reproduces the space and also assumes you want a break between output lines.)

As an illustration of these matters, consider the input

```
He came. He saw.  He conquered.
He ---
```

The first full stop only has one space after it, so is not treated specially. The second full stop has two spaces after it, so these are carried over to the output. The third full stop is at the end of a line, and thus gets two spaces added after it. The output therefore reads

```
He came. He saw.  He conquered.  He ---
```

A tasteful reader would object to this output, as the missing space after the first full stop would offend his sensibilities (though for typeset, rather than typewritten, documents, different aesthetics apply).

A sentence need not end with a full stop: it can end with an exclamation mark or question mark. **Nroff** therefore applies similar rules to these characters.

If you want to avoid complication, use the following two rules for **nroff** input

- start each sentence on a new line
- avoid redundant spaces

If you are not willing to obey the first rule, do not forget to add an extra space after sentences that end before the end of the input line.

Note that to **nroff**, a full stop is simply the character '.'; it is not clever enough to distinguish a full stop at the end of a sentence from any other use of the character '.', e.g. its use in the abbreviation 'etc.'. The moral is that you should avoid putting words like 'etc.' at the ends of input lines, unless they are really the ends of sentences. Otherwise bone-headed **nroff** will add an extra space.

Just as **nroff** takes extra spacing as meaningful, it also takes extra blank lines as meaningful, as we have already mentioned. You must therefore be careful not to use blank lines wantonly. If your input is

```
end of one paragraph.

.PP
Start of next ...
```

Then you will get *two* blank lines between the paragraphs. The blank line in the input gives one, and the **PP** request gives a second one.

RAW TEXT

One purpose of **nroff**'s rules for spacing and blank lines is that they allow raw text to be processed in a reasonable way.

If, for example, a document was prepared without **nroff** in mind, the break between paragraphs might look like this

end of one paragraph.

     Start of next ...

This contains a blank line between the paragraphs and five spaces of indentation before the word 'Start'. **Nroff** reproduces these in the output, and thus the break between paragraphs in the output exactly mirrors the input. Although a user who feeds raw text to **nroff** does not exploit its full facilities he gains the advantages of filling and justification and the division of text into pages. On the other hand he might run into two new problems. Firstly, if his input contains tabular or displayed material, he may be upset by **nroff**'s attempts to 'fill' such material by packing several lines into one. He might therefore need to edit **nf** and **fi** (or **DS** and **DE**) requests into his document. Secondly, if his document does not observe the spacing convention about full stops within lines, he will get inconsistent output: the full stops that happen to occur at the ends of input lines will get two spaces appended, whereas the others will only get one. (A magic **ed** pattern to find full stops that are only followed by one space is

    /\. [A − Z]/

Get Dudley to explain this if you cannot work it out for yourself — doubtless as a bonus he will give you an even cleverer pattern. We could, incidentally, usefully use such a pattern to help edit our Greg Daimler novel, which only has one space after each full stop.)

PAGE SIZE AND SPACING

Computer output devices vary greatly in the sizes of their pages and lines. Moreover within the limits of the physical page size users will want to vary the indentation and vertical spacing. **Nroff** therefore supports requests for controlling page layout. Most of these requests have an argument that is a physical distance. These distances can be described in various possible units, as shown in the following examples.

10i   10 inches

26c   26 centimetres

7m   7 ems; in **nroff** this means 7 characters, but in **troff**, where characters can have variable size, it is 7 times the width of the letter 'M' — hence the name 'em'

7n   7 ens; in **nroff**, ens are the same as ems, but in **troff** an en, which is the width of the letter 'N', is half an em

8   8 default units; for horizontal spacing along the line, the default units are ems, but for vertical spacing down a page the default unit is the height of a line, i.e. the distance from the base of one line to the base of the next

+9   9 default units more than the previous value

−2c   2 centimetres less than the previous value

We have already seen examples similar to the last two of these on the **in** requests

.in +10
.in −10

The first of these caused extra indentation of ten default units (ems); the second reduced the indentation by ten ems, thus reverting to the previous indentation. Examples of **in** which use some of the other units are

.in 1c
.in 3n

Other examples where default units have already been used are the requests

.IP "(2 A)" 10
.ta 8 16 30 48 60

We shall now introduce examples of further requests. Each of these can use any of the above units, although our examples only show one specific case.

Page length

.pl 10i

sets the page length to ten inches. The **pl** request may, however, cause problems if you are using the **ms** macros, since these may insist on a certain page size.

Line length

.nr LL 70   \" if you are using the ms macros
.ll 70   \" if you are not

sets the line length to seventy ems.

Blank lines

.sp 3

outputs three blank lines. Since this is vertical spacing rather than horizontal the default units are heights of lines. If no argument is supplied to **sp** then a single blank line is output — the same effect can be achieved by a blank input line.

Double spacing

.ls 2

causes an extra blank line to be put out after each output line. Thus it gives double spacing — hence the 2. This is useful for draft documents, as it leaves plenty of room for corrections to be pencilled in.

Centring

Finally, there is one spacing request that does not use any units. This is the **ce** request, which centres the text that is supplied on the next input line. The centre is the centre, irrespective of the units of measurement.

The following example shows the use of **ce** and **sp** requests to produce title lines of a document.

```
.ce
\fBBe friends with UNIX\fP
.sp
.ce
by Dudley and Anne
.sp 2
.PP
UNIX helps people get together ...
```

The above input produces the output

<pre>
        Be friends with UNIX

        by Dudley and Anne

    UNIX helps people get together ...
</pre>

ENVIRONMENTS

We have seen that **nroff** provides numerous parameters for controlling the output text: examples are line spacing, tab settings, and the current font. The set of current values of all these parameters is called the *environment*. You can actually maintain up to three alternative environments and switch between them. This is a facility for professionals, but it affects ordinary users when they use the **DS** and **DE** requests. Text within this pair of requests has a different environment from the rest. As a result you may get a few surprises. For example if you put the request

```
.ls 2
```

at the start of your input this will cause double spacing everywhere except within **DS** and **DE**. This is because the latter have a separate environment, which is unaffected by the **ls**.

As a second example, if you are in bold font at the **DE** which ends some displayed text — perhaps because you forgot to switch back to Roman — then the text after the next **DS**, which may be 500 lines further on, will come out in bold face. This is because the **DS** carries on with the environment left by the previous **DE**.

THE START OF A DOCUMENT

If you are preparing a document of any great length you will probably want to do better than our *Be friends with UNIX* example by having a special title page. The recommended form of this is

```
.TL
The document title
.AU
The author(s)
.AI
The author(s) institution or home address
.AB
An abstract outlining the document's content
.AE \" this marks the end of the abstract
.PP \" or .SH followed by a section heading
The text of your document begins here
```

You can, if you wish, leave out any of the above sections. For example the **AI** request and the text that follows it could be omitted. Each of the pieces of text (i.e. the items we have shown in italics) can be as long as you wish.

A specific example of the use of these requests is

```
.TL
Be friends with UNIX
.AU
Dudley
Anne
.AB
This article describes how you can get to meet
your fellow UNIX users, and how to escape the attentions
of the ones you do not like.
.AE
.SH
Getting to know you
.PP
UNIX helps people to get together.
You can use \fBmail\fP and \fBwrite\fP
commands to do this.  ...
```

The output from this, which is shown in Figure 11.2, gives a much more impressive start to the document than the previous effort we showed.

In addition to the title page itself you may wish to put, at the very start of a document, instructions to control the overall document format. If you look at the documentation of the **ms** macros you will find how to control page headings and footers, and even how to divide pages into multiple columns.

By default each page is numbered at the top, and has the current date as a footer at the bottom.

If you do not use the **ms** macros you can still control page headings and footers, but you have to program them for yourself using the appropriate **nroff** requests. Otherwise documents may appear as if they were one enormous page.

Be friends with UNIX

Dudley
Anne

ABSTRACT

This article describes how you can get to meet your fellow UNIX users, and how to escape the attentions of the ones you do not like.

Getting to know you

UNIX helps people to get together. You can use **mail** and **write** commands to do this. ...

Figure 11.2 A title page

MACRO LIBRARIES

The **ms** macros are a good general-purpose aid to document preparation, but if you have specialized needs you may find them inappropriate. If so you have two alternatives:

- use another set of macros
- write your own macros

The first is obviously preferable, since it saves you work by exploiting the efforts of others. Thus it is well worth finding out what macro libraries are available on your UNIX implementation. You should find descriptions of them in Section 7 of your *UNIX Programmer's Manual*.

If you want to write your own macros, your first action should be to look at some existing macros written by experts, for instance the **ms** macros themselves.

You might find these in a file called **/usr/lib/tmac/tmac.s.** If you **cat** this file you will have a shock: it is full of formidably esoteric material such as

```
.de I
.nr PQ \\n(.f
.if t .ft 2
.if "\\$1""q .if n .ul 1000
.if !"\\$1""q .if n .ul 1
.if t .if !"\\$1"" \&\\$1\\f\\n(PQ\\$2
.if n .if \\n(.$=1 \&\\$1
.if n .if \\n(.$>1 \&\\$1\\c
.if n .if \\n(.$>1 \\&\\$2
..
```

Do not despair. Writing a complete macro library as powerful as **ms** is indeed a task beyond ordinary mortals. However it is not too difficult to write a set of a dozen or so macros to augment an existing library in order to meet your special needs.

Having said this is 'not too difficult' we shall stretch the reader's credulity further by saying that in spite of this we have not the space to explain it in the current book.

MANUAL PAGES

We said in Chapter 9 that manual pages are kept in an internal form, which is then converted to a suitable format for the output device. The manual pages are in fact in the form of **nroff** (or really **troff**) input; when you use the **man** command to look at a manual page, what **man** does is to run **nroff** in order to convert the manual page to a suitable format to be output.

Now that you understand a little about **nroff** it might be of interest to look at the manual pages as stored inside the computer. On most UNIX implementations the manual pages for Section 1 of the *UNIX Programmer's Manual* are in a directory called **/usr/man/man1**, though your UNIX may be different. The manual page for **ls** is stored in a file called **ls.1** (or perhaps on other UNIX systems some other name containing **ls**). If you **cat** this you will see an example of **nroff** input.

The manual pages use a macro library called the **man** macros; this is similar but not identical to the **ms** macros. The manual pages also use a lot of the built-in **nroff** requests — the ones with lower case names.

DANGEROUS COMBINATIONS

If you find out more about **nroff** by reading the documentation you will increase your stock of requests. However be careful in mixing **ms** requests (the capital letter ones) with the rest; an example would be to mix the **ms** requests for page headers with your own clever low-level requests to generate headers. The likely result is that the two mechanisms will work at cross purposes and produce chaos.

The modest set of **nroff** requests described in this book can be intermixed quite freely with the **ms** requests — provided you do not ask for anything really daft. Be sure, however, that you use the **ms** version of the **ll** request, as shown in our earlier example of setting the line length.

TYPESETTING

Some documents, though initially prepared for humble printing devices using **nroff**, may subsequently be typeset. Your novel is accepted by a publisher; someone publishes a book about you called *The Collected UNIX letters of /usr/me*; more prosaically, the announcements of your local computer club's meetings, which you prepare on your UNIX system, are to be typeset so that they look more professional. If you want your file to be typeset it is unlikely that you will have the necessary typesetter on your own computer. Instead you will need to send the file, via electronic mail, tape or diskette, to another UNIX system that possesses **troff** and is equipped with suitable hardware.

The result of such an exercise can be a beautiful document. If you have any experience of computing, however, you will realize that nothing ever goes as smoothly as you expect (even when you do not expect much in the first place). Problems of converting **nroff** input for use with **troff** arise mainly because typeset characters are of different sizes: an 'i' is, for example, much less wide than a 'W'. The average width of characters is considerably smaller than an em, which is the width of a character in **nroff** output. A secondary problem is that if you think only in terms of **nroff** you will use the same character for a hyphen, a dash, and a minus sign.

These problems might manifest themselves as follows

- your indentation of 10 default units (ems) looks fine in **nroff** but looks much too wide for **troff**
- alignment of the columns in a table is wrong in **troff** because characters are of different widths
- all dashes and minus signs come out as hyphens, which look absurdly small. (Similarly all quotes may come out as closing inverted commas, as in 'x', because **nroff** users are not accustomed to distinguishing between quotes and apostrophes.)

Even when you cure these problems you still need to adapt your document to take advantage of the enhancements that **troff** offers over **nroff**, such as an increased variety of fonts and the ability to vary the size of characters (e.g. to print titles in a larger type).

The moral is that if you are one of those frightfully organized people who think many steps ahead, it is well worth paying attention to the needs of **troff** when you design your personal house style.

INDEPENDENCE OF PRINTING DEVICES

One advantage of the **ms** macros is that they make your document more *device-independent*, i.e. it can be adapted to any printer. We have already emphasized the undesirability of being tied to one particular printer. Where relevant, the macros automatically tailor their output for the printing device to be used, and indeed this smooths any transition from **nroff** to **troff**. To some extent the macros also allow you to change your style too: if you do not like the style of layout provided by some macros you can change them. Thus you could alter the layout of paragraphs by writing a revised **PP** macro — though be warned that tampering by amateurs can often have catastrophic effects.

When you use the shell command that invokes **troff** or **nroff** you can supply an argument that states which printing device you plan to use; this causes the output of **nroff** to be adapted accordingly. An example is

nroff − ms − T1234x myfile > outputfile

The **outputfile** will then be geared to the model 1234x printer. Our model 1234x is entirely hypothetical; you will need to find out for yourself what special printer options, if any, are available on your own **nroff**. If you find that **nroff** is at odds with your output device, the problem can often be solved by using the right − **T** option.

SUMMARY OF FORMATTING

For most people, producing good documents is a satisfying task. It does however require attention to detail.

Nroff is not an easy formatting system to master, but it has more power than many of its superficially attractive rivals. Most problems are avoided by a careful advance into **nroff** rather than a headlong charge. The stages of your advance might be

- find out about available printing devices, even about typesetters that might be used in the remote future
- look at some samples of **nroff** input produced by colleagues who are masters of **nroff**. Most important, try to find documents of a similar nature to yours
- start by performing some experiments with **nroff** using short documents
- before you begin your first major document, develop your own house style; use this consistently
- use the **ms** macros, except for small documents such as letters, or documents with special needs
- use **checknr** to try to find the errors before you feed anything to **nroff**
- treat disasters along the way as a cause for laughter rather than tears

LIST OF REQUESTS

This concludes our description of **nroff**. Since an ill-written document is still an ill-written document even if it is beautifully formatted, we devote the subsequent Sections of this Chapter to the quality of writing. This final **nroff** Section summarizes all the requests that we have used.

Built-in requests

bp	start a new page
br	break (i.e. start a new line)
ce	place next line(s) in centre of page
fi	fill subsequent text (cancels **nf**)
ft	change font
in	change indentation
ll	set line length

ls	set line spacing
nf	do not fill subsequent text
nr	set 'number register' — we used it to set **LL**
pl	set page length
sp	output blank line(s)
ta	place tab positions

In addition the requests **\fB**, **\fI**, etc., can be used to change font within a line. By default all text is filled and justified.

Requests in **ms** *macros*

DE	end displayed text
DS	start displayed text
IP	indented paragraph
LP	paragraph with no indentation
NH	numbered section heading
PP	paragraph with first line indented
SH	section heading

In addition the requests **AB**, **AE**, **AI**, **AU** and **TL** can be used for the title page.

AIDS TO GOOD WRITING

UNIX provides three aids to good writing: **spell**, **style**, and **diction**. We have already covered the first of these.

The **style** and **diction** programs are, in the words of their authors (Cherry and Vesterman, 1981): "a first step towards helping writers to produce readable documents". Broadly, the **style** program looks at documents as a whole, and **diction** looks at individual words.

We fed one of the Chapters of this book to **style**. The resultant output is shown in Figure 11.3. There is so much information here that the initial effect is off-putting, but perseverance pays.

READABILITY GRADES

The first piece of information is about *readability grades*: four separate measures are shown, though they all give similar readings, varying between 9.9 and 10.7. These measures are all based on lengths of sentences and lengths of words: the only difference between the four measures is that slightly different formulae are used. We suggest that, to start with, you only take notice of the first measure, which is derived from a formula due to Kincaid. A Kincaid measure on its own is meaningless; it is only useful when compared with corresponding measures from other documents. If one document has a lower figure than another, this means it has shorter words and sentences. By and large, it should therefore be easier to read, though there is a limit: a book for toddlers may come up with a figure as low as 5, but most adults, though certainly finding such books easy to read, do not find the style attractive (nor their content, though this is a separate matter).

```
readability grades:
   (Kincaid) 10.2   (auto) 10.2
   (Coleman-Liau)  9.9  (Flesch) 10.7 (56.5)
sentence info:
   no. sent 179 no. wds 3506
   av sent leng 19.6 av word leng 4.63
   no. questions 2 no. imperatives 0
   no. nonfunc wds 1869   53.3%   av leng 6.04
   short sent (<15) 35% (63) long sent (>30)   11% (20)
   longest sent 79 wds at sent 13;
   shortest sent 4 wds at sent 15
sentence types:
   simple  35% (62) complex  45% (81)
   compound   7% (13) compound-complex  13% (23)
word usage:
   verb types as % of total verbs
   tobe  38% (162) aux  23% (97) inf  14% (61)
   passives as % of non-inf verbs  11% (41)
   types as % of total
   prep 9.7% (339) conj 2.7% (93) adv 5.7% (201)
   noun 24.1% (845) adj 13.6% (477) pron 8.6% (301)
   nominalizations   1 % (43)
sentence beginnings:
   subject opener: noun (28) pron (24) pos (4)
                    adj (17) art (34) tot  60%
   prep  11% (20) adv  12% (21)
   verb   3% (5)  sub_conj  12% (22) conj   0% (0)
   expletives   2% (4)
```

Figure 11.3 Output from the **style** *program*

Our figure of 10.2 is already on the low side. A survey of documents in Bell Laboratories came up with a mean Kincaid reading of 13.3. The maximum was 16.9 and the minimum 9.5.

We suggest you apply **style** to your documents and compare your Kincaid reading with those quoted here, and with readings you can derive from files belonging to your friends. If your prose stands out as exceptionally simple or exceptionally complex, this should be a warning to examine your style.

You should expect figures to vary according to the type of document. It might be acceptable for a piece of literary criticism to have a high figure, but technical documents are better with low ones: the reader will have enough trouble understanding new technical concepts, and should not be diverted by having to unravel long sentences, or to look up long words in a dictionary.

SENTENCE INFORMATION

The next two sections of **style**'s output give information about sentence structure. Good authors mix long sentences with short ones. (That is why children's books, with an excess of short sentences, are unattractive to adults.) Thus if you find your **style** figures are much different from those of your fellows, you should examine the nature of your sentences, and how you distribute them.

Do not be too over-awed by the mass of detail that is spewed out by **style**. Items such as 'nonfunc wds' (which are actually nouns, adverbs and non-auxiliary verbs) can be ignored until you have become accustomed to understanding how to interpret the broad message that **style** gives you.

WORD USAGE

Although **style**'s counts of parts of speech are rough and ready, they may still help to tell you that something is wrong with your style. An over-use of adjectives, for example, may be acceptable in holiday brochures, but in most documents it soon annoys the reader. An excess of passive verbs is a danger signal in technical documents, since most books on style, and most experiments on comprehension, show that active verbs are better. Finally almost total lack of pronouns might indicate that a document is too wordy.

SENTENCE OPENERS

We were somewhat surprised at the last line of our output from **style**: our Chapter apparently contains four expletives. Has **style** an especially prim view of what are rude words?

The answer is that expletives are not what we thought. They are words like 'it' and 'there' which are used at the start of sentences in which the subject *follows* the verb, e.g.

There are three files used by the program

Many authors over-use such expletives, and some critics treat them with as much horror as rude words.

If you look at the last five lines of Figure 11.3, you will see a complete analysis of the parts of speech used to start sentences. A good principle of style is to vary the way your sentences begin. If **style** shows that you rarely use certain parts of speech as sentence openers then you may gain by extending your repertoire.

SUMMARY OF STYLE

Style gives you a number of crude statistics. They are not even totally accurate as **style** cannot always tell where sentences begin and end, or whether such words as 'need' or 'beat' are nouns or verbs.

The statistics are nevertheless valuable. If you are an exceptionally gifted author your figures from **style** may be considerably different from the average; indeed a variation from the norm may confirm the exceptional superiority of your style. However for each author whose style stands out for its excellence, there are ten authors whose outpourings are unreadable. If you think you may be one of these, examine the output from **style** and see if it is trying to give you a helpful message.

DICTION

The **diction** program is much simpler than **style** and its message is more readily apparent. **Diction** looks at individual words or phrases and highlights ones that are commonly misused. For example some authorities on style say that the word *very* should be banned. **Diction** displays every sentence containing this word. An example of the output you might see is

it was a[very]warm day.

The word or phrase that **diction** objects to is placed within square brackets.

Diction makes no attempt to understand or to parse its document. When it sees the word *very* it objects, whatever the context. Thus it might display

that is the[very]reason why I kept quiet.

This use of *very* is very unlikely to offend anyone, yet **diction** is not clever enough to distinguish it from any other use of *very*.

Other samples of the output from **diction**, all taken from Chapter 2 of this book, are as follows

(1) *moreover you might have a[number of]sessions in a day*

Here the phrase 'number of' offends **diction**. It prefers alternatives such as 'several' or 'many'. (Note that the input is converted to lower case by **diction**: the original word 'Moreover' has become 'moreover'.)

(2) *[the nature]of messages sent obviously depends on the user community.*

Here **diction** is telling us that the words 'the nature' serve no great purpose, and can be eliminated if the sentence is re-written.

(3) *a machine[which]only allows ...*

Here 'that' is preferred to 'which'.

If you want an explanation of why **diction** has objected to a word or phrase, you will find, in most UNIX implementations, a companion program to **diction**, which provides such explanations. It may be called **explain** or **suggest**.

REACTION

The list of words and phrases that **diction** does not like runs to about 500 entries. Given such a huge list of dislikes, it can hardly fail to find something objectionable even in a small document.

There is, however, one advantage of **diction** over mothers-in-law and fathers-in-law: you do not have to listen to it. If you are annoyed by its carping, you can leave it in solitary confinement in the file system, and never invite it to look at your documents.

Banishment of **diction** is one extreme; paying lip service to its every whim is another. The best approach is a middle course. Experience of the use of **diction** at Bell Laboratories shows that a typical user takes notice of just over half of **diction**'s comments, and cheerfully ignores the rest.

SUMMARY OF ALL AIDS

The message from all the UNIX tools described in this Chapter can be summarized as follows: if you want to produce beautiful and readable documents you need to work hard. In **nroff** UNIX provides an adequate tool for formatting, which allows painstaking people to produce really fine documents, and ordinary people to produce reasonable ones.

UNIX tools to help you with style are less adequate. This is inevitable: human teachers may try for years to get their pupils to write good English, and their labours often end in total failure. It is unreasonable to expect simple programs to do dramatically better. Do not expect **style** and **diction** to help you, therefore, if your use of words is clumsy, your explanations ambiguous and your overall organizing skills non-existent. Nevertheless these programs can assist you with some of the more mechanical aspects of style, and can as a result tip the balance between a document being unread and being acceptable. The authors of these two programs deserve great credit for taking a promising first step into what may in the future be an increasingly fruitful field.

CHAPTER 12

Programming

You taught me language; and my profit on't
Is, I know how to curse: the red plague rid you,
For learning me your language!
SHAKESPEARE, 'THE TEMPEST'

This Chapter introduces the use of UNIX for writing programs. If you are determined never to write any programs you may, of course, skip this Chapter. We do however wish to make some allowance for beginners so we shall start with an introduction to programming languages — thus giving more sophisticated readers a chance to skip too. For any readers who remain, we shall introduce our topic by means of an analogy.

PROGRAMMING LANGUAGES

A Frenchman regards the French language as far superior to any other. An Englishman, on the other hand, regards the English language as superior to French, and infinitely superior to American. At present you communicate with a computer by means of a programming language, rather than a spoken language. There are as many programming languages in the world as spoken languages, and people are equally obstinate in claiming that their programming language is far superior to any other. In truth it is not possible to say one programming language is better than another with the same certainty that one can say that English is so obviously superior to American. All one can say is that some programming languages are more suitable for certain tasks, say manipulating business records, or performing complex numerical calculations.

Because of the diversity of feelings about programming languages, any operating system for general use must support a large number of such languages. These languages are implemented by *language processors* (which can be sub-divided into *compilers* or *interpreters*). Hundreds of different language processors have been written for UNIX, but only a few are likely to be available on any particular implementation. You will therefore have to find out for yourself what language processors, and hence what programming languages, are supported by your UNIX. You will always find, however, that the C language is supported so we shall start by introducing this.

DESIGN OF PROGRAMMING LANGUAGES

The nature of the C language can best be understood by considering what it was designed for.

The ideal programming language has the following properties
(1) it is easy for beginners to use
(2) it is easy for experts to use
(3) it makes programs easy to read
(4) it imposes a discipline on users so that good programming practices must be followed
(5) it is suitable for short programs
(6) it is suitable for medium-sized programs
(7) it is suitable for huge programs, totalling tens or hundreds of thousands of lines
(8) it is suitable for proving programs correct
(9) it is easy to implement on any computer
(10) it makes for *efficient* (i.e. fast) execution of programs

No-one can design a programming language that meets all these criteria. (Nevertheless people keep trying, and a new programming language is born every day.) In practice successful language designers have to concentrate on a few criteria.

The designers of BASIC rated (1) and (5) as the most important criteria.

The designer of Pascal rated (4) as the most important, with (3) and (10) also prominent.

The designers of ADA had to cover (7) and this forced them to compromise many other desirable criteria.

The designers of C rated (10), (6) and (2) as most important — perhaps in that order. If these criteria are important to you — or if you want to exploit the unique role of C as the 'language of UNIX' — then C is your language.

COMPARING PROGRAMS

In order that you may be able to relate C to a language you know already we shall show the same program encoded in BASIC, Pascal and C. This is a program that inputs an integer N, followed by N further numbers, and calculates the average of these N numbers. An example of possible data, assuming N to be 4, is

    4   3.6   2.9   -4.15   28.64

It is, of course, a trivial program, and does not give programming languages a chance to show their full prowess. However it will serve to give a first impression.

The program in BASIC is

```
10   REM  - - -FINDS THE AVERAGE OF N NUMBERS- - -
100 INPUT N
110 LET S = 0
120 FOR K = 1 TO N
130    INPUT X
140    LET S = S+X
150 NEXT K
200 IF N <= 0 THEN 230
210 PRINT "AVERAGE="; S/N
220 GOTO 999
230 PRINT "NO NUMBERS IN DATA"
999 END
```

The purpose of the IF statement in line 200 is to make the program *robust*: if it is supplied with ridiculous data, such as a value of -123 for N, it does not go berserk. Instead it prints the message

    NO NUMBERS IN DATA

In Pascal the program is

program average(input, output);

  { - - - **finds the average of N numbers** - - - }

```pascal
var
    n, k: integer;
    sum, number: real;

begin
    read(n);
    sum := 0;
    for k := 1 to n do
    begin
        read(number);
        sum := sum + number
    end;
    if n > 0 then
        writeln('Average =', sum/n)
    else
        writeln('No numbers in data')
end.
```

In C the program is

```c
/* --- finds the average of N numbers --- */

#include <stdio.h>

main()
{
    int n, k;
    float sum, number;

    scanf("%d",&n);
    sum = 0;
    for (k=1; k <= n; k++)
    {   scanf("%f",&number);
        sum += number;
    }
    if (n > 0)
        printf("Average = %f\n", sum/n);
    else
        printf("No numbers in data\n");
}
```

GENERAL IMPRESSIONS

We shall start by looking at some general properties of C programs, and the way they differ from BASIC and Pascal. We shall then examine the above C program line by line, and explain some of the details. If you are not a programmer you may have trouble with these details but we hope you at least gain some impression of what is going on.

The first impression from looking at the above programs is that C is closer to Pascal than to BASIC. This is more than a superficial property, as the underlying ideas of C really are quite close to Pascal, in spite of the different aims of the languages. One reason for the manifestly different appearance of C from BASIC, is that BASIC programs are prepared line by line in an interactive manner whereas C (and Pascal) programs are not. You prepare your C program in a file, using an editor, and then pass this file to the C language processor. In BASIC, on the other hand, you type your lines directly into the BASIC language processor; BASIC language processors have their own built-in editor, which uses the line-numbers on the front of each line.

Even a first glance at a C program indicates that it comes from the same stable as UNIX, and in particular shares the philosophy that syntax should be concise. To illustrate this it is useful to take Pascal as a base point. The Pascal version of our program is liberally peppered with *reserved words*, which are English words with fixed meanings in Pascal. Examples of reserved words are **program**, **var**, **begin**, **end**, **for**, **to** and **do**. C has fewer reserved words, and those that it does have are the short ones such as **for** and **if**. In many cases C omits Pascal's reserved words, because they are not strictly necessary, or replaces them by single punctuation characters, for example **begin** is '{'. The use of the **for** statement in our examples epitomizes the differences: Pascal's

```
for k := 1 to n do
begin
    ...
```

(where only the reserved words are shown in bold) is, in C

```
for (k = 1; k <= n; k++)
{ ...
```

DETAILS OF THE C PROGRAM

We shall now give an outline of the purpose of each line of our sample C program.

The first line is a comment, and thus the first effective line of the program is the *include* line. This inserts into the program a built-in set of declarations, which are in a file called **stdio.h** that lies within a directory deep in UNIX. The details of this file are unimportant here, but its use illustrates two important principles. Firstly it is normal practice to build C programs out of small and separate modules, thus following the small-is-beautiful philosophy. The *include* facility is part of a mechanism that helps implement this philosophy. A second point illustrated by the *include* line is the flexibility of C. The input/output facilities in C are not built into the language but are implemented via separate modules that you can combine with your program. You thus have freedom to use any input/output facilities you wish. There is, however, a standard module available for those who do not have unusual requirements. This is invoked by our above inclusion of the **stdio.h** file. In contrast to this flexible approach, most programming languages have built-in input/output facilities, and if they do not meet your needs it is your bad luck.

The next line of our C program is

main()

This heralds the start of the main *function* in the program. (A function in C not only corresponds to what other languages call functions, but also includes the mechanism that is called a subroutine or procedure.) In general a C program is split up into a *main* function and lots of subsidiary functions, but our simple program consists only of the *main* function. The body of the *main* function is enclosed between the brackets '{' and '}'.

The next two lines contain the declarations of the variables that are local to the *main* function. In C, as in Pascal, variables can have any name you like (within certain limits) and you have to say in advance which names you are using. More important, you have to specify the *data type* of each variable, i.e. the kind of values it can take. When we write the declaration

int n, k;

we say that n and k are names of variables whose values are *int*egers (whole numbers). The declaration

float sum, number;

says that *sum* and *number* are names of variables whose values are *float*ing-point numbers (numbers that may have fractional parts). Data types and data structures are one of the keys to the power of a programming language, and C offers a rich variety which our sample program only hints at.

The remainder of the C program consists of the statements that need to be executed to calculate the required average. The statements *scanf* and *printf* are concerned with input and output, respectively. The first argument to each of these gives the format of the item to be input or output. We will not go into details, save to say that **%d** means decimal integer format, **%f** means floating-point format, and **\n** means start a new line. (The use of percent signs and backslashes may well remind readers of the joys of metacharacters and wildcards.)

The final point of interest about our sample C program is the two statements

k++
sum += number;

The former increases k by one (and, if used in a context where a value is needed, for example as an array subscript, gives the new value of k). The latter increases *sum* by the value of *number*. The purpose of these two cryptic pieces of notation is partly to save writing but more importantly to make the program execute speedily. Many computers have special instructions or special 'auto-increment' registers which can be used to increment variables. The C notation makes it easier to take advantage of such features. It is a small illustration of a general point about C: since C was initially used to implement UNIX itself (and still fulfils this role) it was vital that each feature of the language allowed for fast and efficient implementation.

IN C YOU CAN ...

C is popular with programmers. The major reason why this is so is not brought out by our trivial sample program. The reason is C's generality: whatever you want to do, you can do it in C. This contrasts with languages where you can only do the things that the language designers wanted you to do, and even then you must do them in the right way.

Using C gives you the impression of being your own boss, rather than being a junior member of a strict religious order. This point is well brought out by Kernighan (1981) in a comparison of C and Pascal. In Kernighan's account, it is not much of a fight: C wins every round handsomely. The knock-out punch in the final round is that in Pascal *there is no escape*: the rules in Pascal are ruthlessly enforced. In C, on the other hand, if you do not like a rule you usually have the means of suspending it, and if you do not like a component of your environment you can change it.

You will doubtless have your own views on whether success and happiness in life lies in keeping to a set of rigid rules. According to your philosophy, you can choose your programming language. To further help your choice you may be interested in a paper by Feuer and Gehani (1982), which is an account of the C versus Pascal fight as seen by two other ringside spectators.

If you want to read a full and definitive account of the C language, you should read the book on C by Kernighan and Ritchie (1978). Initially C was available on one computer, the PDP-11; now it is not only available on all computers that run UNIX, but also on some of those that use other operating systems. The book is relevant to all these implementations.

SYSTEM CALLS

Most of the facilities built into UNIX itself can be invoked from within a C program. This is done by a *system call*. The list of available system calls is given in Section 2 of your *UNIX Programmer's Manual*. One example of a system call is *chmod* which allows a program to change the permissions on a file. It therefore corresponds to the **chmod** command in UNIX, which must indeed have been implemented using the *chmod* system call.

System calls are one reason why, if you aspire to being a UNIX systems programmer, you really must learn C. Although you can build new UNIX commands by using shell scripts and the like, there are certain facilities that are best achieved by writing C programs containing system calls.

EXECUTING A PROGRAM

We have now finished our brief discussion of programming languages and our introduction to C. The remainder of the Chapter is devoted to explaining the mechanics of preparing and executing programs. Our aim is to paint a broad picture of what is available, since detailed descriptions would lead to long Sections of interest to a minority of readers. Please forgive, therefore, the regular requests that you should look up details in your local documentation.

For most programming languages you need to convert your original *source* program into an equivalent binary form that the computer can execute. The latter is called an *executable program*. Once an executable program has been stored in a file, that filename can be used as a UNIX command. Thus, as we have already explained, the built-in UNIX commands (**cat**, **ls**, etc.) correspond to executable programs stored in files somewhere in your search path.

The way you set about executing a program of your own is as follows

(1) prepare the source program in a file.
(2) use a UNIX command to invoke the language processor for your programming language in order to produce an executable program from your source program. We call this *compiling* your program (though, strictly speaking, the language processor may sometimes be an interpreter rather than a compiler).
(3) if the language processor has found any errors in your source program, then edit your program and recompile it.
(4) execute your executable program.

The only programming languages that are not likely to follow the above pattern are interactive languages such as BASIC.

The language processor for the C language is called **cc**. The UNIX command to compile a C program is

    cc *file* ...

For a Fortran 77 program the command is

    f77 *file* ...

(assuming, of course, that **f77** is available on your UNIX).

THE EXECUTABLE PROGRAM

Most language processors create the executable program in a file which by default has the name **a.out** and lies within your current directory. The permissions on the executable program are, of course, set to include execute permission — otherwise you would not be able to execute it.

To execute the **a.out** program you simply use the command

    a.out

Most programs, including our earlier examples of the averaging program, are written to use the standard input and output rather than to work with explicit files. If you want to take input from a given file, rather than from the standard input, you can do this by exploiting the redirection facilities of the UNIX shell. Thus if **a.out** contains our averaging program, and we want to apply it to data in a file **mydata** then we can simply use the command

    a.out < **mydata**

Likewise if we want to send the output to a file rather than to our terminal we say

    a.out > **afile**

An elaborate example that redirects both input and output is

    a.out < /usr/friend/data > **subdirectory/answers**

Session 3 in Appendix A contains a complete example of compiling and executing a program.

KEEPING AN EXECUTABLE PROGRAM

There are three possible results of your using an **a.out** program that you have just created

- your program does not do what it should. In this case you need to correct the source program and recompile it. You will then have a new **a.out** to try.
- your program does its job correctly and you have no further need for it. In this case you can delete your **a.out** file, and also your original source program.
- your program does its job correctly and you wish to keep it for later use.

We shall now discuss this third possibility.

If your program is a short one you do not need to keep your **a.out** file. You can simply recompile the source program when you next need to use it. If, on the other hand, your program is a long one that is regularly used you will want to keep the **a.out** file, thus eliminating the time delay of recompiling the program. To do this you choose a suitable filename, **average** say, and type the command

    mv a.out average

This effectively renames **a.out** as **average** (destroying any previous version of **average**). Sometimes it is desirable to **mv** the **a.out** file to a filename that is in a **bin** directory, as discussed in Chapter 7.

You can, of course, simply leave your executable program in **a.out** but this has two potential disadvantages

- you may want to work on some other programs, and you may then generate a new **a.out** file that overwrites the previous one.

- some UNIX managements treat files called **a.out** as transient, and automatically delete them all at periodic times (e.g. at midnight each Sunday) in order to save space.

In practice only a small minority of **a.out** files are saved and re-used. Sadly most **a.out** programs have one execution and are then slaughtered, usually because they do not work. Indeed the very reason UNIX uses the fixed name **a.out** is that by default executable programs are objects that can be overridden or deleted. There are a few survivors, however: most of the built-in UNIX programs were **a.out** files at some stage in their development.

We should emphasize that the **a.out** files have no special properties. They are just binary files with execute permission. This contrasts with some operating systems which support special 'workfiles'. Given that there is no magic in the name of **a.out**, a few language processors use different default names — **obj** is an example.

COMPILING SEPARATE MODULES

The philosophy of UNIX is that big programs should, where possible, be split into smaller programs. Some of the 'smaller' programs are still, nevertheless, big — **nroff** is an example of one such — and may take a long time to compile. Such programs should be split up into separate units that we call *modules*. The use of separate modules is valuable even in small programs; for example our sample C program was combined with a separate pre-written input/output module. A good compiling system should allow modules to be compiled separately so that if one module is changed it is only necessary to recompile that module, and not the whole program. Most UNIX programming languages have good compiling systems.

The principle used is that a module is converted to a so-called *object code* form, which can then be stored in a file (an *object file*). An object file is a binary file very close in form to the final executable form of the program. A UNIX program called a *loader* (or a *linking loader*) converts object files to their final executable form. The great advantage of the loader is that it can combine together several object files to make a single executable program. A large program can be compiled as follows

(1) compile each module into an object file.
(2) use the loader to combine the object files of all the modules to produce the executable program; then execute this program.
(3) if there turns out to be an error in any module, correct the source file for this module and recompile it to a new object file; then go back to step (2).

Since loading is much faster than recompiling the above method provides an attractive way of dealing with large modular programs.

Only advanced users need to know the details of the loader. The majority can be ignorant even of its name (which is **ld**) since language processors generally invoke the loader automatically.

EXTENSIONS

A potential disadvantage of the above mechanism is that you can have several incarnations of a program, i.e.

- a source file for each module
- an object file for each module
- the executable program

This creates two problems. Firstly it uses a lot of file space; this can only be solved by ruthless deletion of object files and executable programs that do not justify their keep. Secondly there is the problem of keeping track of the names of all the files. UNIX neatly solves this problem by using extensions of filenames. In Chapter 7, when we introduced the idea of extensions, we gave the following examples

average.p   a Pascal program
average.c   a program in the C language
average.spec   a specification of the program

Two further examples are
average.o   the object file for the program
average   the executable file of the program

This use of extensions to indicate the nature of a file is exploited by language processors and indeed you are required to follow some of the conventions we have shown, as we shall see shortly.

COMPILING A MULTI-MODULE PROGRAM

The mechanisms provided by most UNIX language processors for compiling multi-module programs are so delightfully simple that you hardly even need to know what an object file is. We shall illustrate this by considering the compilation of a C program that consists of three modules: **module1.c**, **module2.c**, and **module3.c**.

To compile the program you first use the command

cc module1.c module2.c module3.c

or its equivalent which uses the '?' wildcard of the shell:

cc module?.c

The **cc** language processor deduces that if it compiles more than one file at a time then it is dealing with a multi-module program and the user might want object files retained. In our example it therefore automatically produces an object file (with a **.o** extension) from each source file (**.c** extension) that it compiles. It thus produces the three object files **module1.o**, **module2.o** and **module3.o**. It also produces an **a.out** file in the normal way.

If the user executes this **a.out** file and finds that there is an error in the second module he duly makes the required correction to **module2.c**. He does not want to recompile the other two modules since they are unchanged. He therefore recompiles his program using the command

cc module1.o module2.c module3.o

This recompiles **module2.c**, generating a new object file **module2.o**, and then causes the loader to integrate this new object file with **module1.o** and **module3.o** to generate a new **a.out** file. The overall result is that compilation is considerably faster as the first and third modules are not recompiled.

The whole process of creating an executable program from a group of source modules, or more generally the process of creating files that depend on other files, can be further automated by using a superb UNIX program called **make**. The principle is that you tell **make** how to generate each file using the others; when you call **make** it looks at the datestamps on files, and if file **x** depends on file **y**, then **make** will regenerate **x** if **y** has changed more recently than **x**. You can specify your instructions to **make** by creating a file called **makefile** within your current directory, and then you simply type

make

An example of a simple **makefile**, which compiles our multi-module program, is

a.out: module1.o module2.o module3.o
      cc module1.o module2.o module3.o

The first line, which we call the *dependency line*, says that **a.out** depends on **module1.o**, **module2.o**, and **module3.o**. To generate an **a.out** file from these files it is necessary to execute the command(s) that follow the dependency line. (These command lines are each preceded by tab characters to distinguish them from dependency lines.) In our case there is a single command

cc module1.o module2.o module3.o

Make automatically knows that each file with a **.o** extension depends on the corresponding file with a **.c** extension. It also knows that if file *x*.**c** has changed more recently than *x*.**o**, then it should recompile the former to generate a new version of the latter. Thus there is no need for us to tell it that **module1.o** depends upon **module1.c** and so on. In general you can, however, have several dependency lines, plus their associated command lines, within the same **makefile**.

The uses of the **make** command go far beyond compiling programs. It can be used, for example, to make books out of individual chapters. **Makefiles** also serve as valuable documentation of how files interdepend, and can even supplant the **README** files we suggested in Chapter 7.

LANGUAGES AND PROCESSORS

The **cc** language processor has a host of options for controlling the compilation process and the generation of files — you can, for example, send the final executable program to a filename that is not **a.out**. Other language processors have similar options. You will need to consult the documentation of your chosen language processor for details.

When a program is divided into separately-compiled modules, programming languages offer some notation for referencing one module from another. The method used is totally dependent on the programming language; it often involves concepts such as 'external' or 'common'.

Sadly, most programmers spend a lot of their time detecting and correcting errors. Syntax errors in the use of a programming language are usually easy to correct. Generally the language processor will not even generate an executable file if a source program is syntactically wrong. The C language has a special supporting program called **lint**, which can be used to examine a C source program and look for errors and doubtful syntax that **cc** does not catch.

The more difficult errors arise when a program is syntactically correct but does not do what it should. Programmers are divided on their approach to debugging. Some believe there is no substitute for thought and experimentation; others believe that special debugging systems are valuable. To cater for the latter UNIX provides a family of debugging programs corresponding to the languages it supports. These programs have names such as **adb** and **sdb**, and can be explored in your local documentation.

In addition, for those who enjoy low-level programming, most UNIX systems provide an assembler called **as**. You can, however, do most tasks in C without recourse to such depths.

LIBRARIES

UNIX provides libraries of valuable functions to aid your programming. More-over you can, if you wish, create your own libraries by using a program called **ar**. Libraries have the extension **.a** to distinguish them from other files. The advantage of a library over an object file is that the loader can pick the functions you need from the library rather than including the whole library in your executable program. UNIX uses the term 'archive' for these libraries — hence the use of the letter **a** as their extension.

Section 3 of your *UNIX Programmer's Manual* gives a list of the built-in library routines available. These include the functions in the **stdio** library we mentioned earlier, plus many more. They are mainly designed for use from within C programs, but can sometimes be used in other languages too.

The method of using a library is as follows. You place an *include* line in your program so that the program can reference the objects in the library. This tells your program about the specification of the library, but you also have to tell the compiler to combine the library with your program. The built-in UNIX libraries are stored in the directories **/lib** or **/usr/lib**. The compiler option $-lx$ (it is really an option implemented by the loader rather than the compiler) causes the library file **lib$x$.a** from within **/lib** or **/usr/lib** to be used. As a specific example, if you want to use the built-in library of mathematical subroutines (sine, Bessel functions, etc.), you include a file called **math.h** by placing the line

#**include** < **math.h** >

in your program. Given that this library is stored in the file **libm.a**, you put the $-$**lm** option on the **cc** command to compile your program. You need to put this option at the *end* of your **cc** command since the search of the library must come after the compilation of your program — only then is it known which library facilities are needed.

Lastly a piece of general advice about libraries, which carries over to most other facilities of UNIX: before you plunge into implementing anything, leaf through your UNIX documentation to find out what is already there. Many programmers spend all their time re-inventing the wheel.

FOLLOWING THE UNIX STYLE

When you write programs you should try to follow the general UNIX style so that your programs are easy and natural to use. Remember that nearly all the built-in programs in the UNIX system were written in C, so C provides all the power you need to follow the general style. In particular C provides mechanisms to allow your program to examine the command line that caused it to be executed, e.g.

a.out $-$**x**

This enables the program to implement its own options — in the above case it could look to see if it had an argument that set the **x** option and, if it was there, behave in some special way.

Other languages available on UNIX may provide similar facilities, though inevitably C has the most finely tuned ones.

SUMMARY

To summarize the message of this Chapter

- pick a programming language which is available on your UNIX and suits your needs and your approach to life.

- learn the C language if you ever want to compete with Dudley.
- divide your programs into separate modules and then exploit UNIX's excellent facilities for object files.
- try to design your programs to have a similar style and user interface to the built-in UNIX programs — unless you really hate this style or think the users of your program should be protected from the influence of hrmt.

CHAPTER 13

Rounding off

And I could tell you no more,
Should I preach a whole year!
LONGFELLOW

The purpose of this final Chapter is to round off our description of UNIX by covering some valuable commands that have not naturally fitted into any of the preceding Chapters. At the end of this Chapter we give a summary of UNIX as a whole.

DEVICES

Before we describe any more UNIX commands, we must fulfil a promise made in Chapter 5: to explain more about communication with peripheral devices that may be attached to your computer.

In Chapter 5 we explained that a device may be spooled, thus enabling several people to use it simultaneously. When a device is spooled you do not communicate with it directly; instead you use a program that does the spooling — **lpr** is an example of such a program.

You may have a device on your computer for which spooling is unavailable or inappropriate; you will need to communicate directly with such a device (and thus no other user can use the device at the same time as you). UNIX makes direct communication easy by treating devices exactly as if they were files. Each device is represented by a 'filename' of form

/dev/*devicename*

We shall call these names *device filenames*. If you type the command

ls /dev

you will get a summary of all the device filenames available on your UNIX. Some of your device filenames will be esoteric ones concerned with the inner workings of your UNIX, but you should see some names you recognize. There should always be one or more device filenames of the form **tty***n* where n is some number. These correspond to the terminals attached to your UNIX; they are the same names that are used in the output from the **who** and **write** commands.

There is a command

tty

which will tell you the device filename of the terminal you are using. We shall assume that it is

/dev/tty11

The beauty of UNIX's device filenames is that they can be used exactly like true filenames. For example you can say

cat afile > /dev/tty11

to send output to your terminal. This does not, of course, do anything different from a normal **cat**, since that too sends output to your terminal. However some other user can type the above command and thus redirect **cat**'s output to your terminal rather than his. Indeed the way a command such as

write me

works is to look up **me** in a table of users — the same table used by the **who** command — and then to redirect output to the device filename associated with **me**, in our case **/dev/tty11**.

Writing directly to someone else's terminal is not an act of a civilized person, and the real value of device filenames comes when you have some special device attached to your computer. Assume such a device is a tea-maker, called **/dev/teamaker**. Before using the device you need to get Dudley and his friends to write programs that control it and to put its name in the **/dev** directory of your UNIX. Some devices, such as printers, just output the text sent to them, but Dudley's programs for the tea-maker will need to interpret the text as commands. We shall assume that Dudley has provided the two commands

spoons N   (put N spoonfuls of tea in the pot)
boil   (boil the water)

Given this, we can then reap the rewards of all Dudley's hard work by saying

```
$ cat  >/dev/teamaker
spoons 2
boil
∧ d
$
```

and then go and enjoy our tea.

PERFORMING COMMANDS IN THE FUTURE

We can now begin our description of some further UNIX commands. We start with a remarkable command, the **at** command, which allows you to control the future. You can specify that a given shell program, which is stored in a file, is to be executed at some specified future time. The way you do this is to say

   at *time file*

The *time* is normally a series of four digits representing the time on a twenty-four hour clock. Thus 1430 is 2.30 p.m. There are also more elaborate ways of specifying *time*, and you can even specify, with the time, a date several days or months ahead. If you do not specify a date the command will be executed within the next twenty-four hours.

The *file*, which we call an *at-file*, must be the name of a file that contains a shell program. Given that this program is to be executed in the future, when you may not be logged in, the shell program must not communicate with your terminal. It must not therefore use the standard input or output (or the standard error output).

The **at** command is useful on busy time-sharing systems, where mammoth programs are best run overnight. It is also useful for management functions, for example updating tables or clearing up the file system, which again is best done in the middle of the night when the system is not busy. (The superuser, who does the management, may actually use her own special facility, called **cron**, which is even more powerful than **at**.)

An *at-file* can itself contain an **at** command, and thus **at** commands can perpetuate themselves. A job that runs at three o'clock one morning can therefore itself spawn a similar job that runs at three o'clock the next morning, and this can spawn a further job, thus implementing a daily routine.

Some UNIXes allow the −**m** option on **at**. This causes you to be sent mail to confirm that the **at** has indeed been executed. This option is almost part of the style of UNIX, and other commands of a similar nature to **at** may have the same option; its purpose is to re-assure the user that what he asked for did really happen.

As an example of the usage of **at**, assume that the file **checknovel** contains the two lines

> **checknr chapter* > nrofferror**
> **spell chapter* > spellerror**

This checks for **nroff** errors and spelling errors in all the chapters of a book, and sends the results to two files, **nrofferror** and **spellerror**. The **checknovel** file can be executed at 3 a.m. by the command

> **at 0300 checknovel**

The execution of **at** will use as its current directory the same directory that is now the current directory, so we are assuming that all the **chapter** files are in this directory.

A UNIX command of a similar nature to **at** is **sleep**. The command

> **sleep** *n*

causes a process to go to sleep for *n* seconds. Thus if you had a shell program containing the two commands

> **sleep 600**
> **echo   Wake up**

then executing this program causes the words 'Wake up' to be displayed ten minutes (600 seconds) later. Such a shell program could be run in the background while, in the foreground, you are reading one of Dudley's files that contains a description of his programming adventures.

COMPARING FILES

There are several UNIX commands for comparing files. The **diff** command is perhaps the most frequently used. **Diff** compares two files and identifies all the lines where they differ. It produces its output in a form similar (but not identical) to a sequence of **ed** commands to create one file from the other. Thus if you are a master of **ed**, you will soon be good at unravelling **diff**'s output too.

Consider the command

> **diff f1 f2**

where **f2** is identical to **f1** except that

- a new line, which reads 'You owe me one thousand pounds', has been added after line 122.
- line 100, which contains the text 'I owe you fifty pounds', has been deleted from **f2**.

The output from this **diff** command is

```
100d99
< I owe you fifty pounds
122a122
> You owe me one thousand pounds
```

The number 99 after the **d** in the first line and the number 122 after the **a** in the third line are actually line numbers of the file **f2**. If you really want to edit **f1** to create **f2** imagine these numbers are not there. The '<' and '>' characters indicate lines present in **f1** but not **f2**, and vice-versa.

There are thus two ways that the output from **diff** augments the ordinary **ed** notation. The purpose of the extensions is to provide extra information that you might need. If, however, you do want the output from **diff** to be true **ed** commands, rather than the above approximation to them, you should use the −**e** option. In our example

diff −**e f1 f2**

produces the output

```
122a
You owe me one thousand pounds
.
100d
```

Notice how the edits come out in back-to-front order, so that a change in an earlier line does not upset the line number of a later one. Sometimes when you have two similar files you can profitably delete one of them and use an edit 'script' such as the above to re-create it from the other one when the need arises.

Another command for comparing files is **comm**. **Comm** is designed to work on files that have already been sorted into alphabetical order (e.g. by **sort**). An example would be a list of spelling errors produced by the **spell** command — indeed **spell** uses **sort** to sort its output. The syntax of the **comm** command is

comm [−[**123**]] *file1 file2*

Comm compares *file1* with *file2* and produces three columns of output

Column 1: lines in *file1* but not *file2*
Column 2: lines in *file2* but not *file1*
Column 3: lines that occur in both files

The options specify the columns you want *suppressed*, e.g. −**3** suppresses column 3.

As an example of the use of **comm** assume you are using UNIX to keep the accounts of a business and that you have two files

janlate   late payers in January
feblate   late payers in February

Assuming these files are sorted into alphabetical order, the command

comm −**12 janlate feblate**

will display the third column of **comm**'s output, i.e. the names of those who paid late in both January and February. (The name **comm** suggests this type of use: finding *comm*on lines of files.)

The UNIX commands for comparing files are a good illustration of the value of the material under the 'SEE ALSO' heading of UNIX manual pages. If you type

    man comm

to find out about the **comm** command, the last lines of its output are

    .

    .

    .

    SEE ALSO
        cmp(1), diff(1), uniq(1)

This tells you that if **comm** does not quite serve your purpose you should look at the manual pages for **cmp** (a command that reports a difference in terms of line and byte number), **diff** and **uniq** — all of which are described in Section 1 of the *UNIX Programmer's Manual*.

FILE USAGE

We have emphasized that sooner or later you will always become short of file space. To help you monitor how greedy you are, UNIX provides a command **du**. This tells you how many 'blocks' of disk space are occupied by your current directory and by each of its sub-directories. The size of a block is normally 512 bytes (characters).

To get an overall picture of your disk usage, type **du** when you are in your home directory. Try typing it each time you log in, and watch how your file usage creeps inexorably upwards. You could even put a **du** command in your **.profile** file, so that you are told automatically of your file usage whenever you log in.

CHANGING YOUR PASSWORD

You can change your password at any time by using the **passwd** command. When you first use UNIX one of your earliest acts may be to set a new password. The **passwd** command understands the frailties of human nature, and tries to guard against them. In particular it tries to protect you from theft, carelessness and forgetfulness.

Assume you are called away from your terminal on some urgent matter (see **/dev/teamaker** above), and you leave your terminal logged in. While you are away some felon might sneak up to your terminal and change your password; he would then have control over all your computer possessions. The **passwd** command prevents this by requiring anyone who changes a password to quote the old password.

It fights carelessness and forgetfulness by requiring you to type your new password twice. This helps you remember it, and guards against you mistyping a password and then not knowing what it is. Furthermore **passwd** guards against another human frailty: laziness. It requires you, for your own protection, to type passwords that are at least six characters long. However if you insistently keep setting the same short password, or if your password is a mixture of letters and other characters, it eventually relents this restriction.

The following shows a sample use of **passwd**

```
$ passwd
Changing password for me
Old password: cleverme
New password: genius
Retype new password: genius
$
```

(Although we show the passwords on the above display they do not, in fact, appear on the screen for all to see. They are suppressed in the same way as when you type a password to log in.)

SEVEN DEADLY SINS

Given that the **passwd** command discourages *sloth* in typing passwords, and *covetousness* of your password by others, and that **du** monitors your *gluttony* for file space, UNIX covers three of the Seven Deadly Sins with just two commands. Although you might argue that **diff**, with its apparently tortuous output, causes *anger* rather than curbs it, you at least have **man** to help assuage the anger. *Envy* can be curbed by denying read permission on files, on the basis that what the eye does not see the heart does not grieve for; anyone guilty of *pride* is reduced to humility when they first try to master **ed** or **nroff**. There are, however, no programs to curb *lust*.

PAGINATED PRINTING

We have seen that the **cat** command displays files exactly as they are, and that **nroff** can be used to format a file in order to make it really good to look at. The **pr** command comes between these two. Its main contribution is to divide a file up into pages of standard size, with a heading and page number at the top of each page. As its name implies, **pr** is especially useful for files that are to be printed, rather than displayed on a screen.

If we applied **pr** to the start of our Greg Daimler novel, which is stored in the file **chapter1**, its output would begin as follows

```
Dec 18 11:56 1983   chapter1 Page 1


Greg Daimler entered the room. There were seven bodies on
the floor. He coughed. A body fell from the top of the
bookcase. He looked up. He saw ten more bodies stuck to
the ceiling.
The tractor outside stopped its engine.
The clock struck three.
At this point a door opened.
```

A tall and exceptionally beautiful girl entered the room.
She was wearing a low-cut and very tight dress.

.

.

.

As you can see the page heading has the current date and time, the file name and the page number. Each page has a similar heading, though obviously the page number differs from page to page. In addition to creating page headings, **pr** adds blank lines at the foot of pages. There are a host of options on **pr** to give you control over the exact format of headings, and the size of lines and pages.

If you type the option -2 the printing comes out in two columns; the option -3 causes 3-column output, and so on. This is useful for printing, in a compact form, files that consist of short lines.

If you use a command such as

pr f1 f2 f3

then, following the normal UNIX style, **pr** will print each of the three files in turn.

CONTROLLING YOUR TERMINAL

In Chapter 5, when we discussed terminals, we referred to the **stty** command; this can be used to set options associated with your terminal. If you type

stty

on its own you are told what the current settings are. (On some UNIX implementations you may need to type **stty all** or **stty everything**.)

As an example of the use of **stty** the command

stty $-$**echo**

causes your terminal to stop echoing, i.e. characters you type at the keyboard no longer appear on your display. To restore echoing you type

stty echo

This example is typical of the syntax of **stty**, which is different from that of most other UNIX commands. Since **stty** does not have filenames as its arguments, the normal rules for options are relaxed. Options are represented, much to hrmt's disgust, by long words such as **echo**, rather than by a single letter. If the name of an option is preceded by a minus sign the option is switched off, and if the name of the option is not preceded by a minus sign it is switched on.

In addition to on/off options such as **echo**, **stty** has some options that involve the setting of a number or a character associated with a terminal. An example of this is

stty erase =

This causes the erase key, i.e. the character you type when you have just typed a wrong character and want to delete it, to become an equals sign. After the above use of **stty**, if you typed

Di = aimler

it would be treated as 'Daimler'. Thus the equals sign has taken the place of the previous erase key, the '#' key say, and if you now typed the '#' key it would be treated as an ordinary character.

There is a host of options available on **stty**, but most users settle into a hide-bound way of using their terminal and thus only need to consider using **stty** when they change terminal. If you examine the output from typing **stty** on its own, which, as we have said, displays the current option settings, you will get some idea of the range of options available. A sample display is

```
$ stty
speed 9600 baud
erase = '#'; kill = '@'
even odd −raw −nl echo −lcase −tabs cbreak
width 132 length 24
```

GAMES

To some, a computer is a tool for playing games; as a by-product it can also do some 'useful' things as well. Numerous computer games have been written for UNIX: the games range from sophisticated chess-playing programs to games of fantasy and imagination. On time-sharing UNIX systems the management may try to suppress games — though often the end result of such restriction is to *increase* the amount of game playing. If you explore Section 6 of your *UNIX Programmer's Manual*, you will find what games are officially available on your UNIX.

LOOKING AT THE END OF A FILE

It is often useful to be able to look at the last few lines of a file, for example to find out how far someone has got with a report file they are preparing. You can do this using the editor — specifically its **p** command — but an easier method is to use the command

    tail *file*

This displays the last few lines of the *file*. **Tail** has options to give some extra control over the lines to be displayed, to the extent that it can even display complete files. Some UNIX implementations provide a **head** command which is complementary to **tail**.

If you want to find out about the general nature of a file, you can use the **file** command. This command examines a given file and tries to make an intelligent guess at what it contains — for example a C program or some **nroff** input.

COUNTING

The command

    wc [*file*] ...

gives you three statistics about the given *files*: the number of lines, the number of words and the number of characters. An example of its use is

```
$ wc report
   481    3517    20796 report
```

Here the **report** file contains 481 lines, 3517 words and 20796 characters. The **wc** command is especially valuable as a component of a pipe, e.g.

```
$ who | wc
   9    45    270
```

The **who** command displays the names of all current users, one to a line. Hence the number of lines produced by **who**, in our case 9, is the number of users. The other two figures, 45 and 270 are in this case unwanted statistics. They could be suppressed by the $-l$ option, which means 'line count only', e.g.

```
who | wc  −l
```

The options $-w$ (for words) and $-c$ (for characters) serve a similar purpose to the $-l$ option.

VERSIONS OF UNIX

In this Chapter, as in previous ones, we have tried to describe facilities common to all UNIX implementations but have made occasional remarks about features that will vary between implementations. We shall finish by saying more about the different versions of UNIX. UNIX, like any successful product, is undergoing continuous development and improvement. Paradoxically the best improvements in software are ones that users need not be aware of. Examples of such improvements — we shall call these *evolutionary* improvements — would be

- a performance gain in an existing command
- a new command
- an improved command which offers all the options previously available, but some new ones too.

The worst improvements are *revolutionary* improvements where some existing facility disappears and is replaced by some new and different facility. In this case users find that some of their techniques, perhaps perfected over several years, no longer work. Such "improvements" really do need to be dramatic improvements if their net effect is to make users happier.

Fortunately most UNIX improvements over the years have been evolutionary ones. That is why it is possible to write books on UNIX as a whole rather than on one particular implementation.

UNIX development started at Bell Laboratories in 1969, and was mainly based on the PDP-11 computer. It was not until 1975, and the so-called Sixth Edition, that UNIX was made available widely outside Bell Laboratories. At that stage there was work within Bell Laboratories to make UNIX portable, i.e. able to be moved to computers other than the PDP-11. This was successful, largely because UNIX is almost entirely based on the C language; once C has been implemented on a new computer, UNIX can follow. Thus implementations of UNIX were spawned for numerous computers, and it became a generally available system. In addition to this portability work, UNIX itself was improved and the end product was released as the Seventh Edition of UNIX — the hugely successful release that is popularly known as 'Version Seven' or 'V7'.

At this point a new force was introduced to UNIX development: the University of California at Berkeley worked on implementations for VAX computers. Their work has met with as much user acclaim as that of Bell Laboratories itself, and 'Berkeley UNIX' and 'the Berkeley enhancements' have become widely known. Berkeley UNIX has itself been issued in successive versions: these have numbers such as 4.1BSD and 4.2BSD.

Bell Laboratories have also been developing UNIX. They have used a new numbering system for releases after Version 7. Instead of Version 8, we have had System III, System V, and so on.

If you find all this confusing, just forget it. Just as you can drive a car without knowing the exact model, so you can use and enjoy your UNIX system without being aware of its version number and parentage. Your local documentation will describe the facilities that you have; the best attitude is to be thankful for what is available rather than envious of someone who claims to have a later version than you.

SUMMARY

We shall finish the book by returning to the point we made at the start: that ideas are more important than details. Obviously you will need to learn enough details to use the repertoire of commands that suits you, but you will only exploit the real power of UNIX if you exploit its ideas. In particular you should

- organize your files in a hierarchy of separate directories, with no more than a dozen or so files in each directory.
- exploit the UNIX aids for producing documents, even if your primary use of UNIX is not as an aid to writing. Any project is useless without good documentation.
- use pipes to build your own tailored commands out of other commands.
- where pipes are inadequate, write shell programs to build your own UNIX commands.
- exploit others: before you do a job yourself browse round the file system to see what facilities are already there to help you. See what you can gain from the work of other users: communicate with your fellows using electronic mail.
- no society can work unless the givers are in balance with the takers. Hence if you develop anything that is generally useful, make it available to your fellows. Better still, make each individual component of your work available to others, so that they can build something of their own using your modules.

All these points can be summed up in one: the way to achieve something big is to create small and manageable units and combine them effectively. UNIX has succeeded because it has provided an environment for doing this. Its users have succeeded where they have exploited this environment.

References

Bourne, S. (1983). *The UNIX system*, Addison-Wesley, London.

Cherry, L.L. and W. Vesterman. (1981). *Writing tools — the STYLE and DICTION programs*, Computer Science Technical Report 91, Bell Laboratories, Murray Hill, N.J.

Deitel, H.M. (1983). *An introduction to operating systems*, Addison-Wesley, Reading, Mass.

Feuer, A. and N.H. Gehani. (1982). "A comparison of the programming languages C and PASCAL", *Computer Surveys 14,1*, pp. 73-92.

Kernighan, B.W. (1978). *UNIX for beginners — Second edition.* (In Volume 2 of *UNIX Programmer's Manual.*)

Kernighan, B.W. (1981). *Why Pascal is not my favorite programming language*, Computer Science Technical Report 100, Bell Laboratories, Murray Hill, N.J.

Kernighan, B.W. and P.J. Plauger. (1976). *Software tools*, Addison-Wesley, Reading, Mass.

Kernighan, B.W. and P.J. Plauger. (1981). *Software tools in Pascal*, Addison-Wesley, Reading, Mass.

Kernighan, B.W. and D.M. Ritchie. (1978). *The C programming language*, Prentice-Hall, Englewood Cliffs, N.J.

Knuth, D.E. (1973). *The art of computer programming*, Volume 1, Second edition, Addison-Wesley, Reading, Mass.

Lister, A.M. (1979). *Fundamentals of operating systems*, Second edition, Macmillan, London.

Lucas Phillips, C.E. (1952). *The small garden*, Pan, London (reprinted many times since).

Ritchie, D.M. and K. Thompson. (1974). "The UNIX time-sharing system", *Comm. ACM 17,7*, pp. 365-375; reprinted in *Comm. ACM 26,1* (1983), pp. 84-89.

Wilkes, M.V. (1972). *Time-sharing computer systems*, Macdonald/Elsevier, London.

Appendix A:
sample terminal
sessions

In this Appendix we show some examples of complete UNIX sessions. In each case we follow our normal convention of using bold face type to identify material typed by the user.

SESSION 1: SIMPLE MAIL

In this first simple session we log in and then hear that we have some electronic mail. We read our mail, which consists of a single message that comes from the user **bill**. Having displayed the message from **bill**, the **mail** system asks us what to do next: we delete the message, since it is not worth preserving, and quit the **mail** system. Our next UNIX command is to use **mail** again, this time to reply to **bill**. Finally, as a matter of curiosity, we look to see who is currently logged in and then we log out. Since **bill** is logged in, he should receive our mail straight away.

login: **me**	*type login name*
password: **cleverme**	*(password not on screen)*
You have mail.	
$ mail	*read the mail*
From bill Tue Jul 1 12:51:36	
Welcome to UNIX.	
If you want any help getting	
started, let me know.	
? **d**	*delete mail message*
? **q**	*quit mail system*
$ mail bill	*reply to bill*
Thank you for your offer.	
I may well contact you later.	
.	*terminate message*
$ who	*see who is logged in*
bill tty01 Jul 1 12:45	
me tty11 Jul 1 13:50	
anne tty13 Jul 1 13:22	
dudley tty15 Jul 1 03:20	
$ ∧d	*log out*

SESSION 2: DOCUMENT PREPARATION

Here we use the **ed** editor to prepare a document and place it in the file **mynews**. This document is to be processed by the **nroff** text formatter (using the **ms** macros), and includes the requests **SH**, **LP** and **PP**.

Having typed the document we notice that the word 'announce' has been wrongly spelled as 'announve'. We therefore search for the line containing this word, and replace 'announve' by 'announce'. We then write the document to the file **mynews** and quit the editor. (Up to this point the session closely mirrors Sample Session 1 of the description of **ed** in Chapter 8; if you want to look at further examples of editing, you should look at the remaining sample sessions in Chapter 8.)

Having created the **mynews** file we apply a spelling check to it: the **spell** program is silent, meaning that it detected no errors — it even accepted proper names such as 'Martin' and 'Collins'. We then use **nroff** to format the document, and the resultant output appears on the terminal. There are a few blank lines of *header* at the top of the document, and a few lines of *footer*, which include the current date, at the bottom. (We have cheated a bit in displaying this output: we have made lines shorter and the page shorter in order to fit on a page of this book.) Pleased with what we see, we execute **nroff** again, this time sending its output to a printer. We execute this second **nroff** command in the background, since there is no need to interact with it or to wait for it to finish. We achieve this by typing an ampersand at the end of the command. We then log out, leaving the command to finish its work in its own time. On the printed document the section heading 'Announcement' should come out in bold face.

login: **me**	*type login name*
password: **cleverme**	*type password*
$ **ed**	*enter the editor*
a	*append some text*
.SH \" section heading	
Announcement	
.LP \" left-aligned paragraph	
I am pleased to announve	
my engagement	
to Jane, only daughter of	
Major and Mrs. A.J. Collins of	
25 Cathedral Avenue, Canterbury.	
.PP \" indented paragraph	
The wedding will take place at	
St. Martin's	
Church at 2.30 p.m. on Nov. 3.	
.	*terminate text*
/announve/	*search for 'announve'*
I am pleased to announve	*(result of search)*
s//announce/p	*substitute and print*
I am pleased to announce	*(revised line)*
w mynews	*write the file*
301	*(size of file)*
q	*quit the editor*
$ **spell mynews**	*check spelling*
$ **nroff** −**ms mynews**	*format the document*

Announcement

I am pleased to announce my engagement to Jane, only daughter of Major and Mrs. A.J. Collins of 25 Cathedral Avenue, Canterbury.

The wedding will take place at St. Martin's
Church at 2.30 p.m. on Nov. 3.

                July 1, 1984

$ nroff −ms   mynews | lpr &   *print it (in background)*
$ ∧d   *log out*

SESSION 3: PREPARING A PROGRAM

This is a session that is only of interest to programmers. It shows the preparation
and execution of a program in the C language.

On logging in we first change our current directory to the **project** directory,
which contains the files associated with our programming project. We then list the
files in this directory, to remind ourselves of what is there. As a result we recall that
the file **average.c** contains the program we want to work on. Assume that this file
contains the C program that we introduced in Chapter 12, i.e.

```
/* − − − finds the average of N numbers − − − */

#include <stdio.h>

main()
{
    int n, k;
    float sum, number;

    scanf("%d",&n);
    sum = 0;
    for (k=1; k <= n; k++)
    { scanf("%f",&number);
      sum += number;
    }
    if (n > 0)
        printf("Average =%f\n", sum/n);
    else
        printf("No numbers in data\n");
}
```

We wish to extend this program by adding, at the start, the extra lines

```
        printf("Type count of numbers\n");
        printf("Then type the numbers\n");
```

To accomplish this we use the **ed** editor, and insert these two extra lines before the
first executable line in the program — the first line containing 'scan'. Unfortunately we make an error in typing the second extra line: we omit the closing ')'.
Unaware of our small mistake we write the 'improved' version of the program on

top of the previous version, and compile it using the **cc** language processor. We get an error message.

Our next steps are to use the editor to correct our error, and then to re-compile the corrected program. **Cc** is silent this time, and no news is good news: no syntax errors were detected in our program, and hence an **a.out** executable program will have been produced. We execute this program, supplying as data the number '4', followed by the four numbers that we wish to be averaged. The program produces the correct answer.

Finally we execute the program using the data in the **data** file, and are told the average of the numbers in this file; the extra messages that we have added to our program are still displayed even though the data is not being typed at the terminal. Perhaps our change to the program was rather a foolish one.

login: **me**	*type login name*
password: **cleverme**	*type password*
$ **cd project**	*change directory*
$ **ls**	*list files*
a.out average.c data manual	
$ **ed average.c**	*edit*
295	*(size of file)*
/scan/	*search for 'scan'*
scanf("%d",&n);	*(result of search)*
i	*insert before this*
printf("Type count of numbers\n");	
printf("Then type the numbers\n";	
.	*terminate inserted text*
w	*write the file*
369	*(size of file)*
q	*quit the editor*
$ **cc average.c**	*compile*
"average.c", line 11: syntax error	*(error message)*
$ **ed average.c**	*edit again*
369	*(size of file)*
11	*display line 11*
printf("Then type the numbers\n";	*(line 11)*
s/;/);/p	*replace ';' by ');'*
printf("Then type the numbers\n");	*(result of replacement)*
w	*write the file*
370	*(size of file)*
q	*quit the editor*
$ **cc average.c**	*re-compile*
$ **a.out**	*execute*
Type count of numbers	
Then type the numbers	
4	*count of numbers*
20 20.5 21 20.5	*numbers to be averaged*
Average = 20.500000	*(program gives answer)*
$ **a.out** <**data**	*use data file*

201

Type count of numbers	*(unwanted messages —*
	see commentary)
Then type the numbers	
Average = 167.456051	*(average of data)*
$ ∧**d**	*log out*

SESSION 4: USING THE FILE SYSTEM TREE

Here we wish to assemble some articles for an issue of a magazine of which we are the editor (in the literary sense rather than the **ed** sense). After logging in we create a new directory, **magazine**, for the magazine issue, and we make this our current directory. The magazine is to be built from four existing files:
(1) **editorial**, which is in our home directory
(2) **smut**, which is in **derek**'s home directory
(3) **dirt**, which is in the **mag** directory, a sub-directory within **jill**'s home directory
(4) **grime**, which is in **jack**'s home directory

As editor, we plan to alter the articles in order to fit the style of the magazine. **Jack** and **jill** wish to keep their original articles; they have asked us to make copies of their articles, and then to alter our copies, rather than the originals. **Derek** is more trusting: he gives us write permission on his **smut** file, so that we can change it as we wish.

We decide to bring all four of the articles into our new directory, and to give them the names **article1**, **article2**, **article3** and **article4**. Figure A.1 shows the position of the relevant files, including our new ones, in the file system tree.

Our first act is to move our **editorial** file from our home directory to the **magazine** directory, renaming it as **article1**. Secondly we make the filename **article2** a synonym for **derek**'s existing **smut** file. We do this 'linking' by using the **ln** command. Thereafter any change in **article2** causes a corresponding change in the **smut** file — indeed they are the same file.

Our last act in building the new directory is to make copies of the contributions from **jill** and **jack**. We can do this with the **cp** command. Unfortunately our attempt to copy **jack**'s file fails, because we have not got the necessary permissions to access his **grime** file. There are two possible reasons for this

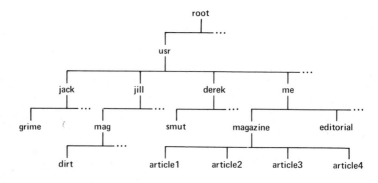

Figure A.1 The file system tree

- we have not got read permission for his **grime** file
- we have not got execute permission for one of the directories on the path to **grime**, e.g. we may lack execute permission for **jack**'s home directory.

We use the $-l$ option on the **ls** command to list the permissions on the **grime** file, and find that the problem is that we have not got read permission for this file. We cannot, of course, change the permissions on a file that **jack** owns, so all we can do is to send him some mail.

Lastly we list the contents of our new directory in order to see that the **article1**, **article2** and **article3** files are indeed there, and to see their size. Notice that, since we have linked to **derek**'s file rather than copied it, he is still the owner (see third field of listing). The number '2' in the second field of the listing of the **article2** file shows that **article2** is one of two synonyms of a file.

login: **me**	*type login name*
password: **cleverme**	*type password*
$ **mkdir magazine**	*create new directory*
$ **cd magazine**	*change to this directory*
$ **mv ../editorial article1**	*move first article*
$ **ln /usr/derek/smut article2**	*link to second article*
$ **cp /usr/jill/mag/dirt article3**	*copy third article*
$ **cp /usr/jack/grime article4**	*try to copy*
cp: cannot open /usr/jack/grime	*(error message)*
$ **ls** $-l$ **/usr/jack/grime**	*look at permissions*
$-$rw$--------$ 1 jack 5708 Jun 30 10:17 grime	
	(only owner can read)
$ **mail jack**	*send mail*
Please let me read your	
grime file.	
.	*terminate message*
$ **ls** $-l$	*list files*
total 14	*(blocks of file space used)*
$-$r w $-$ r $--$ r $--$ 1 me 2112 Jun 27 17:58 article1	
$-$r w $-$ r w $-$ r w $-$ 2 derek 3329 Jun 25 15:37 article2	
$-$r w $-$ r $--$ r $--$ 1 me 799 Jun 5 12:32 article3	
$ ∧**d**	*log out*

Appendix B:
list of commands

This Appendix, which is intended for quick reference, gives specifications of the commands that are explained in this book. We show for each command the syntax, the page number of the tutorial description within the body of the book, a brief specification, and an example. We describe the major options that are available on commands, including some not covered in the main text, but we have made no attempt to give a comprehensive description of every single option. Indeed when the options on a particular command are rarely used we have ignored them altogether. Options vary somewhat between UNIX implementations, and the only definitive statement of the options available to you is given by your local documentation.

At the end of the Appendix we give a further list of commands, which either have not been mentioned in the book or have only been described in general terms. These are mainly specialized commands, but do not regard them in any way as second class: what is an off-beat specialist activity to one user is a vital mainstream activity to another.

Commands are described using the same syntactic notation as the UNIX manual pages. Note that a list of options, each of which can be a single letter or digit, is specified in a manner such as

$[-[\mathbf{xyz}]]$

This means that the option consists of a minus sign followed by any combination of the letters **x**, **y** and **z**, written in any order. Thus possible settings of this option are $-\mathbf{z}$, $-\mathbf{xy}$, $-\mathbf{yx}$, $-\mathbf{xyz}$ and $-\mathbf{yzx}$.

SPECIFICATIONS OF COMMANDS

at *time* [*month day*] [*file*]   execute AT future time   187

the *file*, which should contain one or more shell commands, is remembered; this remembered copy is then executed at the future *time*, either within the next twenty-four hours or at the specified *month* and *day*. If the *file* is omitted, the standard input is used.

Example **at 0920 dec 25 x**   *(executes* **x** *on Xmas morning)*

cat [*file*] ...   conCATenate and output   52

copy *file*s to the standard output.

Example **cat part1 part2 > afile**   *(copies* **part1** *plus* **part2** *to* **afile***)*

cd [*directory*]   Change Directory   59

change current directory to *directory* — if omitted to home directory.

Example **cd novel**

chmod *ddd file* ...   CHange MODe   57

change permission on *file*s to *ddd*. Each *d* is a digit between 0 and 7, and digits relate to owner, group, others, respectively. (There is also an alternative syntax for describing permissions.)

Example **chmod 660 afile**   *(allows owner and group to read and write)*

comm [−[123]] *file1 file2*   find COMMon lines   189

> compare *file1* and *file2*, which are already sorted. The output is in three
> columns: (1) lines only in *file1*; (2) lines only in *file2*; (3) common lines. The
> options can be used to suppress any of these columns.
>
> *Example* **comm −12 lost found**   *(identifies common lines)*

cp *file1 file2*   CoPy   61

> copy *file1* to *file2* (overwriting it if it previously existed). There is also a
> variant of **cp** for copying a sequence of files.
>
> *Example* **cp /usr/john/his mine**   *(makes a copy of someone else's file)*

date   give DATE   51

> output the current date and time.
>
> *Example* **date**

diction [*file*] ...   check DICTION   169

> identify, within the *files*, sentences that contain apparent misuse of English.
> The files may be in **nroff** format.
>
> *Example* **diction chapter6**   *(checks diction of **chapter6**)*

diff [−[beh]] *file1 file2*   find DIFFerences   188

> identify the differences between *file1* and *file2*. The output is based on a
> sequence of **ed** commands to create one file from the other. The **b** option
> lessens the significance of blanks; the **e** option enforces strict **ed** format; the **h**
> option does a 'half-hearted' comparison.
>
> *Example* **diff newx oldx**   *(finds differences between two versions)*

du [−a] [−s] [*file*] ...   summarize Disk Usage   190

> display the amount of disk space, in units of blocks, occupied by the *files*.
> Normally each *file* is a directory file, and **du** gives the total size of the files in
> this directory, and in all its sub-directories. If no *files* are specified, the current
> directory is assumed. The **a** (for all) option gives a more verbose analysis, and
> covers individual files; the **s** (for summary) option gives a more terse analysis.
>
> *Example* **du**   *(gives size of files within current directory)*

echo [−n] [*argument*] ...   ECHO   78

> copy the *argument*s to the standard output. The **n** option suppresses the
> newline at the end of the line, and thus would cause a subsequent **echo** to
> come out on the same line.
>
> *Example* **echo Files starting with f are f∗**   *(gives files starting with 'f')*

ed [*file*]   EDit   92

> edit the *file* (if omitted then editing starts with a null buffer).
>
> *Example* **ed afile**

grep [−*options*] *pattern* [*file*] ...   Globally find Reg. Exp., Print   71

> output all the lines of the *file*s that contain a match of the *pattern*, which is a
> 'regular expression' in **ed** notation. Some of the options are
> c count matching lines
> l give names of files that contain a match
> n give line number of each match
> v give the non-matching, not the matching, lines
> y do not differentiate upper and lower case
>
> *Example* **grep program chapter***   (*matches lines containing 'program'*)

kill *processID*   KILL   82

> kill the background process which is identified by the number supplied as the
> *processID*.
>
> *Example* **kill 4583**

ln *file* [*name*]   LiNk two filenames   64

> add the *name* as a filename in the current directory, and make this
> synonymous with *file*. (If *name* is omitted, the name is assumed to be the last
> component in the *file* pathname.)
>
> *Example* **ln /usr/john/data x**   (*makes* **x** *a synonym for* **john**'s **data** *file*)

lpr [−**m**] *file* ...   output to LinePRinter   83

> arrange for the *file*s to be output on a printer. The printing goes on in the
> background while other work proceeds. The **m** option causes you to be sent
> mail when the printing has been completed.
>
> *Example* **lpr chapter6**   (*prints* **chapter6**)

ls [−[**adlrstu**]] *file* ...   LiSt filenames   51

> if a *file* is a directory (the normal case) give a list of the files within it; if a *file* is
> not a directory just give its name. The most important options are
> a list all files, even those whose names begin with a dot
> d treat a directory file as an ordinary file — therefore do not give its
>   contents
> l give a 'long' listing, which includes file properties (owner, permissions,
>   etc.)
>
> The other options are concerned with the order in which the list of filenames
> is to be sorted.
>
> *Example* **ls −l novel**   (*gives a full listing of the* **novel** *directory*)

mail [*loginname*]   send or read MAIL   127

if a *loginname* is supplied, a message is sent to the user with this name; the message comes from the standard input. If no *loginname* is supplied, this causes the **mail** system to be entered in order to read any incoming mail.

Example   **mail john**   *(sends mail to* **john***)*

man [*section*] *title*   display MANual page   120

search the given *section* of the *UNIX Programmer's Manual* for the page with the given *title*, and output this page. If the *section* is omitted the whole Manual is searched.

Example   **man chess**   *(gives documentation for chess program)*

mesg [**n**] [**y**]   allow/inhibit MESsaGes   128

prevent (if **n**) or allow (if **y**) other people to use **write** to send messages to you. If neither option is specified, a report of the current status is given.

Example   **mesg n**   *(prevents others writing to you)*

mkdir *name* ...   MaKe DIRectory   58

create, within the current directory, new directories with the given *name*s.

Example   **mkdir novel**   *(creates* **novel** *directory)*

mv *file1 file2*   MoVe   61

rename *file1* as *file2*. If *file2* already exists the previous version is overwritten. (There may also be variants of **mv** for renaming directories or sequences of files.)

Example   **mv /novel/x x**   *(moves* **x** *into current directory)*

nroff [−*option*] ... [−**ms**] [*file*] ...   (text formatter)   145

prepare the *file*s, using the special formatting requests within them, and send the result to the standard output. If **troff** is specified rather than **nroff**, output is prepared in a format suitable for a typesetter. The **ms** option specifies that the **ms** macro library of requests is to be used. Other important options are

e   put equal spacing between words in justified lines
nN start page numbering at N
T*name*   prepare output for *name* terminal

Example   **nroff** −**ms chapter6**   *(formats* **chapter6***)*

passwd   set PASSWorD   190

start the dialogue for setting a new password.

Example   **passwd**

pr [−*option*] ... *file* ...   PRint   191

display the *files*, dividing them into pages with headers and footers. The most important option is − *N*, where *N* is a digit: this gives *N*-column output. There are also numerous options concerned with page layout, size, numbering, etc.

Example **pr** − **3 names**   *(displays **names** in 3-column paginated form)*

ps [−[**al**]]   give Process Status   82

give information about your current processes. The **a** option covers all users' processes, and the **l** option gives a long listing.

Example **ps**

pwd   Print Working Directory   59

display the pathname of the current directory (i.e. the 'working' directory).

Example **pwd**

rm [−*options*] *file* ...   ReMove files   62

delete the *files*. The most important options are **i** (for interactive), which asks you to confirm each deletion, and **r**, a drastic option that 'recursively' deletes a directory and all the files within it — including any sub-directories.

Example **rm chapter6**   *(deletes **chapter6**)*

rmdir *directory*   ReMove DIRectory   64

delete the *directory*, which must be empty, i.e. all the files within it must already have been deleted.

Example **rmdir novel**   *(deletes **novel** directory)*

sh [*file*] ...   execute SHell   84

execute the *files* as commands for the **sh** shell.

Example **sh doit**   *(executes shell commands stored in **doit**)*

spell [−**b**] [*file*] ...   check SPELLing   7

apply spelling checks on *files*, and display the words that appear to be wrong. The files may be in **nroff** format. The **b** option is for those in favour of British spelling.

Example **spell** − **b chapter6**   *(checks the spelling of **chapter6**)*

stty [*option*] ...   Set terminal (TTY) options   192

set *option*s controlling the behaviour of your terminal. If no options are given the current settings are reported. Some of the most frequently used options are

even	allow input characters with even parity
−even	do not allow input characters with even parity
odd	allow input characters with odd parity
−odd	do not allow input characters with odd parity
echo	echo input characters on the display
−echo	do not echo input characters on the display
lcase	map lower case input characters into upper case
−lcase	do not map lower case input characters into upper case
nl	only accept newlines to end input lines
−nl	accept carriage returns to end input lines
tabs	do not convert tab characters to spaces for display
−tabs	convert tab characters to spaces for display
erase *c*	set the erase key to be the *c* key
kill *c*	set the kill key to be the *c* key

Example **stty erase =**   *(sets the '=' sign to be the erase key)*

---

style [−*option*] ... [*file*] ...   analyze STYLE   166

give statistical information about the style of *files*, which may be in **nroff** format. The *option*s can be used to display the sentences that have certain properties, e.g.

a	display all sentences and their lengths
e	display sentences that begin with expletives
l *N*	display sentences longer than *N* words
p	display sentences that contain a passive verb
P	display parts of speech
r *N*	display sentences whose readability index exceeds *N*

Example **style chapter6**

---

tail [*file*]   give TAIL   193

display the last few lines of *file*.

Example **tail afile**

---

tty   give terminal (TTY) name   186

give pathname of your terminal. (This fits the UNIX concept of treating devices as files.)

Example **tty**

---

wc [-[clw]] [*file*] ...   give Word Count   193

output counts of the number of words, lines and characters in *files*. If only a subset of these three counts is required, the **c** option can be used to select the count of characters, and the **l** and **w** options can be used to select the counts of lines and words, respectively.

Example **wc chapter6** *(counts words, lines and characters in **chapter6**)*

who [**am I**]   say WHO is logged in   123

give information about all the users currently logged in. If 'am I' is specified, then only information about the current user is given.

Example **who**

write *loginname*   WRITE a message   124

send a message (which comes from the standard input) to the user with the given *loginname*. The main purpose of **write** is for immediate and urgent communication; otherwise **mail** is more civilized.

Example **write john** *(sends message to* **john***)*

FURTHER COMMANDS

Programming

adb, **sdb**	debuggers
as	assembler
cc	C compiler
f77	Fortran 77 compiler
ld	loader
lint	C program checker

In addition there are numerous other language processors, tools for building compilers, etc.

Miscellaneous

ar	maintainer of archive (library)
awk	pattern matching language
cal	calendar creator
calendar	reminder service
cmp	file comparator
csh	alternative shell to **sh**
crypt	encrypter
dd	file copier — useful for mag. tapes etc. (but also see **tar**)
eqn, **neqn**	preprocessors for mathematical typesetting
explain	aid to understanding **diction**
file	file analyzer
find	file bloodhound
games	see Section 6 of *UNIX Programmer's Manual*
learn	teaching system
login	log in a fresh user
make	file builder
sleep	time killer
sort	sorter
tabs	controller of tab positions on terminal
tar	tape archiver

tbl	preprocessor for typesetting of tables
tee	T-junction in pipe
time	command timer
tr	character translator
uniq	deleter of successive duplicate lines
uucp	UNIX to UNIX file copier
vi	screen editor

In addition there may be invaluable local commands, such as a **help** (or **apropos**) system, **checknr** and **finger**.

Index

RATFOR, 45
raw-mode, 38
read permission, 33, 34, 35, 203
read-only file, 36
readability grade, 166
README file, 77, 83, 182
recursive, 210
redirection, 41, 53, 68, 70, 78, 84, 86,
    120, 178, 186
regular expression, **107–10**, 112
remote user, 127, 129
removable file system, 23
resilience, 32
response time, 13
RETURN key, 39, 50, 51, 133
Ritchie, D.M., 10, 177
rm command, **62**, 64, 138, 210
rmdir command, 64, 210
root, **root**, 16, 30, 31, 32, 56, 60, 86,
    136
round-robin, 13
run, 8

scheduling algorithm, 13, 14, 17
screen, 5
screen editor, 92, 115
scrolling, 39
sdb, 182
search (*see also* **grep** command), 7
search path, **86**, 89, 137
search-and-replace, 111
secrecy, 21
section of manual, 119
security, 15, *also see* protection
semantics, 68
session, 15
set command, 89
sh command, 73, 82, **84**, 210
sharing, 12–15, 42
sharing files, 17
shell, **41–5**, 68–90, 93, 113
    different, 73
    programming language, 88
shell program, 84, 90, 195
simultaneous writing, 65
single-user system, 12
sleep command, 188
small-is-beautiful, 10, 20, 28, 43, 195
software tools, 45, 81
sort command, 80, 189
source file, 180
source program, 21, 177

space character, 56, 89, 137
spell command, 7, 59, 69, 89, 121, 188,
    189, 199, 210
spooling, 42, 83
standard error output, 42
standard input, 42, 44, 52, 70, 178
standard output, 42, 44, 52, 86, 178
statistics of file content, 193
statistics of style, 168
storage exhausted, 36
storage medium, xiii
stty command, 41, **192**, 210
style command, 166–9, 211
style of UNIX commands, 68–73, 183,
    188
sub-directory, 27
suggest command, 169
superuser, 13, **15**, 16, 17, 30, 32, 33, 34,
    35, 87, 187
synonym for filename, 64
syntax, 68, 72
system call, 177
system program, 7, 9, 177

tab, 211, 212
tail command, 193, 211
tape, 22, 212
task, 12
tbl, 153
tee command, 45
telephone directory, 26
telephone line, 66
temporary file, 81
terminal, xiii, 5, 41, 52, 82, 90, 123, 130,
    192–3
terminal characteristics, 41
text formatter, *see* **nroff**
Thompson, K., 10
time-out, 66
time-slot, 13, 14
timing, 213
tool, 8, 68, 73
tr command, 80
tree, **29–32**, 56, 59, 60
troff command, 44, 142, 158, 163, 164,
    209
tty, 82, 124, 139, 186
tty command, 186, 211
type-ahead, 40, 135
typesetting, 142, 156, **164**
typewriter, 5
typing, 38

umask, 34
uniq command, 80
University of California, *see* Berkeley
UNIX implementation, 5
UNIX look-alike, xiv
UNIX Programmer's Manual, 9, **118**, 177, 183, 193
UNIX version, 60, 194–5
unlink, 64, 138
up, 130
user-friendly, 3
usr directory, 30, 33, 86
usr/me directory, 51
uucp command, 129

Version Seven, xiv, 195

Vesterman, W., 166
vi editor, 92, 115

wc command, 193, 211
who command, **123**, 186, 194, 198, 212
WIBNI, 43
wildcard, 73, 78, 107, 110, 138
Wilkes, M.V., 13
window, 83
word, 52
word-processing, 9, 142
workfile, 179
working directory, *see* current directory
write command, **124–26**, 128, 186, 212
write permission, 33, 34, 35, 64, 65, 136